GENERATIONS
Your Family in Modern American History

GENERATIONS
Your Family in Modern American History

Jim Watts
The City College of the City University of New York

Allen F. Davis
Temple University

 Alfred A. Knopf
NEW YORK

THIS IS A BORZOI BOOK
PUBLISHED BY ALFRED A. KNOPF, INC.

First Edition
987654
Copyright © 1974 by Alfred A. Knopf, Inc.

Library of Congress Cataloging in Publication Data

Watts, Jim, 1935–   comp.
    Generations: your family in modern American history.

    1.United States—Social conditions—Addresses,
essays, lectures.   2.   United States—Genealogy—
Addresses, essays, lectures.   I.   Davis, Allen
Freeman, 1931–   joint comp.   II.   Title.
HN57.W354   309.1'73   74–8546
ISBN 0–394–31752–1

Manufactured in the United States of America

Designed by Meryl Sussman Levavi

Cover photos: Library of Congress, General Electric, Charles Gatewood,
Philip Teuscher

Grateful acknowledgment is extended to the following for permission to reprint previously published material:

The Association for the Study of Negro Life and History, Inc.: From the July and October 1919 issues of the *Journal of Negro History*, "Letters of Negro Migrants of 1916–1918," collected under the direction of Emmett J. Scott. Copyright © by The Association for the Study of Negro Life and History, Inc.

The Dial Press: Excerpted from "Choosing a Dream: Italians in Hell's Kitchen" by Mario Puzo. Originally appeared in *McCall's* magazine. Reprinted from the book, *The Immigrant Experience,* by Thomas C. Wheeler, by permission of the publisher, The Dial Press.

Doubleday & Company, Inc.: "An 18-Year-Old Looks Back on Life," copyright © 1972 Joyce Maynard from the book *Looking Back* by Joyce Maynard. Reprinted by permission of Doubleday & Company, Inc.

Farrar & Rinehart, Inc.: From *A Bride Goes West* by Nannie T. Alderson and Helena Huntington Smith. Copyright 1942, renewed 1970, by Nannie T. Alderson and Helena Huntington Smith.

The Free Press, a Division of Macmillan Publishing Co., Inc.: From *The American Worker in the Twentieth Century: A History Through Autobiographies* by Eli Ginzberg and Hyman Berman. Copyright © 1963 by The Free Press.

Grove Press, Inc.: From *The Autobiography of Malcolm X* by Alex Haley & Malcolm X. Reprinted by permission of Grove Press, Inc. Copyright © 1965 by Alex Haley & Betty Shabazz.

Harper & Row, Inc.: Pp. 289–90, 292 in *My America* by Louis Adamic. Copyright 1938 by Louis Adamic. •Abridged from pp. 252, 256–59, 261–64, 265–67, 269–72 in *A Choice of Weapons* by Gordon Parks. Copyright © 1965, 1966 by Gordon Parks. Reprinted by permission of Harper & Row, Publishers, Inc.

Holt, Rinehart and Winston, Inc.: Map from *Concentration Camps USA: Japanese Americans and World War II* by Roger Daniels. Copyright © 1971 by Holt, Rinehart and Winston, Inc. Reproduced by permission of Holt, Rinehart and Winston, Inc.

Houghton Mifflin Company: From *State of the Nation* by John Dos Passos. Copyright by Elizabeth H. Dos Passos. •From *Pacific War Diary, 1942–1945* by James J. Fahey. Copyright © 1963 by James J. Fahey.

Japanese American Evacuation and Relocation Records, The Bancroft Library, University of California, Berkeley. Published by permission of the Director, The Bancroft Library, University of California, Berkeley.

Alfred A. Knopf, Inc.: From *Down These Mean Streets,* by Piri Thomas. Copyright © 1967 by Piri Thomas. Reprinted by permission of Alfred A. Knopf, Inc.

The New York Times Company: "Poll Shows 40% Attend Church . . . ," from *The New York Times,* January 13, 1974. •"Tomatoes Were Not Worth Growing—90 Years Ago" by Ruth Tirrell, from *The New York Times,* January 13, 1974 •Chart, "Most Call Crime City's Worst III," from *The New York Times,* January 16, 1974. •"The Football Phenomenon and Its Place on Campus" by Iver Peterson, from *The New York Times,* January 16, 1974. •"A College Student Makes a Big Decision" by Gerald N. Rosenberg, from *The New York Times,* January 16, 1974. •"E.P.A. Finds Biggest Rivers Among the Dirtiest," from *The New York Times,* January 18, 1974. © 1974 by The New York Times Company. Reprinted by permission.

W. W. Norton & Company, Inc.: Reprinted from *The Feminine Mystique* by Betty Friedan. By permission of W. W. Norton & Company, Inc. Copyright © 1974, 1963 by Betty Friedan.

Pantheon Books/ A Division of Random House, Inc.: From *Hard Times: An Oral History of the Great Depression* by Studs Terkel. Copyright © 1970 by Studs Terkel. Reprinted by permission of Pantheon Books.

Prentice-Hall, Inc.: From *The World Since 1500: A Global History* by L. S. Stavrianos, pp. 162–165, 230–235, © 1966. Reprinted by permission of Prentice-Hall, Inc., Englewood Cliffs, New Jersey.

Paul R. Reynolds, Inc.: From "My-Furthest-Back-Person—The African" by Alex Haley. Copyright © 1972 by Alex Haley. Reprinted by permission of Paul R. Reynolds, Inc.

The Saturday Evening Post: From "Heroism: 'Commando' Kelly's One Man's War" by Sergeant Charles E. Kelly [and Pete Martin]. Reprinted by permission from *The Saturday Evening Post* © 1944 The Curtis Publishing Company.

Evelyn Singer Agency, Inc.: From *Jews Without Money* by Michael Gold. Published 1930 by Horace Liveright, Inc. By permission of the Evelyn Singer Agency, Inc.

Time Incorporated: From "The American Century" by Henry Luce, Farrar & Rinehart, Inc., © 1941 Time Inc. Reprinted by permission.

acknowledgments

My contributions to this book grew out of nine years of teaching experience at the City College of New York, a singular institution whose success, despite continuing struggles, is too little appreciated. In addition, a National Endowment for the Humanities Younger Humanist Fellowship has given me the opportunity to study and reflect upon modes of experimental teaching.

My understanding of the importance of coming to terms with roots was developed through long talks with an extraordinary man, my late father, Jake Watts, of Oswego, New York. I also wish to acknowledge the inspiration, sometimes knowingly, often not, provided by Mary Sullivan Hughes Watts, Maurice Bice, Mikki Blackman, Norman Blackman, Norene Dove, Adrienne Rich, Walter Scholes, George Strand, Arthur Thompson, and, especially, Judy Watts. Professor Sheila Herstein of the Cohen Library, CCNY, provided expertise and understanding of the project. Colleagues at City College who participated in the planning and teaching of an experimental course in family history included Bob Hajdu, Gail Kaplan, Sue Levine, Lucy Quimby, and Bob Twombly. This book owes much to their uncluttered thinking and commitment to effective teaching.

JIM WATTS

A number of students at Temple University have contributed to *Generations* by studying the history of their families and sharing their discoveries with me. This book also owes a great debt to my family—Harold F. Davis, my father, who talked to me about my own family and helped me relate the past to the present, and Greg, Paul, and Bobbie, who went on many expeditions in search of ancestors. Leone Cobb not only taught me how to use the semicolon, but also helped me rediscover my hometown. Barry Kramer, Sally Benson, and Hannah Newman listened and made suggestions, while William Cutler and Ronald Grele gave advice on oral history, and Alice Kessler Harris, who read the manuscript at one point, made some important changes. Brenda Shepler and Donna Ervin typed the manuscript with speed and care.

Finally, both Jim and I would like to express appreciation to the staff at Alfred A. Knopf for their thoughtful and efficient work. In particular, we would like to thank Lynn Goldberg, who contributed to the book with her imagination and her search for pictures, and Elaine Romano, who rescued the book after months of frustration and improved it in a great many ways.

ALLEN F. DAVIS

contents

introduction

If you have grown up and gone to school in the United States, you have studied American history for almost as long as you can remember. From the first or second grade when you colored pictures of Lincoln and cut out cherry trees and hatchets, to later grades when you memorized the special meaning of dates like 1607 or 1863, American history has been a required subject. You have been buffeted by facts about Puritans, the westward movement, the age of Jackson, Civil War battles, overseas expansion, the New Deal, and the New Frontier, but the facts have probably had little meaning and surely have been forgotten more quickly than they were memorized. Although there is a certain intellectual excitement in sorting out the conflicting interpretations of past events, that kind of intellectual game often leaves out the human element.

Perhaps a few historical facts have remained with you because of a personal experience—a visit to a local battle site or a historic house, a tour of a restored village, coming across some old news clippings or letters preserved by a relative, or perhaps just seeing some striking old pictures. They gave you a glimpse of a different kind of past, one remote from that in history books and inhabited by real people with problems and hopes and desires. But the glimpse was, no doubt, fleeting and soon disappeared. Perhaps while reading a novel or watching a movie, you got another brief look at the past as a panorama of human suffering, lust and love, failure and triumph; but that is not supposed to be history—or is it?

All of us, through our parents, grandparents, great-grandparents, and other ancestors, are a part of history stretching back into a dim and distant past. You will probably search in vain for a really famous person in your family background. Everyone, however, has ancestors whose lives were altered by the forces of history—by wars, depressions, population movements, shifts in national bound-

aries, changes in farming methods, the process of industrialization. You can begin to understand some of the dimensions of human existence, some of the process of change, by looking at your own family, studying your own particular ethnic group, and examining the community in which you live.

The best way to begin the study of the past is with yourself. Where do you fit in? What makes you similar to your friends? What makes you different? How do you explain your own special situation? Does it have something to do with the generation in which you were born? The accident of birth, for example, caused those born in the 1930s, a time of low birth rate, to have had much greater employment opportunities than you can expect to have if you were born in the 1950s, a time of high birth rate. Perhaps it is not so much time and generation as sex, race, or religion that you see as crucial in defining your place and identity. Then, being a woman or being a black, an Italian or a Jew will become the most important fact in your life. And social class, too, can be significant in defining your life style, especially if you are either very rich or very poor.

Probably the most crucial influence on your life was your own family. Whether you grew up in a nuclear family (made up of husband, wife, and children) or an extended family (a group of assorted relatives living together and functioning as a unit), you have, no doubt, been radically affected by your interaction with your parents, brothers and sisters, and other relatives. These interactions constitute a unique story, a history. There are "official" records of this history—deeds, marriage certificates, divorce decrees, various court records, the discharge papers of one released from the army. But behind these recorded events are human stories of pathos and triumph and tragedy. A baby dies, a son leaves home, a daughter marries, children rebel against their parents. There is bitterness and remorse and failure, or perhaps resignation. All of these are universals which touch every family at one point or another.

This book should help you to understand yourself and your family, and in the process to appreciate how your family has been affected by the events of the past. One of those events, the movement of peoples, is an especially important theme in this book. Perhaps your family came from Ireland in the great migration after the potato famine in the 1840s; or maybe they were Jews who left Russia in the early 1900s. Possibly you are descended from the slaves who survived the passage from Africa, or perhaps you can trace your ancestry back to the migration from England in the seventeenth and eighteenth centuries. Whatever your own special background, unless you are a pure-blooded Indian, your ancestors went through the process of being uprooted from one culture and establishing themselves in another. (Even if your background can be traced to the native Americans, you too have a heritage of movement and change.) The wrenching moves from one land to another that your parents or grandparents made, the hopes and fears, dreams and heartaches they had, make up one almost universal human component of the American past.

There are, of course, some for whom the effects of immigration are too distant to be felt. But even if your parents or grandparents are not recent immigrants, the chances are that your family has moved from farm to city, from small city to metropolis, from East to West, or from South to North. Americans have always been a mobile people and they continue to be even in the 1970s. It is a rare American family that has lived for more than one or two generations in the same community, let alone in the same house. Every move meant leaving friends and often possessions, although it did not necessarily mean leaving the memories of a place behind. The human dimension of American mobility can be probed by asking questions of your family.

Geographic mobility is only one of the experiences shared by all Americans. Another is the American Dream, the belief that America is a land of opportunity where poor men and women, if they work hard, can improve their situation or at least create a better life for their children. Almost everyone, except those who came as slaves, believed this dream in the past, but how many really succeeded in creating a better life in a new land?

A person's success, or lack of it, has been affected by many factors, not the least of which, in the twentieth century, have been the Great Depression and the war that followed it. These large historical forces are much discussed in history books, mainly from the viewpoint of their effect on political processes and society in the abstract. Both events had very personal sides to them, however, as any member of your family who lived through those decades can attest. For nearly everyone who experienced the depression of the thirties, the hope for a continuously improving life was shattered. True, that hope was revived for some of the prosperity and sense of purpose that World War II gave back to the country. But not everyone shared in this wartime optimism—certainly not those black Americans who fought for a freedom they did not have at home, nor those Japanese-Americans interned in concentration camps for the accident of their ethnic heritage—and even for those who did, the memory of bad times was too vivid to ever allow them freedom from naggingly practical concerns. If there is a gap between generations today manifested in what parents and children are concerned with and in what their expectations for the future are, surely it has been conditioned by the differences between the periods of history through which the two generations have lived. Those differences can be laid out and, if not reconciled, at least understood through an examination of your own family's recollections of living through the past.

The strategy of this book, then, is to help you gather information and to ask questions about yourself and your family and about the movements and events that have influenced your history. We ask you to start with yourself and then to find out about your parents' generation and your grandparents' as well. We ask you to contemplate the experience of movement and disruption that is almost universal in the country's history. We also ask that you study the impact of those two major events of the twentieth century—the depression and World War II—on your family and community. At the end we try to get you to look at the world you are presently living in and to ask questions about it. So the structure of this book is circular. It starts with you and the present, goes back several generations, and then comes forward to the present again.

GENERATIONS
Your Family in Modern American History

My Furthest-Back Person—the African
ALEX HALEY

It is more difficult to find information about some families than about others, but almost everyone can learn something about his heritage and background, and everyone can get caught up in the search. The following is an account of how Alex Haley, best known for his work about the black leader Malcolm X, traced his own family back to his slave ancestors. His quest is an unusual story, in many ways a unique one, but some of its excitement and fascinating detective work may well await you in your study of your own family's history. Your resources will be more limited than Haley's, so you probably will not be able to duplicate his method. Still, you may be able to uncover an even more exciting story; certainly, it will be a more meaningful one, because it will be, after all, about *your* past. Notice Haley's method—and his persistence—as you read his account, and keep them in mind for when you are asked to look for your own past.

My Grandma Cynthia Murray Palmer lived in Henning, Tenn. (pop. 500), about 50 miles north of Memphis. Each summer as I grew up there, we would be visited by several women relatives who were mostly around Grandma's age, such as my Great Aunt Liz Murray who taught in Oklahoma, and Great Aunt Till Merriwether from Jackson, Tenn., or their considerably younger niece, Cousin Georgia Anderson from Kansas City, Kan., and some others. Always after the supper dishes had been washed, they would go out to take seats and talk in the rocking chairs on the front porch, and I would scrunch down, listening, behind Grandma's squeaky chair, with the dusk deepening into night and the lightning bugs flicking on and off above the now shadowy honeysuckles. Most often they talked about our family—the story had been passed down for generations—until the whistling blur of lights of the southbound Panama Limited train *whooshing* through Henning at 9:05 P.M. signaled our bedtime.

So much of their talking of people, places and events I didn't understand: For instance, what was an "Ol' Massa," an "Ol' Missus" or a "plantation"? But early I gathered that white folks had done lots of bad things to our folks, though I couldn't figure out why. I guessed that all that they talked about had happened a long time ago, as now or then Grandma or another, speaking of someone in the past, would excitedly thrust a finger toward me, exclaiming, "Wasn't big as *this* young 'un!" And it would astound me that anyone as old and grey-haired as they could relate to my age. But in time my head began both a recording and picturing of the more graphic scenes

Can you recall any such discussions of your family history?

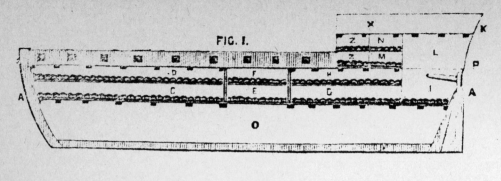

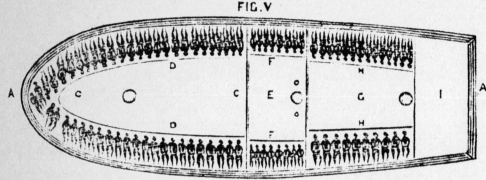

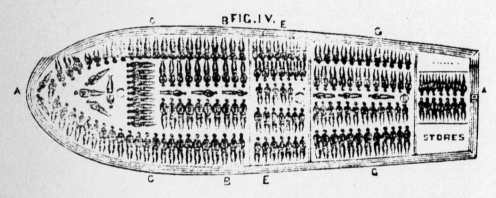

From the seventeenth century through the beginning of the nineteenth century, when the importation of slaves to the United States was terminated, nearly 15 million blacks were transported here on ships. The schematic diagram above shows that traders planned not for safety, much less comfort, but for maximum numbers, so that as many as half those transported died enroute. When, and under what conditions, did your ancestors arrive in the New World?

they would describe, just as I also visualized David killing Goliath with his slingshot, Old Pharaoh's army drowning, Noah and his ark, Jesus feeding that big multitude with nothing but five loaves and two fishes, and other wonders that I heard in my Sunday school lessons at our New Hope Methodist Church.

The furthest-back person Grandma and the others talked of—always in tones of awe, I noticed—they would call "The African." They said that some ship brought him to a place that they pronounced "'Naplis." They said that then some "Mas' John Waller" bought him for his plantation in "Spotsylvania County, Va." This African kept on escaping, the fourth time trying to kill the "hateful po' cracker" slave-catcher, who gave him the punishment choice of castration or of losing one foot. This African took a foot being chopped off with an ax against a tree stump, they said, and he was about to die. But his life was saved by "Mas' John's" brother—"Mas'

Who is the "furthest-back" person that is still remembered in your family?

William Waller," a doctor, who was so furious about what had happened that he bought the African for himself and gave him the name "Toby."

Crippling about, working in "Mas' William's" house and yard, the African in time met and mated with "the big house cook named Bell," and there was born a girl named Kizzy. As she grew up her African daddy often showed her different kinds of things, telling her what they were in his native tongue. Pointing at a banjo, for example, the African uttered, *"ko"*; or pointing at a river near the plantation, he would say, *"Kamby Bolong."* Many of his strange words started with a *"k"* sound, and the little, growing Kizzy learned gradually that they identified different things.

Is the foreign language you know that of your ancestors? If not, why didn't you learn that language?

When addressed by other slaves as "Toby," the master's name for him, the African said angrily that his name was *"Kin-tay."* And as he gradually learned English, he told young Kizzy some things about himself—for instance, that he was not far from his village, chopping wood to make himself a drum, when four men had surprised, overwhelmed, and kidnapped him.

So Kizzy's head held much about her African daddy when at age 16 she was sold away onto a much smaller plantation in North Carolina. Her new "Mas' Tom Lea" fathered her first child, a boy she named George. And Kizzy told her boy all about his African grandfather. George grew up to be such a gamecock fighter that he was called "Chicken George," and people would come from all over and "bet big money" on his cockfights. He mated with Matilda, another of Lea's slaves; they had seven children, and he told them the stories and strange sounds of their African great-grandfather. And one of those children, Tom, became a blacksmith who was bought away by a "Mas' Murray" for his tobacco plantation in Alamance County, N. C.

Tom mated there with Irene, a weaver on the plantation. She also bore seven children, and Tom now told them all about their African great-great-grandfather, the faithfully passed-down knowledge of his sounds and stories having become by now the family's prideful treasure.

The youngest of that second set of seven children was a girl, Cynthia, who became my maternal Grandma (which today I can only see as fated). Anyway, all of this is how I was growing up in Henning at Grandma's, listening from behind her rocking chair as she and the other visiting old women talked of that African (never then comprehended as *my* great-great-great-great-grandfather) who said his name was *"Kin-tay,"* and said *"ko"* for banjo, *"Kamby Bolong"* for river, and a jumble of other *"k"*-beginning sounds that Grandma privately muttered, most often while making beds or cooking, and who also said that near his village he was kidnaped while chopping wood to make himself a drum.

The story had become nearly as fixed in my head as in Grandma's by the time Dad and Mama moved me and my two younger brothers, George and Julius, away from Henning to be with them at the small black agricultural and mechanical college in Normal, Ala., where Dad taught.

To compress my next 25 years: When I was 17 Dad let me enlist as a mess boy in the U.S. Coast Guard. I became a ship's cook out in the South Pacific during World War II, and at night down by my bunk I began trying to write sea adventure stories, mailing them off to magazines and collecting rejection slips for eight years before some editors began purchasing and publishing occasional stories. By 1949 the Coast Guard had made me its first "journalist"; finally with 20 years' service, I retired at the age of 37, determined to make a full time career of writing. I wrote mostly magazine articles; my first book was "The Autobiography of Malcolm X."

Then one Saturday in 1965 I happened to be walking past the National Archives building in Washington. Across the interim years I had thought of Grandma's old stories—otherwise I can't think what diverted me up the Archives' steps. And when a main reading room desk attendant asked if he could help me, I wouldn't have dreamed of admitting to him some curiosity hanging on from boyhood about my slave forebears. I kind of mumbled that I was interested in census records of Alamance County, North Carolina, just after the Civil War.

The microfilm rolls were delivered, and I turned them through the machine with a building sense of intrigue, viewing in different census takers' penmanship an endless parade of names. After about a dozen microfilmed rolls, I was beginning to tire, when in utter astonishment I looked upon the names of Grandma's parents: Tom Murray, Irene Murray . . . older sisters of Grandma's as well—every one of them a name that I'd heard countless times on her front porch.

It wasn't that I hadn't believed Grandma. You just *didn't* not believe my Grandma. It was simply so uncanny actually seeing those names in print and in official U.S. Government records.

During the next several months I was back in Washington whenever possible, in the Archives, the Library of Congress, the Daughters of the American Revolution Library. (Whenever black attendants understood the idea of my search, documents I requested reached me with miraculous speed.) In one source or another during 1966 I was able to document at least the highlights of the cherished family story. I would have given anything to have told Grandma, but, sadly, in 1949 she had gone. So I went and told the only survivor of those Henning front-porch storytellers: Cousin Georgia Anderson, now in her 80's in Kansas City, Kan. Wrinkled, bent, not well herself, she was so overjoyed, repeating to me the old stories and sounds; they were like Henning echoes: "Yeah, boy, that African say his name was *'Kin-tay';* he say the banjo was *'ko,'* an' the river *'Kamby-Bolong,'* an' he was off choppin' some wood to make his drum when they grabbed 'im!" Cousin Georgia grew so excited we had to stop her, calm her down, "You go 'head, boy! Your grandma an' all of 'em—they up there watching what you do!"

That week I flew to London on a magazine assignment. Since by now I was steeped in the old, in the past, scarcely a tour guide missed me—I was awed at so many historical places and treasures I'd heard of and read of. I came upon the Rosetta stone in the British Museum, marveling anew at how Jean Champollion, the French archaeologist, had miraculously deciphered its ancient demotic and hieroglyphic texts . . .

The thrill of that just kept hanging around in my head. I was on a jet returning to New York when a thought hit me. Those strange, unknown-tongue sounds, always part of our family's old story . . . they were obviously bits of our original African *"Kin-tay's"* native tongue. What specific tongue? Could I somehow find out?

Back in New York, I began making visits to the United Nations Headquarters lobby; it wasn't hard to spot Africans. I'd stop any I could, asking if my bits of phonetic sounds held any meaning for them. A couple of dozen Africans quickly looked at me, listened, and took off—understandably dubious about some Tennessean's accent alleging "African" sounds.

My research assistant, George Sims (we grew up together in Henning), brought me some names of ranking scholars of African linguistics. One was particularly intriguing: a Belgian- and English-educated Dr. Jan

Have you ever tried to research your own family history? Why or why not?

Why have blacks in particular become so conscious of their heritage? Would other groups do well to follow their example?

How did looking for his own history help the author's appreciation of history?

Vansina; he had spent his early career living in West African villages, studying and tape-recording countless oral histories that were narrated by certain very old African men; he had written a standard textbook, "The Oral Tradition."

So I flew to the University of Wisconsin to see Dr. Vansina. In his living room I told him every bit of the family story in the fullest detail that I could remember it. Then, intensely, he queried me about the story's relay across the generations, about the gibberish of *"k"* sounds Grandma had fiercely muttered to herself while doing her housework, with my brothers and me giggling beyond her hearing at what we had dubbed "Grandma's noises."

Dr. Vansina, his manner very serious, finally said, "These sounds your family has kept sound very probably of the tongue called 'Mandinka.'"

I'd never heard of any "Mandinka." Grandma just told of the African saying *"ko"* for banjo, or *"Kamby Bolong"* for a Virginia river.

Among Mandinka stringed instruments, Dr. Vansina said, one of the oldest was the *"kora."*

"Bolong," he said, was clearly Mandinka for "river." Preceded by *"Kamby,"* it very likely meant "Gambia River."

Dr. Vansina telephoned an eminent Africanist colleague, Dr. Philip Curtin. He said that the phonetic *"Kin-tay"* was correctly spelled *"Kinte,"* a very old clan that had originated in Old Mali. The Kinte men traditionally were blacksmiths, and the women were potters and weavers.

I knew I must get to the Gambia River.

The first native Gambian I could locate in the U.S. was named Ebou Manga, then a junior attending Hamilton College in upstate Clinton, N. Y. He and I flew to Dakar, Senegal, then took a smaller plane to Yundum Airport, and rode in a van to Gambia's capital, Bathurst. Ebou and his father assembled eight Gambia government officials. I told them Grandma's stories, every detail I could remember, as they listened intently, then reacted. *"'Kamby Bolong'* of course is Gambia River!" I heard. "But more clue is your forefather's saying his name was *'Kinte.'"* Then they told me something I would never even have fantasized—that in places in the back country lived very old men, commonly called *griots,* who could tell centuries of the histories of certain very old family clans. As for *Kintes,* they pointed out to me on a map some family villages, Kinte-Kundah, and Kinte-Kundah Janneh-Ya, for instance.

The Gambian officials said they would try to help me. I returned to New York dazed. It is embarrassing to me now, but despite Grandma's stories, I'd never been concerned much with Africa, and I had the routine images of African people living mostly in exotic jungles. But a compulsion now laid hold of me to learn all I could, and I began devouring books about Africa, especially about the slave trade. Then one Thursday's mail contained a letter from one of the Gambian officials, inviting me to return there.

Monday I was back in Bathurst. It galvanized me when the officials said that a *griot* had been located who told the *Kinte* clan history—his name was Kebba Kanga Fofana. To reach him, I discovered, required a modified safari; renting a launch to get upriver, two land vehicles to carry supplies by a roundabout land route, and employing finally 14 people, including three interpreters and four musicians, since a *griot* would not speak the revered clan histories without background music.

The boat Baddibu vibrated upriver, with me acutely tense: Were these Africans maybe viewing me as but another of the pith-helmets? After about two hours, we put in at James Island, for me to see the ruins of the once British-operated James Fort. Here two centuries of slave ships had

What would drive a man to such lengths to find his past?

5

loaded thousands of cargoes of Gambian tribespeople. The crumbling stones, the deeply oxidized swivel cannon, even some remnant links of chain seemed all but impossible to believe. Then we continued upriver to the left-bank village of Albreda, and there put ashore to continue on foot to Juffure, village of the *griot*. Once more we stopped, for me to see *toubob kolong,* "the white man's well," now almost filled in, in a swampy area with abundant, tall, saw-toothed grass. It was dug two centuries ago to "17 men's height deep" to insure survival drinking water for long-driven, famishing coffles of slaves.

Why would these remnants of the past have affected him so?

Walking on, I kept wishing that Grandma could hear how her stories had led me to the *"Kamby Bolong."* (Our surviving storyteller Cousin Georgia died in a Kansas City hospital during this same morning, I would learn later.) Finally, Juffure village's playing children, sighting us, flashed an alert. The 70-odd people came rushing from their circular, thatch-roofed, mud-walled huts, with goats bounding up and about, and parrots squawking from up in the palms. I sensed him in advance somehow, the small man amid them, wearing a pillbox cap and an off-white robe—the *griot.* Then the interpreters went to him, as the villagers thronged around me.

And it hit me like a gale wind: every one of them, the whole crowd, was *jet black.* An enormous sense of guilt swept me—a sense of being some kind of hybrid . . . a sense of being impure among the pure. It was an awful sensation.

How has his growing sense of African heritage affected his self-image as an American black?

The old *griot* stepped away from my interpreters and the crowd quickly swarmed around him—all of them buzzing. An interpreter named A. B. C. Salla came to me; he whispered: "Why they stare at you so, they have never seen here a black American." And that hit me: I was symbolizing for them twenty-five millions of us they had never seen. What did they think of me—of us?

Then abruptly the old *griot* was briskly walking toward me. His eyes boring into mine, he spoke in Mandinka, as if instinctively I should understand—and A. B. C. Salla translated:

"Yes . . . we have been told by the forefathers . . . that many of us from this place are in exile . . . in that place called America . . . and in other places."

I suppose I physically wavered, and they thought it was the heat; rustling whispers went through the crowd, and a man brought me a low stool. Now the whispering hushed—the musicians had softly begun playing *kora* and *balafon,* and a canvas sling lawn seat was taken by the *griot,* Kebba Kanga Fofana, aged 73 "rains" (one rainy season each year). He seemed to gather himself into a physical rigidity, and he began speaking the *Kinte* clan's ancestral oral history; it came rolling from his mouth across the next hours . . . 17th- and 18th-century *Kinte* lineage details, predominantly what men took wives; the children they "begot," in the order of their births; those children's mates and children.

Events frequently were dated by some proximate singular physical occurrence. It was as if some ancient scroll were printed indelibly within the *griot's* brain. Each few sentences or so, he would pause for an interpreter's translation to me. I distill here the essence:

The *Kinte* clan began in Old Mali, the men generally blacksmiths ". . . who conquered fire," and the women potters and weavers. One large branch of the clan moved to Mauretania from where one son of the clan, Kairaba Kunta Kinte, a Moslem Marabout holy man, entered Gambia. He lived first in the village of Pakali N'Ding; he moved next to Jiffarong village; ". . . and then he came here, into our own village of Juffure."

6

African tribes often assign one of their members the highly honored task of mentally keeping their history. What need might the retelling of the past serve?

In Juffure, Kairaba Kunta Kinte took his first wife, ". . . a Mandinka maiden, whose name was Sireng. By her, he begot two sons, whose names were Janneh and Saloum. Then he got a second wife, Yaisa. By her, he begot a son, Omoro."

The three sons became men in Juffure. Janneh and Saloum went off and found a new village, Kinte-Kundah Janneh-Ya. "And then Omoro, the youngest son, when he had 30 rains, took as a wife a maiden, Binta Kebba.

"And by her, he begot four sons—Kunta, Lamin, Suwadu, and Madi . . ."

Sometimes, a "begotten," after his naming, would be accompanied by some later-occurring detail, perhaps as ". . . in time of big water (flood), he slew a water buffalo." Having named those four sons, now the *griot* stated such a detail.

"About the time the king's soldiers came, the eldest of these four sons, Kunta, when he had about 16 rains, went away from this village, to chop wood to make a drum . . . and he was never seen again . . ."

7

Goose-pimples the size of lemons seemed to pop all over me. In my knapsack were my cumulative notebooks, the first of them including how in my boyhood, my Grandma, Cousin Georgia and the others told of the African *"Kin-tay"* who always said he was kidnapped near his village—while chopping wood to make a drum . . .

I showed the interpreter, he showed and told the *griot,* who excitedly told the people; they grew very agitated. Abruptly then they formed a human ring, encircling me, dancing and chanting. Perhaps a dozen of the women carrying their infant babies rushed in toward me, thrusting the infants into my arms—conveying, I would later learn, "the laying on of hands . . . through this flesh which is us, we are you, and you are us." The men hurried me into their mosque, their Arabic praying later being translated outside: "Thanks be to Allah for returning the long lost from among us." Direct descendants of Kunta Kinte's blood brothers were hastened, some of them from nearby villages, for a family portrait to be taken with me, surrounded by actual ancestral sixth counsins. More symbolic acts filled the remaining day.

What caused their excitement? Might it have had something to do with finding a piece of their own lost history?

When they would let me leave, for some reason I wanted to go away over the African land. Dazed, silent in the bumping Land Rover, I heard the cutting staccato of talking drums. Then when we sighted the next village, its people came thronging to meet us. They were all—little naked ones to wizened elders—waving, beaming, amid a cacophony of crying out; and then my ears identified their words: *"Meester Kinte! Meester Kinte!"*

Let me tell you something: I am a man. But I remember the sob surging up from my feet, flinging up my hands before my face and bawling as I had not done since I was a baby . . . the jet-black Africans were jostling, staring . . . I didn't care, with the feelings surging. If you really knew the odyssey of us millions of black Americans, if you really knew how we came in the seeds of our forefathers, captured, driven, beaten, inspected, bought, branded, chained in foul ships, if you really knew, you needed weeping . . .

Back home, I knew that what I must write, really, was our black sage, where any individual's past is the essence of the millions'. Now flat broke, I went to some editors I knew, describing the Gambian miracle, and my desire to pursue the research; Doubleday contracted to publish, and Reader's Digest to condense the projected book; then I had advances to travel further.

Do you agree with this statement? Would finding your own history give you this sense?

What ship brought Kinte to Grandma's "'Naplis" (Annapolis, Md., obviously)? The old *griot's* time reference to "king's soldiers" sent me flying to London. Feverish searching at last identified, in British Parliament records, "Colonel O'Hare's Forces," dispatched in mid-1767 to protect the then British-held James Fort whose ruins I'd visited. So Kunta Kinte was down in some ship probably sailing later that summer from the Gambia River to Annapolis.

Now I feel it was fated that I had taught myself to write in the U.S. Coast Guard. For the sea dramas I had concentrated on had given me years of experience searching among yellowing old U.S. maritime records. So now in English 18th-century marine records I finally tracked ships reporting themselves in and out to the Commandant of the Gambia River's James Fort. And then early one afternoon I found that a Lord Ligonier under a Captain Thomas Davies had sailed on the Sabbath of July 5, 1767. Her cargo: 3,265 elephants' teeth, 3,700 pounds of beeswax, 800 pounds of cotton, 32 ounces of Gambian gold, and 140 slaves; her destination: "Annapolis."

That night I recrossed the Atlantic. In the Library of Congress the Lord Ligonier arrival was one brief line: "Shipping In The Port Of Annapolis—1748–1775." I locate the author, Vaughan W. Brown in his Baltimore brokerage office. He drove to Historic Annapolis, the city's historical society, and found me further documentation of her arrival on Sept. 29, 1767. (Exactly two centuries later, Sept. 29, 1967, standing, staring seaward from an Annapolis pier again I knew tears). More help came in the Maryland Hall of Records. Archivist Phebe Jacobsen found the Lord Ligonier's arriving customs declaration listing, "98 Negroes"—so in her 86-day crossing, 42 Gambians had died, one among the survivors being 16-year-old Kunta Kinte. Then the microfilmed Oct. 1, 1767, Maryland Gazette contained, on page two, an announcement to prospective buyers from the ship's agents, Daniel of St. Thos. Jenifer and John Ridout (the Governor's secretary):"from the River GAMBIA, in AFRICA . . . a cargo of choice, healthy SLAVES . . ."

How far back can you go?

one

THE SELF EXAMINED

Everyone, regardless of his background or position in life, is interested in himself. Part of the fascination of reading a novel or watching a movie is, after all, the feeling of identification with the characters depicted. Autobiography has much the same appeal, for in following the author's memories and self-analysis, it is easy to move to one's own memories and to probe for meaning and understanding from one's own past. Usually autobiographies are written by the famous, but certainly one does not have to be famous to write and think autobiographically. In fact, without realizing it, we do it every day. The old man recalling stories of his youth for his grandson; the mother suggesting in pride or in anger that when she was a girl, "things were different"; brothers and sisters sharing their conflicting memories of the same event—all are examples of thinking in this manner.

The two selections that follow—one by a girl who grew up in an affluent suburb, the other by a boy raised in an inner-city slum—are examples of autobiographic accounts by ordinary people. In one sense they are unrepresentative of the kind of self-evaluation that most people undertake in trying to make sense out of their backgrounds: in general, people do not take the trouble to write down their family legends or their recollections of childhood and adolescence. But in another, more important sense they are typical because the factors that they represent as having had the most influence on their lives have probably had a similar impact on lives like our own. For both, the influence of the community where they were born and grew up was a marked one. It determined, for instance, how they spent their free time—in front of a television set or on the streets with a gang. Their respective socioeconomic classes, too, played a recognizable part in shaping their lives and their expectations for the future, since, obviously, being affluent or very poor affects not only the physical conditions of life but attitudes that grow from these conditions. And, although both are not consciously aware of it, the sex roles they were expected to assume had a large influence on the course of their actions.

Perhaps you will find that you have little in common with either of the authors. If, for example, you have moved many times, you may lack their sense of belonging to a particular community. But, then, examining the differences that you feel between yourself and the authors may prove just as significant in providing clues to yourself as recognizing those social factors that you share with them. And, there are many other factors besides. In the past, religion and ethnicity were important in establishing the identities of a vast number of immigrant Americans and, with race, continue to have an influence—for some, a major one—on the quality of life. In the end, of course, our experience is shaped not only by abstract social forces but also by the people with whom we associate. Perhaps, then, you can point to a particular individual—a parent, teacher, or friend—who gave your life its particular impetus.

Obviously, your life is too complex to be totally explained in terms of a few social factors. Yet by studying and thinking about some of the intertwined lines of influence, you can begin to appreciate the history of which you are a part. Through this self-examination, moreover, you will be taking the first step toward understanding your society.

an 18-year-old looks back on life
JOYCE MAYNARD

What kinds of things do you remember from four years ago? ten years ago? Do you recall a song, a house, a friend, a television program, or perhaps a major historical event—for example, the Vietnam War or riots on college campuses and striking students? Everyone has his own special memories, but each generation shares certain experiences that are different from those of its parents. The following essay was written by a college student born in 1953. To what extent do you share her ideas about what influenced her? Is television as important in your life as it seems to have been in hers? Does the impact of TV, and the media in general, contribute to separating your generation from your parents'? Do you have the same hopes—and sense of resignation—as this young woman?

Every generation thinks it's special—my grandparents because they remember horses and buggies, my parents because of the Depression. The over-30's are special because they knew the Red Scare of Korea, Chuck Berry and beatniks. My older sister is special because she belonged to the first generation of teen-agers (before that, people in their teens were *adolescents*), when being a teen-ager was still fun. And I—I am 18, caught in the middle. Mine is the generation of unfulfilled expectations. "When you're older," my mother promised, "you can wear lipstick." But when the time came, of course, lipstick wasn't being worn. "When we're big, we'll dance like that," my friends and I whispered, watching Chubby Checker twist on "American Bandstand." But we inherited no dance steps, ours was a limp, formless shrug to watered-down music that rarely made the feet tap. "Just wait till we can vote," I said, bursting with 10-year-old fervor, ready to fast, freeze, march and die for peace and freedom as Joan Baez, barefoot, sang "We Shall Overcome." Well, now we can vote, and we're old enough to attend rallies and knock on doors and wave placards, and suddenly it doesn't seem to matter any more.

My generation is special because of what we missed rather than what we got, because in a certain sense we are the first and the last. The first to take technology for granted. (What was a space shot to us, except an hour cut from Social Studies to gather before a TV in the gym as Cape Canaveral counted down?) The first to grow up with TV. My sister was 8 when we got our set, so to her it seemed magic and always somewhat foreign. She had known books already and would never really replace them. But for me, the TV set was, like the kitchen sink and the telephone, a fact of life.

Do you share her feeling that it doesn't matter any more?

Was it for you?

12

We inherited a previous generation's hand-me-downs and took in the seams, turned up the hems, to make our new fashions. We took drugs from the college kids and made them a high-school commonplace. We got the Beatles, but not those lovable look-alikes in matching suits with barber cuts and songs that made you want to cry. They came to us like a bad joke—aged, bearded, discordant. And we inherited the Vietnam war just after the crest of the wave—too late to burn draft cards and too early not to be drafted. The boys of 1953—my year—will be the last to go.

How does the transformation of the Beatles symbolize the changes that occurred between the early and the late 1960s? Were you aware of these changes?

Demonstration, especially antiwar protest, was a common form of social activism in the 1960s. Do you think this kind of activism died because of a lack of causes or because people came to regard mass protest as ineffective? Do you feel politically effective now?

So where are we now? Generalizing is dangerous. Call us the apathetic generation and we will become that. Say times are changing, nobody cares about prom queens and getting into the college of his choice any more—say that (because it sounds good, it indicates a trend, gives a symmetry to history) and you make a movement and a unit out of a generation unified only in its common fragmentation. If there is a reason why we are where we are, it comes from where we have been.

Like overanxious patients in analysis, we treasure the traumas of our childhood. Ours was more traumatic than most. The Kennedy assassination has become our myth: Talk to us for an evening or two—about movies or summer jobs or Nixon's trip to China or the weather—and the subject will come up ("Where were *you* when you heard?"), as if having lived through Jackie and the red roses, John-John's salute and Oswald's on-camera murder justifies our disenchantment.

Where were you?

We haven't all emerged the same, of course, because our lives were lived in high-school corridors and drive-in hamburger joints as well as in the pages of Time and Life, and the images on the TV screen. National events and personal memory blur so that, for me, Nov. 22, 1963, was a birthday party that had to be called off and Armstrong's moonwalk was my first full can of beer. If you want to know who we are now; if you wonder how we'll vote, or whether we will, or whether, 10 years from now, we'll end up just like all those other generations that thought they were special—with 2.2 kids and a house in Connecticut—if that's what you're wondering, look to the past because, whether we should blame it or not, we do.

• • •

If I had spent at the piano the hours I gave to television, on all those afternoons when I came home from school, I would be an accomplished pianist now. Or if I'd danced, or read, or painted . . . But I turned on the set instead, every day, almost, every year, and sank into an old green easy chair, smothered in quilts, with a bag of Fritos beside me and a glass of milk to wash them down, facing life and death with Dr. Kildare, laughing at Danny Thomas, whispering the answers—out loud sometimes—with "Password" and "To Tell the Truth." Looking back over all those afternoons, I try to convince myself they weren't wasted. I must have learned something; I must, at least, have changed.

What I learned was certainly not what TV tried to teach me. From the reams of trivia collected over years of quiz shows, I remember only the questions, never the answers. I loved "Leave it to Beaver" for the messes Beaver got into, not for the inevitable lecture from Dad at the end of each show. I saw every episode two or three times, witnessed Beaver's aging, his legs getting longer and his voice lower, only to start all over again with young Beaver every fall. (Someone told me recently that the boy who played Beaver Cleaver died in Vietnam. The news was a shock—I kept coming back to it for days until another distressed Beaver fan wrote to tell me that it wasn't true after all.)

Would you react the same way? Why?

I got so I could predict punch lines and endings, not really knowing whether I'd seen the episode before or only watched one like it. There was the bowling-ball routine, for instance: Lucy, Dobie Gillis, Pete and Gladys—they all used it. Somebody would get his finger stuck in a bowling ball (Lucy later updated the gimmick using Liz Taylor's ring) and then they'd have to go to a wedding or give a speech at the P.T.A. or have the boss to dinner, concealing one hand all the while. We weren't supposed to ask questions like "Why don't they just tell the truth?" These shows were built on deviousness, on the longest distance between two points, and on a kind of symmetry which decrees that no loose ends shall be left untied, no lingering doubts allowed. (The Surgeon General is off the track in worrying about TV violence, I think. I grew up in the days before lawmen became peacemakers. What carries over is not the gunfights but the memory that everything always turned out all right.) Optimism shone through all those half hours I spent in the dark shadows of the TV room—out of evil shall come good.

Does TV still reflect the same optimism today?

Most of all, the situation comedies steeped me in American culture. I emerged from years of TV viewing indifferent to the museums of France, the architecture of Italy, the literature of England. A perversely home-bound American, I pick up paperbacks in bookstores, checking before I buy to see if the characters have foreign names, whether the action takes place in London or New York. Vulgarity and banality fascinate me. More intellectual friends (who watch no TV) can't understand what I see in "My Three Sons." "Nothing happens," they say. "The characters are dull, plastic, faceless. Every show is the same." I guess that's why I watch them—boring repetition is, itself, a rhythm—a steady pulse of flashing Coca-Cola signs, McDonald's Golden Arches and Howard Johnson roofs.

Do you feel the same need for repetitiveness and predictability?

I don't watch TV as an anthropologist, rising loftily above my subject to analyze. Neither do I watch, as some kids now tune in to reruns of "The Lone Ranger" and "Superman" (in the same spirit they enjoy comic books and pop art) for their camp. I watch in earnest. How can I do anything else? Five thousand hours of my life have gone into this box.

• • •

Ask us whose face is on the $5 bill and we may not know the answer. But nearly everyone my age remembers a cover of Life magazine that came out in the spring of 1965, part of a series of photographs that enter my dreams and my nightmares still. They were the first shots ever taken of an unborn fetus, curled up tightly in a sack of veins and membranes, with blue fingernails and almost transparent skin that made the pictures look like double exposures. More than the moon photographs a few years later, that grotesque figure fascinated me as the map of a new territory. It was often that way with photographs in Life—the issue that reported on the "In Cold Blood" murders; a single picture of a boy falling from an airplane and another of a woman who had lost 200 pounds. (I remember the faces of victims and killers from seven or eight years ago, while the endless issues on Rome and nature studies are entirely lost.)

Photographs are the illustrations for a decade of experiences. Just as, when we think of "Alice in Wonderland," we all see Tenniel's drawings, and when we think of the Cowardly Lion, we all see Bert Lahr, so, when we think of Lyndon Johnson's airborne swearing-in as President in 1963, we have a common image furnished by magazines, and when we think of fetuses, now, those cabbages we were supposed to have come from and smiling, golden-haired cherubs have been replaced forever by the cover of Life. Having had so many pictures to grow up with, we share a common visual idiom and have far less room for personal vision. The movie versions of books decide for us what our heroes and villains will look like, and we are powerless to change the camera's decree. So, while I was

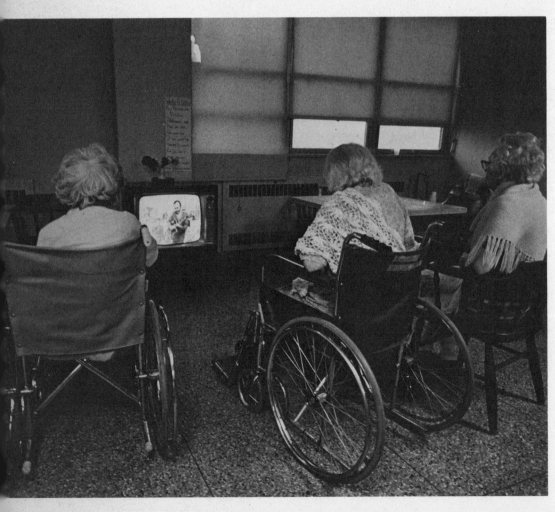

An American born in the 1950s who lives to be seventy may watch more than 50,000 hours of television in his or her lifetime. People, regardless of age or class, seem mesmerized by its offerings—no matter how thin. What common need does TV seem to satisfy? What function does it serve for you?

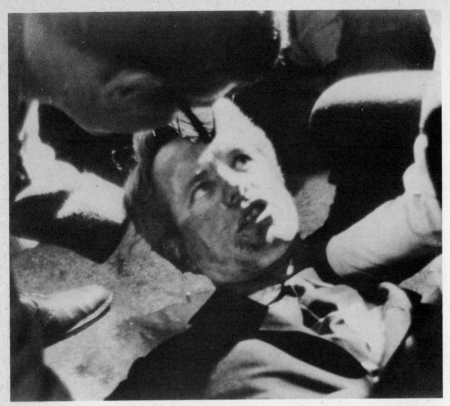

The newspaper and magazine media often carry their messages through photographs that, in freezing action, magnify a scene's impact. This picture of the dying Robert Kennedy is an example. What other photographs can you think of that have had an impact on you?

stunned and fascinated by that eerie fetus (where is he now, I wonder, and are those pictures in his family album?) I'm saddened too, knowing what it did to me. If I were asked to pinpoint major moments in my growing up, experiences that changed me, the sight of that photograph would be one.

• • •

Everyone is raised on nursery rhymes and nonsense stories. But it used to be that when you grew up, the nonsense disappeared. Not for us—it is at the core of our music and literature and art and, in fact, of our lives. Like characters in an Ionesco play, we take absurdity unblinking. In a world where military officials tell us "We had to destroy the village in order to save it," Dylan lyrics make an odd kind of sense. They aren't meant to be understood; they don't jar our sensibilities because we're used to *non sequiturs*. We don't take anything too seriously these days. (Was it a thousand earthquake victims or a million? Does it matter?) The casual butcher's-operation in the film "M*A*S*H" and the comedy in Vonnegut and the album cover showing John and Yoko, bareback, are all part of the new absurdity. The days of the Little Moron joke and the elephant joke and the knock-knock joke are gone. It sounds melodramatic, but the joke these days is life.

You're not supposed to care too much any more. Reactions have been scaled down from screaming and jelly-bean-throwing to nodding your head and maybe—if the music really gets to you (and music's the only thing that does any more)—tapping a finger. We need a passion transfusion, a shot of

Can you think of anything around you that strikes you as absurd?

Is music the only thing that gets to you?

18

energy in the veins. It's what I'm most impatient with, in my generation—this languid, I-don't-give-a-s—— -ism that stems in part, at least, from a culture of put-ons in which any serious expression of emotion is branded sentimental and old-fashioned. The fact that we set such a premium on being cool reveals a lot about my generation; the idea is not to care. You can hear it in the speech of college students today: cultivated monotones, low volume, punctuated with four-letter words that come off sounding only bland. I feel it most of all on Saturday morning, when the sun is shining and the crocuses are about to bloom and, walking through the corridors of my dorm, I see there isn't anyone awake.

Does this describe you and your friends?

•   •   •

We feel cheated, many of us—the crop of 1953—which is why we complain about inheriting problems we didn't cause. (Childhood notions of justice, reinforced by Perry Mason, linger on. Why should I clean up someone else's mess? Who can I blame?) We're excited also, of course: I can't wait to see how things turn out. But I wish I weren't quite so involved, I wish it weren't my life that's being turned into a suspense thriller.

When my friends and I were little, we had big plans. I would be a famous actress and singer, dancing on the side. I would paint my own sets and compose my own music, writing the script and the lyrics and reviewing the performance for the New York Times. I would marry and have three children (they don't allow us dreams like that any more) and we would live, rich and famous (donating lots to charity, of course, and periodically adopting orphans), in a house we designed ourselves. When I was older I had visions of good works. I saw myself in South American rain forests and African deserts, feeding the hungry and healing the sick, with an obsessive selflessness, I see now, as selfish, in the end, as my original plans for stardom.

Now my goal is simpler. I want to be happy. And I want comfort—nice clothes, a nice house, good music and good food, and the feeling that I'm doing some little thing that matters. I'll vote and I'll give to charity, but I won't give myself. I feel a sudden desire to buy land—not a lot, not as a business investment, but just a small plot of earth so that whatever they do to the country I'll have a place where I can go—a kind of fallout shelter, I guess. As some people prepare for their old age, so I prepare for my 20's. A little house, a, comfortable chair, peace and quiet—retirement sounds tempting.

Would you call this optimism? Is your goal similar?

Down These Mean Streets
Piri Thomas

Growing up affluent in suburbia as Joyce Maynard did is one extreme in the range of possible American experiences. There are millions of Americans, however, who have lived at the other extreme, growing up poor in the city. In the following article, Piri Thomas gives an account of coming of age on the mean streets of Spanish Harlem. His world is one of gangs, drugs, and violence, where mere survival is a day-to-day struggle. To what extent is your experience similar to that of Piri Thomas? The constant need to assert one's rights and to establish one's identity through gangs and fighting is primarily a male experience. Yet everyone, in one way or another, must announce, as the author does, "Hey, World—here I am."

YEE-AH!! Wanna know how many times I've stood on a rooftop and yelled out to anybody
"Hey, World—here I am. Hallo, World—this is Piri. That's me.
"I wanna tell ya I'm here—you bunch of mother-jumpers—I'm here, and I want recognition, whatever that mudder-fuckin word means."

Man! How many times have I stood on the rooftop of my broken-down building at night and watched the bulb-lit world below.
Like somehow it's different at night, this my Harlem. There ain't no bright sunlight to reveal the stark naked truth of garbage-lepered streets.
Gone is the drabness and hurt, covered by a friendly night.
It makes clean the dirty-faced kids.

Have you ever felt ambivalent about the place where you grew up?

20

Where you grew up may have had an influence on what you did. Even the smallest details, for example, how you got to school, were probably influenced by your locale. The sum of these details gave a distinctive pace or beat to your life. What rhythms are implicit in these three photos of school transportation? Which suggests your own background, and do you identify or rebel against that rhythm?

This is a bright *mundo* [world], my streets, my *barrio de noche* [ghetto of
   night],
With its thousands of lights, hundreds of millions of colors
Mingling with noises, swinging street sounds of cars and curses,
Sounds of joys and sobs that make music.
If anyone listens real close, he can hear its heart beat—

YEE-AH! I feel like part of the shadows that make company for me in this
   warm *amigo* darkness.
I am "My Majesty Piri Thomas," with a high on anything and like a stoned
   king, I gotta survey my kingdom.
I'm a skinny, dark-face, curly-haired, intense Porty-Ree-can—
Unsatisfied, hoping, and always reaching.

I got a feeling of aloneness and a bitterness that's growing and growing
Day by day into some kind of hate without *un nombre* [a name].
Yet when I look down at the streets below, I can't help thinking
It's like a great big dirty Christmas tree with lights but no fuckin presents.
And man, my head starts growing bigger than my body as it gets crammed
   full of hate.

**Is his experience
of alienation the
same as Joyce
Maynard's?**

And I begin to listen to the sounds inside me.
Get angry, get hating angry, and you won't be scared.
What have you got now? Nothing.
What will you ever have? Nothing
. . . Unless you cop for yourself!

21

Games sometimes acquire a distinctive character because of their surroundings. How might this basketball game be transformed if it were played in uniforms, in a gymnasium? How would the baseball game pictured on the next page be played on a city street?

Hanging around on the block is a sort of science. You have a lot to do and a lot of nothing to do. In the winter there's dancing, pad combing, movies, and the like. But summer is really the kick. All the blocks are alive, like many-legged cats crawling with fleas. People are all over the place. Stoops are occupied like bleacher sections at a game, and beer flows like there's nothing else to drink. The block musicians pound out gone beats on tin cans and conga drums and bongos. And kids are playing all over the place—on fire escapes, under cars, in alleys, back yards, hallways.

We rolled marbles along the gutter edge, trying to crack them against the enemy marbles, betting five and ten marbles on being able to span the rolled distance between your marbles and the other guy's. We stretched to the limit skinny fingers with dirty gutter water caked between them, completely oblivious to the islands of dog filth, people filth, and street filth that lined the gutter.

That gutter was more dangerous than we knew. There was a kid we called Dopey, a lopsided-looking kid who was always drooling at the mouth. Poor Dopey would do anything you'd tell him, and one day somebody told him to drink dirty street water. He got sick, and the ambulance from City Hospital came and took him away. The next time we saw Dopey, he was in a coffin box in his house. He didn't look dopey at all; he looked like any of us, except he was stone dead.

All of us went to Dopey's funeral. We were sweeter to him in death than we ever had been in life. I thought about death, that bogeyman we all knew as kids, which came only to the other guy, never to you. You would live forever. There in front of Dopey's very small, very cheap coffin I promised myself to live forever; that no matter what, I'd never die.

For a few days after Dopey's funeral we talked about how Dopey now was in a big hole in the ground till his bones grew rotten and how none of us was afraid of death or dying. I even described how I'd die and breathe my last. I did the whole bit, acting out every detail. I had a kid hold my head in his lap while I spoke about leaving for the last roundup in the ranch house up

Does this match your idea of a ghetto?

Does the idea of death affect you in the same way?

22

yonder, an idea I got from a Johnny Mack Brown cowboy flicker. It was swell acting. I ended with a long, shuddering expelling of breath, a rolling of the eyeballs, whites showing carefully, and jaws falling slack amidst cries of "Holy Jesus" and "Man, what a fuckin' actor that guy is!" Then I arose from my flat sidewalk slab of death, dusted myself off, looked around and said "Hey, man, let's play Johnny-on-the-Pony, one-two-three."

At thirteen or fourteen we played a new game—copping girls' drawers. It became part of our street living—and sometimes a messy part. Getting yourself a chick was a rep builder. But I felt that bragging to other fellas about how many cherries I'd cracked or how many panties came down on rooftops or back yards was nobody's business but my own, and besides, I was afraid my old lady would find out and I'd get my behind wasted. And anyway it was better to play mysterious with the guys at bullshit sessions, just play it cool as to who and how you copped.

It was all part of becoming *hombre* [a man], of wanting to have a beard to shave, a driver's license, a draft card, a "stoneness" which enabled you to go into a bar like a man. Nobody really digs a kid. But a man—cool. Nobody can tell you what to do—and nobody better. You'd smack him down like Whiplash does in the cowboy flick or really light him up like Scarface in that gangster picture—swoon, crack, bang, bang, bang—short-nose, snub-nose pistol, and a machine gun, and a poor fuckin' loud-mouth is laid out.

That was the way I felt. And sometimes what I did, although it was real enough, was only a pale shadow of what I felt. Like playing stickball . . .

I stood at the side of the sewer that made home plate in the middle of the street, waiting impatiently for the Spalding ball to be bounced my way, my broomstick bat swinging back and forth.

"Come on, man, pitch the ball!" I shouted.

"Take it easy, buddy," the pitcher said.

I was burning, making all kinds of promises to send that rubber ball smashing into his teeth whenever he decided to let it go.

What does "becoming a man" mean to you? Is there anything comparable in "becoming a woman"?

23

"Come on, Piri, lose that ball—smack it clear over to Lexington Avenue."

"Yeah, yeah, watch me."

The ball finally left that hoarder's hand. It came in on one bounce, like it was supposed to, and slightly breaking into a curve. It was all mine.

"Waste it, *panín* [pal]," shouted my boy Waneko.

I gritted my teeth and ran in to meet the ball. I felt the broomstick bat make connection and the ball climb and climb like it was never coming back. It had "home run" all over it. One runner came in and I was right behind him. My boys pushed out their hands to congratulate me. We had twelve *bolos* [dollars] on the game. I slapped skin with them, playing it cool all the way. Man, that was the way to be.

• • •

We were moving—our new pad was back in Spanish Harlem—to 104th Street between Lex and Park Avenue.

Moving into a new block is a big jump for a Harlem kid. You're torn up from your hard-won turf and brought into an "I don't know you" block where every kid is some kind of enemy. Even when the block belongs to your own people, you are still an outsider who has to prove himself a down stud with heart.

As the moving van rolled to a stop in front of our new building, number 109, we were all standing there, waiting for it—Momma, Poppa, Sis, Paulie, James, José, and myself. I made out like I didn't notice the cats looking us over, especially me—I was gang age. I read their faces and found no trust, plenty of suspicion, and a glint of rising hate. I said to myself, *These cats don't mean nothin'. They're just nosy.* But I remembered what had happened to me in my old block, and that it had ended with me in the hospital.

This was a tough-looking block. That was good, that was cool; but my turf had been tough, too. *I'm tough,* a voice within said. *I hope I'm tough enough. I am tough enough. I've got* mucho corazón [*much heart*], *I'm king wherever I go. I'm a killer to my heart. I not only* can *live, I will live, no punk out, no die out, walk bad; be down, cool breeze, smooth.* My mind raced, and thoughts crashed against each other, trying to reassemble themselves into a pattern of rep. I turned slowly and with eyelids half-closed I looked at the rulers of this new world and with a cool shrug of my shoulders I followed the movers into the hallway of number 109 and dismissed the coming war from my mind.

The next morning I went to my new school, called Patrick Henry, and strange, mean eyes followed me.

"Say, pops," said a voice belonging to a guy I later came to know as Waneko, "where's your territory?"

In the same tone of voice Waneko had used, I answered, "I'm on it, dad, what's shaking?"

"Bad, huh?" He half-smiled.

"No, not all the way. Good when I'm cool breeze and bad when I'm down."

"What's your name, kid?"

"That depends. 'Piri' when I'm smooth and 'Johnny Gringo' when stomping time's around."

"What's your name now?" he pushed.

"You name me, man," I answered, playing my role like a champ.

He looked around, and with no kind of words, his boys cruised in. Guys I would come to know, to fight, to hate, to love, to take care of. Little Red,

Waneko, Little Louie, Indio, Carlito, Alfredo, Crip, and plenty more. I stiffened and said to myself, *Stomping time, Piri boy, go with heart.*

I fingered the garbage-can handle in my pocket—my homemade brass knuckles. They were great for breaking down large odds into small, chopped-up ones.

Waneko, secure in his grandstand, said, "We'll name you later, *panín.*"

I didn't answer. Scared, yeah, but wooden-faced to the end, I thought, *Chevere, panín* [Great, pal].

It wasn't long in coming. Three days later, at about 6 p.m., Waneko and his boys were sitting around the stoop at number 115. I was cut off from my number 109. For an instant I thought, *Make a break for it down the basement steps and through the back yards—get away in one piece!* Then I thought, *Caramba! Live punk, dead hero. I'm no punk kid. I'm not copping any pleas.* I kept walking, hell's a-burning, hell's a-churning, rolling with cheer. *Walk on, baby man, roll on without fear. What's he going to call?*

"Whatta ya say, Mr. Johnny Gringo?" drawled Waneko.

Think, man, I told myself, *think your way out of a stomping. Make it good.* "I hear you 104th Street coolies are supposed to have heart," I said. "I don't know this for sure. You know there's a lot of streets where a whole 'click' is made out of punks who can't fight one guy unless they all jump him for the stomp." I hoped this would push Waneko into giving me a fair one. His expression didn't change.

"Maybe we don't look at it that way."

Crazy, man. I cheer inwardly, the cabrón [chump] *is falling into my setup. We'll see who gets messed up first, baby!* "I wasn't talking to you," I said. "Where I come from, the pres is president 'cause he got heart when it comes to dealing."

Waneko was starting to look uneasy. He had bit on my worm and felt like a sucker fish. His boys were now light on me. They were no longer so much interested in stomping me as in seeing the outcome between Waneko and me. "Yeah," was his reply.

I smiled at him. "You trying to dig where I'm at and now you got me interested in you. I'd like to see where you're at."

Waneko hesitated a tiny little second before replying, "Yeah."

I knew I'd won. Sure, I'd have to fight; but one guy, not ten or fifteen. If I lost I might still get stomped, and if I won I might get stomped. I took care of this with my next sentence. "I don't know you or your boys," I said, "but they look cool to me. They don't feature as punks."

I had left him out purposely when I said "they." Now his boys were in a separate class. I had cut him off. He would have to fight me on his own, to prove his heart to himself, to his boys, and most important, to his turf. He got away from the stoop and asked, "Fair one, Gringo?"

"Uh-uh," I said, "roll all the way—anything goes." I thought, *I've got to beat him bad and yet not bad enough to take his prestige all away.* He had *corazón.* He came on me. *Let him draw first blood,* I thought, *it's his block.* Smish, my nose began to bleed. His boys cheered, his heart cheered, his turf cheered. "Waste this chump," somebody shouted.

Okay, baby, now it's my turn. He swung. I grabbed innocently, and my forehead smashed into his nose. His eyes crossed. His fingernails went for my eye and landed in my mouth—crunch, I bit hard. I punched him in the mouth as he pulled away from me, and he slammed his foot into my chest.

We broke, my nose running red, my chest throbbing, his finger—well, that

Is facing violence mainly a ghetto experience or is it a universally male one?

What else is involved here besides a physical challenge?

Why these rules and emphasis upon fair play in an essentially chaotic situation?

was his worry. I tied up with body punching and slugging. We rolled onto the street. I wrestled for acceptance, he for rejection or, worse yet, acceptance on his terms. It was time to start peace talks. I smiled at him. "You got heart, baby," I said.

He answered with a punch to my head. I grunted and hit back, harder now. I had to back up my overtures of peace with strength. I hit him in the ribs, I rubbed my knuckles in his ear as we clinched. I tried again. "You deal good," I said.

"You too," he muttered, pressuring out. And just like that, the fight was over. No more words. We just separated, hands half up, half down. My heart pumped out, *You've established your rep. Move over, 104th Street. Lift your wings, I'm one of your baby chicks now.*

Five seconds later my spurs were given to me in the form of introductions to streetdom's elite. There were no looks of blankness now; I was accepted by heart.

"What's your other name, Johnny Gringo?"

"Piri."

"Okay, Pete, you wanna join my fellows?"

"Sure, why not?"

But I knew I had first joined their gang when I cool-looked them on moving day. *I was cool, man,* I thought. *I could've wasted Waneko any time. I'm good, I'm damned good, pure* corazón. *Viva me!* Shit, I had been scared, but that was over. I was in; it was *my* block now.

Not that I could relax. In Harlem you always lived on the edge of losing rep. All it takes is a one-time loss of heart.

What do you think of the idea of "coolness"—emotionless strength—as a male ideal?

• • •

"You wan' some?" I heard a voice near me say.

I opened my eye a little. I saw a hand, and between its fingers was a stick of pot. I didn't look up at the face. I just plucked the stick from the fingers. I heard the feminine voice saying, "You gonna like thees pot. Eet's good stuff."

I felt its size. It was king-sized, a bomber. I put it to my lips and began to hiss my reserve away. It was going, going, going. I was gonna get a

When you were in high school, what kind of activity was most important to you? Was it, as the picture on the preceding page suggests, an informal activity like "hanging out" on a street corner? Or was it spending time in classes or other more formal groups? How did your community, economic and social class, or sex influence how you spent your time?

gone high. I inhaled. I held my nose, stopped up my mouth. I was gonna get a gone high . . . a gone high . . . a gone high . . . and then the stick was gone, burnt to a little bit of a roach.

Were drugs a part of your experience of growing up?

I got to thinking way-out thoughts on a way-out kick. The words went wasting each other in a mad race inside my head. *Hey world, do you know these mean streets is like a clip machine? It takes, an' keeps on taking, till it makes a cat feel like every day is something that's gotta be forgotten. But there's good things, too, man. Like standing together with your boys, and feeling like king. Like being down for anything, even though you're scared sweat will stand out all over you and your brave heart wants to crawl out through your pores.*

Man! You meet your boys and make it to a jump, where you can break night dancing. You walk down them streets and you feel tall and tough. You dig people watching you an' walk a little more boppy. You let your tailormade hang cool between tight lips, unlit, and when you talk, your voice is soft and deep. Your shoulders brush against your boys. Music pours out of candy stores, restaurants and open windows and you feel good-o at the greatness of the sounds. You see the five-story crumbling building where the dance is happening. You flick your eyeballs around from force of habit, to see if any of the Jolly Rogers [another gang] are around. The shit's on. But nobody like that's around, so you all make it up the stairs, and the sounds of shoes beating them long, dead wooden steps make it sound like a young army going to war. It's only nine guys, but each is a down stud. You think about how many boys you got an' it's more than you need.

The set is on the fifth floor and the floor is creaking an' groaning under the weight of all the coolies that are swinging. You dig the open door of the roof and smell burning pot. It smells like burned leaves. You and your boys dig each other for the same idea and, like one, make it up to the roof. Joints are pulled out of the brims of hats and soon there's no noise except the music and the steady hiss of cats blasting away on kick-sticks.

Then it comes—the tight feeling, like a rubber band being squeezed around your forehead. You feel your Adam's apple doing an up-an'-down act—gulp, gulp, gulp—and you feel great—great, dammit! So fine, so smooth. You like this feeling of being air-light, with your head tight. You like the sharpness of your ears as they dig the mambo music coming up the stairs. You hear every note clear. You have the power to pick out one instrument from another. Bongos, congas, flute, piano, maracas, marimba. You keep in time with your whole body and swinging soul, and all of a sudden you're in the middle, hung up with a chick; and the music is soft and she's softer, and you make the most of grinding against her warmth. Viva, viva, viva!

Then the Jolly Rogers walk in and everybody starts dealing. Your boys are fighting and you fall in with them. Bottles are hitting everything but the walls. You feel somebody put his damn fist square in your damn mouth and split your damn lip and you taste your own sweet blood—and all of a sudden you're really glad you came. You're glad you smoked pot, you're glad somebody punched you in the mouth; you're glad for another chance to prove how much heart you got. You scream mad and your mouth is full of "motherfuckers!" and you swing out hard. Ah, chevere! That broke his fuckin' nose.

Everybody's screaming; there's sounds of feet kicking fallen bad men; there's sounds of chicks screaming "Po-leece" outta open windows.

Then the police siren is heard. It sounds like a stepped-on bitch. A blank is put on the rumble and everybody puts the law into effect. The fight stops and everybody makes it outta the place like it had caught fire. We still hate each other, but we hate the cops worse.

Everybody splits and beats it over hills and over dales—and over rooftops. You feel so good that when the cops make it up them five flights, they ain't gonna find nothing but a sad Puerto Rican record playing a sad bolero called "Adiós, motherfuckers."

Yeah. But the best is the walk back to the block, with the talk about the heart shown in the rumble, the questions put down and the answers given. The look of pride and the warmth of hurts received and given. And each cat makes it to his pad to cop a nod and have his dreams, sweetened by his show of corazón. *Yeah, man, we sure messed them Jolly Rogers up . . .*

Is there anything in this fantasy ideal with which you can identify?

ASSIGNMENT 1
A BRIEF AUTOBIOGRAPHICAL ESSAY

Worlds separate Joyce Maynard and Piri Thomas—the comfortable if uninspiring middle-class suburbs and the violent mean streets of the inner city. Yet as different as their experiences are, both essayists share a common link: each has been able to identify key factors that explain his or her life. What about you?

Unlike Piri Thomas, you may have grown up in an environment fairly free of physical danger. And perhaps you do not, like Joyce Maynard, see television as a dominating force in your development. Yet, if you think about it, you will recall significant experiences—events, people, places, ideas—that have shaped and defined you. You may even have discovered some overriding personal meaning in social class, racial, or ethnic self-identification, or struggled through a crisis that represented a dramatic turning point in your life.

Try writing a brief account of your own life. Follow the method used by Maynard and Thomas; that is, select pertinent factual material, put it in narrative form, and give it some interpretation. As a guide, aim for about 1,000 words, though you may certainly write more if you get carried away.

two

THE AMERICAN DREAM

America has always been a land of legendary promise and opportunity. Of course, the promise often has disintegrated into disappointment, the opportunity turned to defeat. Still, the myth persists that *anyone* in America, regardless of race, creed, sex, or color, has an equal opportunity to achieve success—this is the "American Dream." Truth aside, the myth has had its impact on most Americans.

The dream of success has meant different things to different people. To some the American Dream has meant simply a decent job, enough to eat, and a chance to survive; to others it has meant the opportunity to become a powerful executive, a famous actress, a millionaire. Ethnic background, race, and sex certainly influence what hopes and dreams people have. And though it is true that industrialism and the rise of the city have probably ended those days when sons automatically followed fathers' footsteps and daughters emulated mothers, it is still a fact that who your father is, socially and economically, can make a tremendous difference in determining who you are and what opportunities you may have open to you.

But there are some contemporary social critics who argue that, of late, the long-established American drive for success has declined markedly. Young people today, they contend, are more interested in security than in opportunity, in comfortable life styles than in the high risks and tensions that may lead to success. Some commentators even detect among today's youth a rejection of all material things and a search for a simple existence divorced from the drive for achievement that has so often been seen as the core of American life. At the very least, there seems to be enough of a schism in goals and aspirations among the young to cause their parents some concern. As James Michener remarked a few years ago: "Many a father who has spent the years from 22 to 52 in a mad race to accumulate now finds himself powerless to answer his children who ask, 'Why did you do it, Pop? What good did you get out of it? What have you to show for the rat race except two cars and three picture windows?'" Perhaps you have asked your parents similar startling questions—or do you share their goals and dreams?

As you read the following selections, written by people that are roughly of your parents' generation, ask yourself if you have anything in common with the goals and experiences related in them. Mario Puzo speaks of the role ethnic identity has played in delimiting his ideas of success—largely a negative one, since he reacts against the narrowness of his family's world. Malcolm X describes the nightmarish aspects of the American Dream for the millions of members of his race who are entrapped in a cycle of poverty and despair. Betty Friedan tells of how her dreams for the future were narrowly circumscribed by the role of wife and mother she felt she had to assume. Has ethnicity, race, or sex shaped your expectations for the future? Did they help account for what your parents considered "making it" in American society? Is their dream of success fading in your own generation, and if so, is it so much a generational difference as it is a natural change in society?

Many other questions will come to mind as you delve into what has constituted the American Dream and how it has evolved. Try to determine for yourself if there is anything of value worth retaining of the dream, or whether a new dream for the future is needed.

Choosing a Dream:
Italians in Hell's Kitchen
Mario Puzo

In this essay, Mario Puzo, the author of *The Godfather*, looks back at his youth in New York City and tries to depict some of the forces that had an impact on his life. Not everyone grew up in an Italian neighborhood and dreamed of becoming a writer, but Puzo does recall attitudes and incidents that have a universal appeal. For example, he has an ambivalent attitude toward his family, both loving and resenting them, and he looks back nostalgically on his earlier life as a happier period. He recalls things that perhaps your parents and others from their generation will remember—trolley cars, crowding around the crystal radio set, and how World War II provided one way of escaping family and background. Do you share his optimism about the American experience? Did your father or mother have similar dreams and aspirations? Do you feel that he is right in stating that although a great deal has changed in forty years, one thing has remained the same—"the contempt of the young for their elders"?

As a child and in my adolescence, living in the heart of New York's Neapolitan ghetto, I never heard an Italian singing. None of the grown-ups I knew were charming or loving or understanding. Rather they seemed coarse, vulgar, and insulting. And so later in my life when I was exposed to all the clichés of lovable Italians, singing Italians, happy-go-lucky Italians, I wondered where the hell the moviemakers and story-writers got all their ideas from.

At a very early age I decided to escape these uncongenial folk by becoming an artist, a writer. It seemed then an impossible dream. My father and mother were illiterate, as were their parents before them. But practising my art I tried to view the adults with a more charitable eye and so came to the conclusion that their only fault lay in their being foreigners; I was an American. This didn't really help because I was only half right. I was the foreigner. They were already more "American" than I could ever become.

But it did seem then that the Italian immigrants, all the fathers and mothers that I knew, were a grim lot; always shouting, always angry, quicker to quarrel than embrace. I did not understand that their lives were a long labor to earn their daily bread and that physical fatigue does not sweeten human natures.

And so even as a very small child I dreaded growing up to be like the adults around me. I heard them saying too many cruel things about their

Why had his family remained illiterate over the generations?

What could he mean by this?

Italians, like other immigrant groups, tended to cluster in ethnic ghettoes. This one, on New York's Lower East Side, is much like the one Puzo inhabited in the 1930s, but there were other Little Italy's in dozens of large American cities. In what ways might a person raised in an ethnic ghetto be significantly different from someone who grew up without ethnic reinforcement?

dearest friends, saw too many of their false embraces with those they had just maligned, observed with horror their paranoiac anger at some small slight or a fancied injury to their pride. They were, always, too unforgiving. In short, they did not have the careless magnanimity of children.

In my youth I was contemptuous of my elders, including a few under thirty. I thought my contempt special to their circumstances. Later when I wrote about these illiterate men and women, when I thought I understood them, I felt a condescending pity. After all, they had suffered, they had labored all the days of their lives. They had never tasted luxury, knew little more economic security than those ancient Roman slaves who might have been their ancestors. And alas, I thought, with new-found artistic insight, they were cut off from their children because of the strange American tongue, alien to them, native to their sons and daughters.

Already an artist but not yet a husband or father, I pondered omnisciently on their tragedy, again thinking it special circumstance rather than a constant in the human condition. I did not yet understand why these men and women were willing to settle for less than they deserved in life and think that "less" quite a bargain. I did not understand that they simply could not afford to dream; I myself had a hundred dreams from which to choose. For I was already sure that I would make my escape, that I was one of the chosen. I would be rich, famous, happy. I would master my destiny.

And so it was perhaps natural that as a child, with my father gone, my mother the family chief, I, like all the children in all the ghettos of America, became locked in a bitter struggle with the adults responsible for me. It was inevitable that my mother and I became enemies.

Is it inevitable for parents and children to become enemies?

As a child I had the usual dreams. I wanted to be handsome, specifically as cowboy stars in movies were handsome. I wanted to be a killer hero in a world-wide war. Or if no wars came along (our teachers told us another was impossible), I wanted at the very least to be a footloose adventurer. Then I branched out and thought of being a great artist, and then, getting ever more sophisticated, a great criminal.

What were your childhood ambitions? Did they match those your parents had for you?

33

My mother, however, wanted me to be a railroad clerk. And that was her *highest* ambition; she would have settled for less. At the age of sixteen when I let everybody know that I was going to be a great writer, my friends and family took the news quite calmly, my mother included. She did not become angry. She quite simply assumed that I had gone off my nut. She was illiterate and her peasant life in Italy made her believe that only a son of the nobility could possibly be a writer. Artistic beauty after all could spring only from the seedbed of fine clothes, fine food, luxurious living. So then how was it possible for a son of hers to be an artist? She was not too convinced she was wrong even after my first two books were published many years later. It was only after the commercial success of my third novel that she gave me the title of poet.

My family and I grew up together on Tenth Avenue, between Thirtieth and Thirty-first streets, part of the area called Hell's Kitchen. This particular neighborhood could have been a movie set for one of the Dead End Kid flicks or for the social drama of the East Side in which John Garfield played the hero. Our tenements were the western wall of the city. Beneath our windows were the vast black iron gardens of New York Central Railroad, absolutely blooming with stinking boxcars freshly unloaded of cattle and pigs for the city slaughterhouse. Steers sometimes escaped and loped through the heart of the neighborhood followed by astonished young boys who had never seen a live cow.

The railroad yards stretched down to the Hudson River, beyond whose garbagey waters rose the rocky Palisades of New Jersey. There were railroad tracks running downtown on Tenth Avenue itself to another freight station called St. Johns Park. Because of this, because these trains cut off one side of the street from the other, there was a wooden bridge over Tenth Avenue, a romantic-looking bridge despite the fact that no sparkling water, no silver flying fish darted beneath it; only heavy dray carts drawn by tired horses, some flat-boarded trucks, tin lizzie automobiles and, of course, long strings of freight cars drawn by black, ugly, engines.

What was really great, truly magical, was sitting on the bridge, feet dangling down, and letting the engine under you blow up clouds of steam that made you disappear, then reappear all damp and smelling of fresh ironing. When I was seven years old I fell in love for the first time with the tough little girl who held my hand and disappeared with me in that magical cloud of steam. This experience was probably more traumatic and damaging to my later relationships with women than one of those ugly childhood adventures Freudian novelists use to explain why their hero has gone bad.

My father supported his wife and seven children by working as a trackman laborer for the New York Central Railroad. My oldest brother worked for the railroad as a brakeman, another brother was a railroad shipping clerk in the freight office. Eventually I spent some of the worst months of my life as the railroad's worst messenger boy.

My oldest sister was just as unhappy as a dressmaker in the garment industry. She wanted to be a school teacher. At one time or another my other two brothers also worked for the railroad—it got all six males in the family. The two girls and my mother escaped, though my mother felt it her duty to send all our bosses a gallon of homemade wine on Christmas. But everybody hated their jobs except my oldest brother who had a night shift and spent most of his working hours sleeping in freight cars. My father finally got fired because the foreman told him to get a bucket of water for the crew and not to take all day. My father took the bucket and disappeared forever.

What kind of memories do you have of the place where you grew up? What memories do your parents have?

34

Immigrants may have dreamed of more opportunity in America but, like these Italian-American builders of the Boston-Westchester Railroad, they often had to settle for the lowest-paid, least-respected jobs. Few had the skills for more desirable work, though they often hoped their children would do better. Is upward socioeconomic mobility as important to you as it may have been to your parents and grandparents if they believed in the American Dream?

Nearly all the Italian men living on Tenth Avenue supported their large families by working on the railroad. Their children also earned pocket money by stealing ice from the refrigerator cars in summer and coal from the open stoking cars in the winter. Sometimes an older lad would break the seal of a freight car and take a look inside. But this usually brought down the "Bulls," the special railroad police. And usually the freight was "heavy" stuff, too much work to cart away and sell, something like fresh produce or boxes of cheap candy that nobody would buy.

The older boys, the ones just approaching voting age, made their easy money by hijacking silk trucks that loaded up at the garment factory on Thirty-first Street. They would then sell the expensive dresses door to door, at bargain prices no discount house could match. From this some graduated into organized crime, whose talent scouts alertly tapped young boys versed in strongarm. Yet despite all this, most of the kids grew up honest, content with fifty bucks a week as truck drivers, deliverymen, and white-collar clerks in the civil service.

I had every desire to go wrong but I never had a chance. The Italian family structure was too formidable.

I never came home to an empty house; there was always the smell of supper cooking. My mother was always there to greet me, sometimes with a policeman's club in her hand (nobody ever knew how she acquired it). But she was always there, or her authorized deputy, my older sister, who preferred throwing empty milk bottles at the heads of her little brothers when they got bad marks on their report cards. During the great Depression of the 1930s, though we were the poorest of the poor, I never remember

Was there an occupation that one or both of your parents were shunted into because of their racial or ethnic background? Did they resent the lack of opportunity?

How important do you think the family is in determining a child's conduct in life?

not dining well. Many years later as a guest of a millionaire's club, I realized that our poor family on home relief ate better than some of the richest people in America.

My mother would never dream of using anything but the finest imported olive oil, the best Italian cheeses. My father had access to the fruits coming off ships, the produce from railroad cars, all before it went through the stale process of middlemen; and my mother, like most Italian women, was a fine cook in the peasant style.

My mother was as formidable a personage as she was a cook. She was not to be treated cavalierly. My oldest brother at age sixteen had his own tin lizzie Ford and used it to further his career as the Don Juan of Tenth Avenue. One day my mother asked him to drive her to the market on Ninth Avenue and Fortieth Street, no more than a five-minute trip. My brother had other plans and claimed he was going to work on a new shift on the railroad. Work was an acceptable excuse even for funerals. But an hour later when my mother came out of the door of the tenement she saw the tin lizzie loaded with three pretty neighborhood girls, my Don Juan brother about to drive them off. Unfortunately there was a cobblestone lying loose in the gutter. My mother dropped her black leather shopping bag and picked up the stone with both hands. As we all watched in horror, she brought the boulder down on the nearest fender of the tin lizzie, demolishing it. Then she picked up her bag and marched off to Ninth Avenue to do her shopping. To this day, forty years later, my brother's voice still has a surprised horror and shock when he tells the story. He still doesn't understand how she could have done it.

Do you think mothers play as important a role in the family structure now?

My mother had her own legends and myths on how to amass a fortune. There was one of our uncles who worked as an assistant chef in a famous Italian-style restaurant. Every day, six days a week, this uncle brought home, under his shirt, six eggs, a stick of butter, and a small bag of flour. By doing this for thirty years he was able to save enough money to buy a fifteen-thousand-dollar house on Long Island and two smaller houses for his son and daughter. Another cousin, blessed with a college degree, worked as a chemist in a large manufacturing firm. By using the firm's raw materials and equipment he concocted a superior floor wax which he sold door to door in his spare time. It was a great floor wax and with his low overhead, the price was right. My mother and her friends did not think this stealing. They thought of it as being thrifty.

The wax-selling cousin eventually destroyed his reputation for thrift by buying a sailboat; this was roughly equivalent to the son of a Boston brahmin spending a hundred grand in a whorehouse.

Was the American notion of thrift and hard work exaggerated among recent immigrants?

As rich men escape their wives by going to their club, I finally escaped my mother by going to the Hudson Guild Settlement House. Most people do not know that a settlement house is really a club combined with social services. The Hudson Guild, a five-story field of joy for slum kids, had ping pong rooms and billiard rooms, a shop in which to make lamps, a theater for putting on amateur plays, a gym to box and play basketball in. And then there were individual rooms where your particular club could meet in privacy. The Hudson Guild even suspended your membership for improper behavior or failure to pay the tiny dues. It was a heady experience for a slum kid to see his name posted on the billboard to the effect that he was suspended by the Board of Governors.

• • •

For many Americans of immigrant descent, success has meant earning enough money to be able to leave a ghetto for the suburbs. By this standard these Italian-Americans, enjoying a game of boccie on a court by their suburban homes, have "made it." Would your parents agree with this assessment? Do you share that value?

The Hudson Guild was also responsible for absolutely the happiest times of my childhood. When I was about nine or ten they sent me away as a Fresh Air Fund kid. This was a program where slum children were boarded on private families in places like New Hampshire for two weeks.

As a child I knew only the stone city. I had no conception of what the countryside could be. When I got to New Hampshire, when I smelled grass and flowers and trees, when I ran barefoot along the dirt country roads, when I drove the cows home from pasture, when I darted through fields of corn and waded through clear brooks, when I gathered warm brown speckled eggs in the henhouse, when I drove a hay wagon drawn by two great horses—when I did all these things—I nearly went crazy with the joy of it. It was quite simply a fairy tale come true.

The family that took me in, a middle-aged man and woman, childless, were Baptists and observed Sunday so religiously that even checker playing was not allowed on the Lord's day of rest. We went to church on Sunday for a good three hours, counting Bible class, then again at night. On Thursday evenings we went to prayer meetings. My guardians, out of religious scruple, had never seen a movie. They disapproved of dancing, they were no doubt political reactionaries; they were everything that I came later to fight against.

And yet they gave me those magical times children never forget. For two weeks every summer from the time I was nine to fifteen I was happier than I have ever been before or since. The man was good with tools and built me a little playground with swings, sliding ponds, seesaws. The woman had a beautiful flower and vegetable garden and let me pick from it. A cucumber or strawberry in the earth was a miracle. And then when they saw how much I loved picnics, the sizzling frankfurters on a stick over the wood fire, the yellow roasted corn, they drove me out on Sunday afternoons to a lovely green grass mountainside. Only on Sundays it was never called a picnic, it was called "taking our lunch outside." I found it then—and now—a sweet hypocrisy.

*   *   *

From this Paradise I was flung into Hell. That is, I had to help support my family by working on the railroad. After school hours of course. This

Why was the country so important to him? Were you ever exposed to a way of life entirely different from your own?

was the same railroad that had supplied free coal and free ice to the whole Tenth Avenue when I was young enough to steal with impunity. After school finished at 3 P.M. I went to work in the freight office as a messenger. I also worked Saturdays and Sundays when there was work available.

I hated it. One of my first short stories was about how I hated that job. But of course what I really hated was entering the adult world. To me the adult world was a dark enchantment, unnatural. As unnatural to the human dream as death. And as inevitable.

The young are impatient about change because they cannot grasp the power of time itself; not only as the enemy of flesh, the very germ of death, but time as a benign cancer. As the young cannot grasp really that love must be a victim of time, so too they cannot grasp that injustices, the economic and family traps of living, can also fall victim to time.

Do you accept this view of time and the young?

• • •

America may be a fascistic, warmongering, racially prejudiced country today. It may deserve the hatred of its revolutionary young. But what a miracle it once was! What has happened here has never happened in any other country in any other time. The poor who had been poor for centuries—hell, since the beginning of Christ—whose children had inherited their poverty, their illiteracy, their hopelessness, achieved some economic dignity and freedom. You didn't get it for nothing, you had to pay a price in tears, in suffering, but why not? And some even became artists.

Do you agree?

Not even my gift for retrospective falsification [remembering the good and not the bad] can make my eighteenth to twenty-first years seem like a happy time. I hated my life. I was being dragged into the trap I feared and had foreseen even as a child. It was all there, the steady job, the nice girl who would eventually get knocked up, and then the marriage and fighting over counting pennies to make ends meet. I noticed myself acting more unheroic all the time. I had to tell lies in pure self-defense, I did not forgive so easily.

But I was delivered. When World War II broke out I was delighted.

Many Italian-Americans of your parents' generation viewed Frank Sinatra and Joe DiMaggio (pictured on the preceding page) as symbols of the American Dream come true. Few of that generation, however, achieved the wealth and fame of these two superstars. Like the people shown here, most settled for considerably less. By their own standards, were the men and women who failed to reach that height of success failures? Did they, in fact, settle for less?

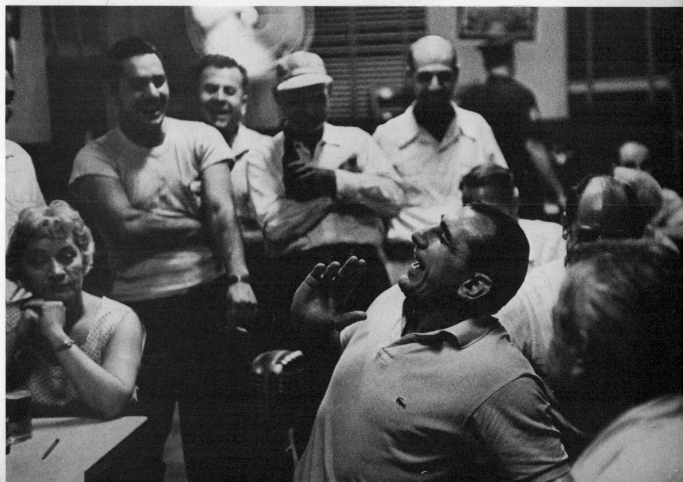

There is no other word, terrible as it may sound. My country called. I was delivered from my mother, my family, the girl I was loving passionately but did not love. And delivered WITHOUT GUILT. Heroically. My country called, ordered me to defend it. I must have been one of millions, sons, husbands, fathers, lovers, making their innocent getaway from baffled loved ones. And what an escape it was. The war made all my dreams come true. I drove a jeep, toured Europe, had love affairs, found a wife, and lived the material for my first novel. But of course that was a just war as Vietnam is not, and so today it is perhaps for the best that the revolutionary young make their escape by attacking their own rulers.

Did any member of your family serve in a war? Did he or she experience the war in this way?

Then why five years later did I walk back into the trap with a wife and child and a civil service job I was glad to get? After five years of the life I had dreamed about, plenty of women, plenty of booze, plenty of money, hardly any work, interesting companions, travel, etc., why did I walk back into that cage of family and duty and a steady job?

For the simple reason, of course, that I had never really escaped, not my mother, not my family, not the moral pressures of our society. Time again had done its work. I was back in my cage and I was, I think, happy. In the next twenty years I wrote three novels. Two of them were critical successes but I didn't make much money. The third novel, not as good as the others, made me rich. And free at last. Or so I thought.

Can you ever really escape your family background?

Then why do I dream of those immigrant Italian peasants as having been happy? I remember how they spoke of their forebears, who spent all their lives farming the arid mountain slopes of Southern Italy. "He died in that house in which he was born," they say enviously. "He was never more than an hour from his village, not in all his life," they sigh. And what would they make of a phrase like "retrospective falsification"?

No, really, we are all happier now. It is a better life. And after all, as my mother always said, "Never mind about being happy. Be glad you're alive."

When I came to my "autobiographical novel," the one every writer does about himself, I planned to make myself the sensitive, misunderstood hero, much put upon by his mother and family. To my astonishment my mother took over the book and instead of my revenge I got another comeuppance. But it is, I think, my best book. And all those old-style grim conservative Italians whom I hated, then pitied so patronizingly, they also turned out to be heroes. Through no desire of mine. I was surprised. The thing that amazed me most was their courage. Where were their Congressional Medals of Honor? Their Distinguished Service Crosses? How did they ever have the balls to get married, have kids, go out to earn a living in a strange land, with no skills, not even knowing the language? They made it without tranquillizers, without sleeping pills, without psychiatrists, without even a dream. Heroes. Heroes all around me. I never saw them.

Was it more "heroic" to have been living then than now?

But how could I? They wore lumpy work clothes and handlebar moustaches, they blew their noses on their fingers and they were so short that their high-school children towered over them. They spoke a laughable broken English and the furthest limit of their horizon was their daily bread. Brave men, brave women, they fought to live their lives without dreams. Bent on survival, they narrowed their minds to the thinnest line of existence.

It is no wonder that in my youth I found them contemptible. And yet they had left Italy and sailed the ocean to come to a new land and leave their sweated bones in America. Illiterate Colombos, they dared to seek the promised land. And so they, too, dreamed a dream.

Puzo speaks of the immigrant generation of Italians as "happy" though their lives were grim. Can you detect anything in this photograph of an Italian-American religious festival in 1915 that suggests what he means? Is happiness, in Puzo's sense, part of the American Dream of success?

• • •

But maybe the young are on the right track this time. Maybe they know that the dreams of our fathers were malignant. Perhaps it is true that the only real escape is in the blood magic of drugs. All the Italians I knew and grew up with have escaped, have made their success. We are all Americans now, we are all successes now. And yet the most successful Italian man I know admits that though the one human act he never could understand was suicide, he understood it when he became a success. Not that he ever would do such a thing; no man with Italian blood ever commits suicide or becomes a homosexual in his belief. But suicide has crossed his mind. And so to what avail the finding of the dream? He went back to Italy and tried to live like a peasant again. But he can never again be unaware of more subtle traps than poverty and hunger.

There is a difference between having a good time in life and being happy. My mother's life was a terrible struggle and yet I think it was a happy life. One tentative proof is that at the age of eighty-two she is positively indignant at the thought that death dares approach her. But it's not for everybody that kind of life.

Thinking back I wonder why I became a writer. Was it the poverty or the books I read? Who traumatized me, my mother or the Brothers Karamazov? Being Italian? Or the girl sitting with me on the bridge as the engine steam deliciously made us vanish? Did it make any difference that I grew up Italian rather than Irish or black?

No matter. The good times are beginning, I am another Italian success story. Not as great as DiMaggio or Sinatra but quite enough. It will serve. Yet I can escape again. I have my retrospective falsification (how I love that phrase). I can dream now about how happy I was in my childhood, in my tenement, playing in those dirty but magical streets—living in the poverty that made my mother weep. True, I was a deposed dictator at fifteen but they never hanged me. And now I remember, all those impossible dreams strung out before me, waiting for me to choose, not knowing that the life I was living then, as a child, would become my final dream.

Do you think your generation will abandon this dream of success? Is it still worth dreaming?

the autobiography of Malcolm X
Malcolm X and Alex Haley

For many Americans, especially those born black, the American Dream almost always became a nightmare. Malcolm X, in this excerpt from his autobiography, describes the horror of his youth. He recalls pistol shots and a burning house, the murder of his father, the moves and uprooting, and the poverty, conflict, and insanity that led to the breakup of his family. And yet he has some fond memories along with a sense of family loyalty and pride. Is this kind of nightmare, this perversion of the American Dream, unique to the black experience? Have you seen it happening in your own family? Is there any experience in your family background that would contribute to a greater understanding of the nightmare Malcolm X describes here?

When my mother was pregnant with me, she told me later, a party of hooded Ku Klux Klan riders galloped up to our home in Omaha, Nebraska, one night. Surrounding the house, brandishing their shotguns and rifles, they shouted for my father to come out. My mother went to the front door and opened it. Standing where they could see her pregnant condition, she told them that she was alone with her three small children, and that my father was away, preaching, in Milwaukee. The Klansmen shouted threats and warnings at her that we had better get out of town because "the good Christian white people" were not going to stand for my father's "spreading trouble" among the "good" Negroes of Omaha with the "back to Africa" preachings of Marcus Garvey.

My father, the Reverend Earl Little, was a Baptist minister, a dedicated organizer for Marcus Aurelius Garvey's U.N.I.A. (Universal Negro Improvement Association). With the help of such disciples as my father, Garvey, from his headquarters in New York City's Harlem, was raising the banner of black-race purity and exhorting the Negro masses to return to their ancestral African homeland—a cause which had made Garvey the most controversial black man on earth.

Still shouting threats, the Klansmen finally spurred their horses and galloped around the house, shattering every window pane with their gun butts. Then they rode off into the night, their torches flaring, as suddenly as they had come.

My father was enraged when he returned. He decided to wait until I was born—which would be soon—and then the family would move. I am not sure why he made this decision, for he was not a frightened Negro, as most

Why didn't his father turn to the law?

42

The Ku Klux Klan, a white terrorist group that originated in the South during Reconstruction, went through a second period of growth directly after World War I. Catholics, Jews, and foreigners, as well as blacks, were subject to its attacks. Has your family ever been under attack by a similar group?

then were, and many still are today. My father was a big, six-foot-four, very black man. He had only one eye. How he had lost the other one I have never known. He was from Reynolds, Georgia, where he had left school after the third or maybe fourth grade. He believed, as did Marcus Garvey, that freedom, independence and self-respect could never be achieved by the Negro in America, and that therefore the Negro should leave America to the white man and return to his African land of origin. Among the reasons my father had decided to risk and dedicate his life to help disseminate this philosophy among his people was that he had seen four of his six brothers die by violence, three of them killed by white men, including one by lynching. What my father could not know then was that of the remaining three, including himself, only one, my Uncle Jim, would die in bed, of natural causes. Northern white police were later to shoot my Uncle Oscar. And my father was finally himself to die by the white man's hands.

It has always been my belief that I, too, will die by violence. I have done all that I can to be prepared.

How did Malcolm X die?

• • •

. . . The teaching of Marcus Garvey stressed becoming independent of the white man. We went next, for some reason, to Lansing, Michigan. My father bought a house and soon, as had been his pattern, he was doing free-lance Christian preaching in local Negro Baptist churches, and during the week he was roaming about spreading word of Marcus Garvey.

He had begun to lay away savings for the store he had always wanted to own when, as always, some stupid local Uncle Tom Negroes began to funnel stories about his revolutionary beliefs to the local white people. This time, the get-out-of-town threats came from a local hate society called The Black Legion. They wore black robes instead of white. Soon, nearly everywhere my father went, Black Legionnaires were reviling him as an "uppity nigger" for wanting to own a store, for living outside the Lansing Negro district, for spreading unrest and dissension among "the good niggers."

As in Omaha, my mother was pregnant again, this time with my youngest sister. Shortly after Yvonne was born came the nightmare night

Why weren't blacks more united at this time?

in 1929, my earliest vivid memory. I remember being suddenly snatched awake into a frightening confusion of pistol shots and shouting and smoke and flames. My father had shouted and shot at the two white men who had set the fire and were running away. Our home was burning down around us. We were lunging and bumping and tumbling all over each other trying to escape. My mother, with the baby in her arms, just made it into the yard before the house crashed in, showering sparks. I remember we were outside in the night in our underwear, crying and yelling our heads off. The white police and firemen came and stood around watching as the house burned down to the ground.

•   •   •

After that, my memories are of the friction between my father and mother. They seemed to be nearly always at odds. Sometimes my father would beat her. It might have had something to do with the fact that my mother had a pretty good education. Where she got it I don't know. But an educated woman, I suppose, can't resist the temptation to correct an uneducated man. Every now and then, when she put those smooth words on him, he would grab her.

My father was also belligerent toward all of the children, except me. The older ones he would beat almost savagely if they broke any of his rules—and he had so many rules it was hard to know them all. Nearly all my whippings came from my mother. I've thought a lot about why. I actually believe that as anti-white as my father was, he was subconsciously so afflicted with the white man's brainwashing of Negroes that he inclined to favor the light ones, and I was his lightest child. Most Negro parents in those days would almost instinctively treat any lighter children better than they did the darker ones. It came directly from the slavery tradition that the "mulatto," because he was visibly nearer to white, was therefore "better."

Is it plausible that a man so conscious of his black heritage would think this way?

•   •   •

Back when I was growing up, the "successful" Lansing Negroes were such as waiters and bootblacks. To be a janitor at some downtown store was to be highly respected. The real "elite," the "big shots," the "voices of the race," were the waiters at the Lansing Country Club and the shoeshine boys at the state capitol. The only Negroes who really had any money were the ones in the numbers racket, or who ran the gambling houses, or who in some other way lived parasitically off the poorest ones, who were the masses. No Negroes were hired then by Lansing's big Oldsmobile plant, or the Reo plant. (Do you remember the Reo? It was manufactured in Lansing, and R. E. Olds, the man after whom it was named, also lived in Lansing. When the war came along, they hired some Negro janitors.) The bulk of the Negroes were either on Welfare, or W.P.A., or they starved.

•   •   •

My mother at this time seemed to be always working—cooking, washing, ironing, cleaning, and fussing over us eight children. And she was usually either arguing with or not speaking to my father. One cause of friction was that she had strong ideas about what she wouldn't eat—and didn't want *us* to eat—including pork and rabbit, both of which my father loved dearly. He was a real Georgia Negro, and he believed in eating plenty of what we in Harlem today call "soul food."

I've said that my mother was the one who whipped me—at least she did whenever she wasn't ashamed to let the neighbors think she was killing

When Malcolm X was a child, blacks were largely excluded from automobile assembly-line work. Now they make up a sizable proportion of automobile workers. Is this an indication that the American Dream is becoming accessible to blacks? Is this an improvement?

me. For if she even acted as though she was about to raise her hand to me, I would open my mouth and let the world know about it. If anybody was passing by out on the road, she would either change her mind or just give me a few licks.

Thinking about it now, I feel definitely that just as my father favored me for being lighter than the other children, my mother gave me more hell for the same reason. She was very light herself but she favored the ones who were darker. Wilfred, I know, was particularly her angel. I remember that she would tell me to get out of the house and "Let the sun shine on you so you can get some color." She went out of her way never to let me become afflicted with a sense of color-superiority. I am sure that she treated me this way partly because of how she came to be light herself.

Did favoritism ever affect any of the punishments you received?

• • •

One afternoon in 1931 when Wilfred, Hilda, Philbert, and I* came home, my mother and father were having one of their arguments. There had lately been a lot of tension around the house because of Black Legion threats. Anyway, my father had taken one of the rabbits which we were raising, and ordered my mother to cook it. We raised rabbits, but sold them to whites. My father had taken a rabbit from the rabbit pen. He had pulled off the rabbit's head. He was so strong, he needed no knife to behead chickens or rabbits. With one twist of his big black hands he simply twisted off the head and threw the bleeding-necked thing back at my mother's feet.

My mother was crying. She started to skin the rabbit, preparatory to cooking it. But my father was so angry he slammed on out of the front door and started walking up the road toward town.

It was then that my mother had this vision. She had always been a strange woman in this sense, and had always had a strong intuition of things about to happen. And most of her children are the same way, I think. When something is about to happen, I can feel something, sense something. I never have known something to happen that has caught me completely off guard—except once. And that was when, years later, I discovered facts I couldn't believe about a man who, up until that discovery, I would gladly have given my life for.

* Malcolm X was one of eight children.—Ed.

Almost 5,000 blacks were the victims of lynchings in the fifty years following Reconstruction, many in the North and West. Most died by hanging, but there were other hideous mob actions, like that against Malcolm X's father. Is the decline in such overt violence a sign of improved racial relations?

My father was well up the road when my mother ran screaming out onto the porch. "*Early*! *Early*!" She screamed his name. She clutched up her apron in one hand, and ran down across the yard and into the road. My father turned around. He saw her. For some reason, considering how angry he had been when he left, he waved at her. But he kept on going.

She told me later, my mother did, that she had a vision of my father's end. All the rest of the afternoon, she was not herself, crying and nervous and upset. She finished cooking the rabbit and put the whole thing in the warmer part of the black stove. When my father was not back home by our bedtime, my mother hugged and clutched us, and we felt strange, not knowing what to do, because she had never acted like that.

I remember waking up to the sound of my mother's screaming again. When I scrambled out, I saw the police in the living room; they were trying to calm her down. She had snatched on her clothes to go with them. And all of us children who were staring knew without anyone having to say it that something terrible had happened to our father.

My mother was taken by the police to the hospital, and to a room where a sheet was over my father in a bed, and she wouldn't look, she was afraid to look. Probably it was wise that she didn't. My father's skull, on one side, was crushed in, I was told later. Negroes in Lansing have always whispered that he was attacked, and then laid across some tracks for a streetcar to run over him. His body was cut almost in half.

He lived two and a half hours in that condition. Negroes then were stronger than they are now, especially Georgia Negroes. Negroes born in Georgia had to be strong simply to survive.

It was morning when we children at home got the word that he was dead. I was six. I can remember a vague commotion, the house filled up with people crying, saying bitterly that the white Black Legion had finally gotten him. My mother was hysterical. In the bedroom, women were holding smelling salts under her nose. She was still hysterical at the funeral.

I don't have a very clear memory of the funeral, either. Oddly, the main thing I remember is that it wasn't in a church, and that surprised me, since my father was a preacher, and I had been where he preached people's funerals in churches. But his was in a funeral home.

And I remember that during the service a big black fly came down and landed on my father's face, and Wilfred sprang up from his chair and he shooed the fly away, and he came groping back to his chair—there were folding chairs for us to sit on—and the tears were streaming down his face. When we went by the casket, I remember that I thought that it looked as if my father's strong black face had been dusted with flour, and I wished they hadn't put on such a lot of it.

What effect might this have had on a young boy?

• • •

So there we were. My mother was thirty-four years old now, with no husband, no provider or protector to take care of her eight children. But some kind of a family routine got going again. And for as long as the first insurance money lasted, we did all right.

Wilfred, who was a pretty stable fellow, began to act older than his age. I think he had the sense to see, when the rest of us didn't, what was in the wind for us. He quietly quit school and went to town in search of work. He took any kind of job he could find and he would come home, dog-tired, in the evenings, and give whatever he had made to my mother.

Hilda, who always had been quiet, too, attended to the babies. Philbert and I didn't contribute anything. We just fought all the time—each other at home, and then at school we would team up and fight white kids. Sometimes the fights would be racial in nature, but they might be about anything.

Reginald came under my wing. Since he had grown out of the toddling stage, he and I had become very close. I suppose I enjoyed the fact that he was the little one, under me, who looked up to me.

My mother began to buy on credit. My father had always been very strongly against credit. "Credit is the first step into debt and back into slavery," he had always said. And then she went to work herself. She would go into Lansing and find different jobs—in housework, or sewing—for white people. They didn't realize, usually, that she was a Negro. A lot of white people around there didn't want Negroes in their houses.

She would do fine until in some way or other it got to people who she was, whose widow she was. And then she would be let go. I remember how she used to come home crying, but trying to hide it, because she had lost a job that she needed so much.

What options were open to his mother? Do black women have more options today?

Once when one of us—I cannot remember which—had to go for something to where she was working, and the people saw us, and realized she was actually a Negro, she was fired on the spot, and she came home crying, this time not hiding it.

When the state Welfare people began coming to our house, we would come from school sometimes and find them talking with our mother, asking a thousand questions. They acted and looked at her, and at us, and around in our house, in a way that had about it the feeling—at least for me—that we were not people. In their eyesight we were just *things*, that was all.

My mother began to receive two checks—a Welfare check and, I believe, a widow's pension. The checks helped. But they weren't enough, as many of us as there were. When they came, about the first of the month, one always was already owed in full, if not more, to the man at the grocery store. And, after that, the other one didn't last long.

We began to go swiftly downhill. The physical downhill wasn't as quick as the psychological. My mother was, above everything else, a proud woman, and it took its toll on her that she was accepting charity. And her feelings were communicated to us.

She would speak sharply to the man at the grocery store for padding the bill, telling him that she wasn't ignorant, and he didn't like that. She would talk back sharply to the state Welfare people, telling them that she was a grown woman, able to raise her children, that it wasn't necessary for them to keep coming around so much, meddling in our lives. And they didn't like that.

But the monthly Welfare check was their pass. They acted as if they owned us, as if we were their private property. As much as my mother would have liked to, she couldn't keep them out. She would get particularly incensed when they began insisting upon drawing us older children aside, one at a time, out on the porch or somewhere, and asking us questions, or telling us things—against our mother and against each other.

What statement is the author making about the effects of welfare on the recipient and the donor? Do you agree?

48

• • •

Then, about in late 1934, I would guess, something began to happen. Some kind of psychological deterioration hit our family circle and began to eat away our pride. Perhaps it was the constant tangible evidence that we were destitute. We had known other families who had gone on relief. We had known without anyone in our home ever expressing it that we had felt prouder not to be at the depot where the free food was passed out. And, now, we were among them. At school, the "on relief" finger suddenly was pointed at us, too, and sometimes it was said aloud.

It seemed that everything to eat in our house was stamped Not To Be Sold. All Welfare food bore this stamp to keep the recipients from selling it. It's a wonder we didn't come to think of Not To Be Sold as a brand name.

Sometimes, instead of going home from school, I walked the two miles up the road into Lansing. I began drifting from store to store, hanging around outside where things like apples were displayed in boxes and barrels and baskets, and I would watch my chance and steal me a treat. You know what a treat was to me? Anything!

Or I began to drop in about dinnertime at the home of some family that we knew. I knew that they knew exactly why I was there, but they never embarrassed me by letting on. They would invite me to stay for supper, and I would stuff myself.

Especially, I liked to drop in and visit at the Gohannas' home. They were nice, older people, and great churchgoers. I had watched them lead the jumping and shouting when my father preached. They had, living with them—they were raising him—a nephew whom everyone called "Big Boy," and he and I got along fine. Also living with the Gohannas was old Mrs. Adcock, who went with them to church. She was always trying to help anybody she could, visiting anyone she heard was sick, carrying them something. She was the one who, years later, would tell me something that I remembered a long time: "Malcolm, there's one thing I like about you. You're no good, but you don't try to hide it. You are not a hypocrite."

The more I began to stay away from home and visit people and steal from the stores, the more aggressive I became in my inclinations. I never wanted to wait for anything.

• • •

When I began to get caught stealing now and then, the state Welfare people began to focus on me when they came to our house. I can't remember how I first became aware that they were talking of taking me away. What I first remember along that line was my mother raising a storm about being able to bring up her own children. She would whip me for stealing, and I would try to alarm the neighborhood with my yelling. One thing I have always been proud of is that I never raised my hand against my mother.

In the summertime, at night, in addition to all the other things we did, some of us boys would slip out down the road, or across the pastures, and go "cooning" watermelons. White people always associated watermelons with Negroes, and they sometimes called Negroes "coons" among all the other names, and so stealing watermelons became "cooning" them. If white boys were doing it, it implied that they were only acting like Negroes. Whites have always hidden or justified all of the guilts they could by ridiculing or blaming Negroes.

One Halloween night, I remember that a bunch of us were out tipping over those old country outhouses, and one old farmer—I guess he had

Mario Puzo looks upon his poverty-stricken childhood as one of the happiest times of his life. Account for the difference of attitude in Malcolm X.

How is his growing aggressiveness related to his poverty?

tipped over enough in his day—had set a trap for us. Always, you sneak up from behind the outhouse, then you gang together and push it, to tip it over. This farmer had taken his outhouse off the hole, and set it just in *front* of the hole. Well, we came sneaking up in single file, in the darkness, and the two white boys in the lead fell down into the outhouse hole neck deep. They smelled so bad it was all we could stand to get them out, and that finished us all for that Halloween. I had just missed falling in myself. The whites were so used to taking the lead, this time it had really gotten them in the hole.

Thus, in various ways, I learned various things. I picked strawberries, and though I can't recall what I got per crate for picking, I remember that after working hard all one day, I wound up with about a dollar, which was a whole lot of money in those times. I was so hungry, I didn't know what to do. I was walking away toward town with visions of buying something good to eat, and this older white boy I knew, Richard Dixon, came up and asked me if I wanted to match nickels. He had plenty of change for my dollar. In about a half hour, he had all the change back, including my dollar, and instead of going to town to buy something, I went home with nothing, and I was bitter. But that was nothing compared to what I felt when I found out later that he had cheated. There is a way that you can catch and hold the nickel and make it come up the way you want. This was my first lesson about gambling: if you see somebody winning all the time, he isn't gambling, he's cheating. Later on in life, if I were continuously losing in any gambling situation, I would watch very closely. It's like the Negro in America seeing the white man win all the time. He's a professional gambler; he has all the cards and the odds stacked on his side, and he has always dealt to our people from the bottom of the deck.

Is this an accurate analogy?

• • •

It was about this time that the large, dark man from Lansing began visiting. I don't remember how or where he and my mother met. It may

In 1895 Booker T. Washington, a leading black intellectual, proposed that black advancement would come only if blacks carved out a place of economic service for themselves in their communities that would not antagonize whites. Toward this end he established Tuskegee Institute (pictured on the left) as a training ground for black farmers, mechanics, and domestic servants. The blacks shown here—a blacksmith and a trainman—are in lines of work that Washington would have approved.

In the 1930s, the period Malcolm X recalls here, unemployment was a much more severe problem for blacks than for whites, with three to four times as many blacks forced on to relief rolls as whites. Do you see any correlation between the kinds of jobs blacks occupied and why they were so hard-hit by the depression? What do you think of the philosophy that blacks should concentrate on making small economic gains?

have been through some mutual friends. I don't remember what the man's profession was. In 1935, in Lansing, Negroes didn't have anything you could call a profession. But the man, big and black, looked something like my father. I can remember his name, but there's no need to mention it. He was a single man, and my mother was a widow only thirty-six years old. The man was independent; naturally she admired that. She was having a hard time disciplining us, and a big man's presence alone would help. And if she had a man to provide, it would send the state people away forever.

We all understood without ever saying much about it. Or at least we had no objection. We took it in stride, even with some amusement among us, that when the man came, our mother would be all dressed up in the best that she had—she still was a good-looking woman—and she would act differently, lighthearted and laughing, as we hadn't seen her act in years.

It went on for about a year, I guess. And then, about 1936, or 1937, the man from Lansing jilted my mother suddenly. He just stopped coming to see her. From what I later understood, he finally backed away from taking on the responsibility of those eight mouths to feed. He was afraid of so many of us. To this day, I can see the trap that Mother was in, saddled with all of us. And I can also understand why he would shun taking on such a tremendous responsibility.

But it was a terrible shock to her. It was the beginning of the end of reality for my mother. When she began to sit around and walk around talking to herself—almost as though she was unaware that we were there—it became increasingly terrifying.

The state people saw her weakening. That was when they began the definite steps to take me away from home. They began to tell me how nice it was going to be at the Gohannas' home, where the Gohannas and Big Boy and Mrs. Adcock had all said how much they liked me, and would like to have me live with them.

I liked all of them, too. But I didn't want to leave Wilfred. I looked up to and admired my big brother. I didn't want to leave Hilda, who was like my second mother. Or Philbert; even in our fighting, there was a feeling of brotherly union. Or Reginald, especially, who was weak with his hernia condition, and who looked up to me as his big brother who looked out for him, as I looked up to Wilfred. And I had nothing, either, against the babies, Yvonne, Wesley, and Robert.

As my mother talked to herself more and more, she gradually became less responsive to us. And less responsible. The house became less tidy. We began to be more unkempt. And usually, now, Hilda cooked.

We children watched our anchor giving way. It was something terrible that you couldn't get your hands on, yet you couldn't get away from. It was a sensing that something bad was going to happen. We younger ones leaned more and more heavily on the relative strength of Wilfred and Hilda, who were the oldest.

When finally I was sent to the Gohannas' home, at least in a surface way I was glad. I remember that when I left home with the state man, my mother said one thing: "Don't let them feed him any pig."

· · ·

Eventually my mother suffered a complete breakdown, and the court orders were finally signed. They took her to the State Mental Hospital at Kalamazoo.

It was seventy-some miles from Lansing, about an hour and a half on the bus. A Judge McClellan in Lansing had authority over me and all of my

What does this say about why, in many black families, the mother is the head of the household?

brothers and sisters. We were "state children," court wards; he had the full say-so over us. A white man in charge of a black man's children! Nothing but legal, modern slavery—however kindly intentioned.

My mother remained in the same hospital at Kalamazoo for about twenty-six years. Later, when I was still growing up in Michigan, I would go to visit her every so often. Nothing that I can imagine could have moved me as deeply as seeing her pitiful state. In 1963, we got my mother out of the hospital, and she now lives there in Lansing with Philbert and his family.

It was so much worse than if it had been a physical sickness, for which a cause might be known, medicine given, a cure effected. Every time I visited her, when finally they led her—a case, a number—back inside from where we had been sitting together, I felt worse.

My last visit, when I knew I would never come to see her again—there—was in 1952. I was twenty-seven. My brother Philbert had told me that on his last visit, she had recognized him somewhat. "In spots," he said.

But she didn't recognize me at all.

She stared at me. She didn't know who I was.

Her mind, when I tried to talk, to reach her, was somewhere else. I asked, "Mama, do you know what day it is?"

She said, staring, "All the people have gone."

I can't describe how I felt. The woman who had brought me into the world, and nursed me, and advised me, and chastised me, and loved me, didn't know me. It was as if I was trying to walk up the side of a hill of feathers. I looked at her. I listened to her "talk." But there was nothing I could do.

I truly believe that if ever a state social agency destroyed a family, it destroyed ours. We wanted and tried to stay together. Our home didn't have to be destroyed. But the Welfare, the courts, and their doctor, gave us the one-two-three punch. And ours was not the only case of this kind.

I knew I wouldn't be back to see my mother again because it could make me a very vicious and dangerous person—knowing how they had looked at us as numbers and as a case in their book, not as human beings. And knowing that my mother in there was a statistic that didn't have to be, that existed because of a society's failure, hypocrisy, greed, and lack of mercy and compassion. Hence I have no mercy or compassion in me for a society that will crush people, and then penalize them for not being able to stand up under the weight.

On the whole, has society been more destructive or supportive of your family? In what ways?

I have rarely talked to anyone about my mother, for I believe that I am capable of killing a person, without hesitation, who happened to make the wrong kind of remark about my mother. So I purposely don't make any opening for some fool to step into.

Back then when our family was destroyed, in 1937, Wilfred and Hilda were old enough so that the state let them stay on their own in the big four-room house that my father had built. Philbert was placed with another family in Lansing, a Mrs. Hackett, while Reginald and Wesley went to live with a family called Williams, who were friends of my mother's. And Yvonne and Robert went to live with a West Indian family named McGuire.

Do you think the state could have acted differently?

Separated though we were, all of us maintained fairly close touch around Lansing—in school and out—whenever we could get together. Despite the artificially created separation and distance between us, we still remained very close in our feelings toward each other.

The Feminine Mystique
betty friedan

The American Dream of success has usually been assumed to be a masculine ideal. To make a lot of money or rise to a position of power and influence, to dream of changing the world, or even merely to have a career has usually been the male prerogative. Prior to the contemporary women's liberation movement, the woman was left to dream of becoming a wife and mother. In the following selection, Betty Friedan, one of the early leaders of the women's movement, describes the problems of identity and self-image for women today. Has it always been this way? Is it easier for women now to find a sense of identity and purpose than it was for your mother's generation? Or do you still see a particular dilemma faced by women when they are twenty-one and have to decide what to do with their lives? Also, given the strength of the liberation movement, how do you think males are reacting—is there more resistance than understanding? Give this some thought as you read what Betty Friedan has to say.

I discovered a strange thing, interviewing women of my own generation over the past ten years. When we were growing up, many of us could not see ourselves beyond the age of twenty-one. We had no image of our own future, of ourselves as women.

I remember the stillness of a spring afternoon on the Smith campus in 1942, when I came to a frightening dead end in my own vision of the future. A few days earlier, I had received a notice that I had won a graduate fellowship. During the congratulations, underneath my excitement, I felt a strange uneasiness; there was a question that I did not want to think about.

"Is this really what I want to be?" The question shut me off, cold and alone, from the girls talking and studying on the sunny hillside behind the college house. I thought I was going to be a psychologist. But if I wasn't sure, what did I want to be? I felt the future closing in—and I could not see myself in it at all. I had no image of myself, stretching beyond college. I had come at seventeen from a Midwestern town, an unsure girl; the wide

An entire industry has grown up around a woman's "need" for cosmetics. A trip to the beauty salon was, and in some cases still is, a weekly ritual. Why might women of your mother's generation have participated in this ritual?

horizons of the world and the life of the mind had been opened to me. I had begun to know who I was and what I wanted to do. I could not go back now. I could not go home again, to the life of my mother and the women of our town, bound to home, bridge, shopping, children, husband, charity, clothes. But now that the time had come to make my own future, to take the deciding step, I suddenly did not know what I wanted to be.

I took the fellowship, but the next spring, under the alien California sun of another campus, the question came again, and I could not put it out of my mind. I had won another fellowship that would have committed me to research for my doctorate, to a career as professional psychologist. "Is this really what I want to be?" The decision now truly terrified me. I lived in a terror of indecision for days, unable to think of anything else.

The question was not important, I told myself. No question was important to me that year but love. We walked in the Berkeley hills and a boy said: "Nothing can come of this, between us. I'll never win a fellowship like yours." Did I think I would be choosing, irrevocably, the cold loneliness of that afternoon if I went on? I gave up the fellowship, in relief. But for years afterward, I could not read a word of the science that once I had thought of as my future life's work; the reminder of its loss was too painful.

Why was she afraid of success? Are men ever indecisive in this way?

55

I never could explain, hardly knew myself, why I gave up this career. I lived in the present, working on newspapers with no particular plan. I married, had children, lived according to the feminine mystique as a suburban housewife. But still the question haunted me. I could sense no purpose in my life, I could find no peace, until I finally faced it and worked out my own answer.

What does she mean by "feminine mystique"?

I discovered, talking to Smith seniors in 1959, that the question is no less terrifying to girls today. Only they answer it now in a way that my generation found, after half a lifetime, not to be an answer at all. These girls, mostly seniors, were sitting in the living room of the college house, having coffee. It was not too different from such an evening when I was a senior, except that many more of the girls wore rings on their left hands. I asked the ones around me what they planned to be. The engaged ones spoke of weddings, apartments, getting a job as a secretary while husband finished school. The others, after a hostile silence, gave vague answers about this job or that, graduate study, but no one had any real plans. A blonde with a ponytail asked me the next day if I had believed the things they had said. "None of it was true," she told me. "We don't like to be asked what we want to do. None of us know. None of us even like to think about it. The ones who are going to be married right away are the lucky ones. They don't have to think about it."

Is the question equally as terrifying in the 1970s?

But I noticed that night that many of the engaged girls, sitting silently around the fire while I asked the others about jobs, had also seemed angry about something. "They don't want to think about not going on," my ponytailed informant said. "They know they're not going to use their education. They'll be wives and mothers. You can say you're going to keep on reading and be interested in the community. But that's not the same. You won't really go on. It's a disappointment to know you're going to stop now, and not go on and use it."

In counterpoint, I heard the words of a woman, fifteen years after she left college, a doctor's wife, mother of three, who said over coffee in her New England kitchen:

> The tragedy was, nobody ever looked us in the eye and said you have to decide what you want to do with your life, besides being your husband's wife and children's mother. I never thought it through until I was thirty-six, and my husband was so busy with his practice that he couldn't entertain me every night. The three boys were in school all day. I kept on trying to have babies despite an Rh discrepancy. After two miscarriages, they said I must stop. I thought that my own growth and evolution were over. I always knew as a child that I was going to grow up and go to college, and then get married, and that's as far as a girl has to think. After that, your husband determines and fills your life. It wasn't until I got so lonely as the doctor's wife and kept screaming at the kids because they didn't fill my life that I realized I had to make my own life. I still had to decide what I wanted to be. I hadn't finished evolving at all. But it took me ten years to think it through.

The feminine mystique permits, even encourages, women to ignore the question of their identity. The mystique says they can answer the question "Who am I?" by saying "Tom's wife . . . Mary's mother." But I don't think the mystique would have such power over American women if they did not fear to face this terrifying blank which makes them unable to see themselves after twenty-one. The truth is—and how long it has been true, I'm not sure, but it was true in my generation and it is true of girls growing up today—an American woman no longer has a private image to tell her who she is, or can be, or wants to be.

KEEP YOUR SHIRT ON

'TILL YOU SEE

hartog

I'M JUST HIS WIFE

BUT AFTER ALL, it was *my* idea that he get himself a smoother, Barbasol Face. Now I have to compete with other women at parties to get near that handsome man! It's unfair. I married him despite the rough skin and bristly beard he used to have because of old-fashioned shaving methods.

THAT CHEEK TO CHEEK WALK is hard to resist when a man has a Barbasol Face. For modern Barbasol contains beneficial oils that not only soften the beard, but also soothe the skin, helping to leave it soft and fresh and smooth.

YOU FACE YOUR MIRROR every morning with a smile when Barbasol's handy. Tender skin? Don't worry. Here's the coolest, smilingest, most comforting shave a man can have. You'll agree after a trial of ten days or so. 25¢ and 50¢ tubes, 75¢ jar. Barbasol Blades, 5 for 10¢, 15 for 25¢.

Barbasol

For modern shaving —
No Brush—No Lather—No Rub-in

Some of the advertising copy of a generation ago, particularly that directed toward men, presented a clear picture of women as sexual objects. The advertisement for men's shirts on the left is a blatant example. More subtle is the advertisement for shaving cream that suggests that a man who uses the product will be the cause of intense sexual rivalry among women—with the man's wife making a poor showing in the match. How does such advertising illustrate the point that women of Friedan's generation lacked an identity of their own?

Is the public image of woman changing any?

The public image, in the magazines and television commercials, is designed to sell washing machines, cake mixes, deodorants, detergents, rejuvenating face creams, hair tints. But the power of that image, on which companies spend millions of dollars for television time and ad space, comes from this: American women no longer know who they are. They are sorely in need of a new image to help them find their identity. As the motivational researchers keep telling the advertisers, American women are so unsure of who they should be that they look to this glossy public image to decide every detail of their lives. They look for the image they will no longer take from their mothers.

In my generation, many of us knew that we did not want to be like our mothers, even when we loved them. We could not help but see their disappointment. Did we understand, or only resent, the sadness, the emptiness, that made them hold too fast to us, try to live our lives, run our fathers' lives, spend their days shopping or yearning for things that never seemed to satisfy them, no matter how much money they cost? Strangely, many mothers who loved their daughters—and mine was one—did not want their daughters to grow up like them either. They knew we needed something more.

But even if they urged, insisted, fought to help us educate ourselves, even if they talked with yearning of careers that were not open to them, they could not give us an image of what we could be. They could only tell us that their lives were too empty, tied to home; that children, cooking, clothes, bridge, and charities were not enough. A mother might tell her daughter, spell it out, "Don't be just a housewife like me." But that daughter, sensing that her mother was too frustrated to savor the love of

Women may not have wanted their daughters to grow up like them, but they often reinforced stereotyped roles through what they permitted their children to do. Thus, a boy's free time might be filled with a job like a paper route, while a girl was expected to help with the housework. Compare your upbringing in this respect with that of your mother or father.

her husband and children, might feel: "I will succeed where my mother failed, I will fulfill myself as a woman," and never read the lesson of her mother's life.

Recently, interviewing high-school girls who had started out full of promise and talent, but suddenly stopped their education, I began to see new dimensions to the problem of feminine conformity. These girls, it seemed at first, were merely following the typical curve of feminine adjustment. Earlier interested in geology or poetry, they now were interested only in being popular; to get boys to like them, they had concluded, it was better to be like all the other girls. On closer examination, I found that these girls were so terrified of becoming like their mothers that they could not see themselves at all. They were afraid to grow up. They had to copy in identical detail the composite image of the popular girl—denying what was best in themselves out of fear of femininity as they saw it in their mothers. One of these girls, seventeen years old, told me:

Are there any ethnic, regional, or religious differences in how girls grow up to be women in America?

> I want so badly to feel like the other girls. I never get over this feeling of being a neophyte, not initiated. When I get up and have to cross a room, it's like I'm a beginner, or have some terrible affliction, and I'll never learn. I go to the local hangout after school and sit there for hours talking about clothes and hairdos and the twist, and I'm not that interested, so it's an effort. But I found out I could make them like me—just do what they do, dress like them, talk like them, not do things that are different. I guess I even started to make myself not different inside.
>
> I used to write poetry. The guidance office says I have this creative ability and I should be at the top of the class and have a great future. But things like that aren't what you need to be popular. The important thing for a girl is to be popular.
>
> Now I go out with boy after boy, and it's such an effort because I'm not myself with them. It makes you feel even more alone. And besides, I'm afraid of where it's going to lead. Pretty soon, all my differences will be smoothed out, and I'll be the kind of girl that could be a housewife.
>
> I don't want to think of growing up. If I had children, I'd want them to stay the same age. If I had to watch them grow up, I'd see myself growing older, and I wouldn't want to. My mother says she can't sleep at night, she's sick with worry over what I might do. When I was little, she wouldn't let me cross the street alone, long after the other kids did.
>
> I can't see myself as being married and having children. It's as if I wouldn't have any personality myself. My mother's like a rock that's been smoothed by the waves, like a void. She's put so much into her family that there's nothing left, and she resents us because she doesn't get enough in return. But sometimes it seems like there's nothing there. My mother doesn't serve any purpose except cleaning the house. She isn't happy, and she doesn't make my father happy. If she didn't care about us children at all, it would have the same effect as caring too much. It makes you want to do the opposite. I don't think it's really love. When I was little and I ran in all excited to tell her I'd learned how to stand on my head, she was never listening.
>
> Lately, I look into the mirror, and I'm so afraid I'm going to look like my mother. It frightens me, to catch myself being like her in gestures or speech or anything. I'm not like her in so many ways, but if I'm like her in this one way, perhaps I'll turn out like my mother after all. And that terrifies me.

Is this still important today?

Can you?

And so the seventeen-year-old was so afraid of being a woman like her mother that she turned her back on all the things in herself and all the opportunities that would have made her a different woman, to copy from the outside the "popular" girls. And finally, in panic at losing herself, she turned her back on her own popularity and defied the conventional good behavior that would have won her a college scholarship. For lack of an image that would help her grow up as a woman true to herself, she retreated into the beatnik vacuum.

Is refusing the opportunity for a career a retreat?

In the version of the American Dream permitted to women of past generations, success in life was measured by the kind of marriage they made. To what extent is this still the case?

●　●　●

The only other kind of women I knew, growing up, were the old-maid high-school teachers; the librarian; the one woman doctor in our town, who cut her hair like a man; and a few of my college professors. None of these women lived in the warm center of life as I had known it at home. Many had not married or had children. I dreaded being like them, even the ones who taught me truly to respect my own mind and use it, to feel that I had a part in the world. I never knew a woman, when I was growing up, who used her mind, played her own part in the world, and also loved, and had children.

Did you have any more positive images when growing up?

60

Mine was the first college generation to run head-on into the new mystique of feminine fulfillment. Before then, while most women did indeed end up as housewives and mothers, the point of education was to discover the life of the mind, to pursue truth and to take a place in the world. There was a sense, already dulling when I went to college, that we would be New Women. Our world would be much larger than home. Forty per cent of my college class at Smith had career plans. But I remember how, even then, some of the seniors, suffering the pangs of that bleak fear of the future, envied the few who escaped it by getting married right away.

Did your mother go to college? Do you think that fact made a difference in her outlook?

The ones we envied then are suffering that terror now at forty. "Never have decided what kind of woman I am. Too much personal life in college. Wish I'd studied more science, history, government, gone deeper into philosophy," one wrote on an alumnae questionnaire, fifteen years later. "Still trying to find the rock to build on. Wish I had finished college. I got married instead." "Wish I'd developed a deeper and more creative life of my own and that I hadn't become engaged and married at nineteen. Having expected the ideal in marriage, including a hundred-per-cent devoted husband, it was a shock to find this isn't the way it is," wrote a mother of six.

• • •

It is my thesis that the core of the problem for women today is not sexual but a problem of identity—a stunting or evasion of growth that is perpetuated by the feminine mystique. It is my thesis that as the Victorian culture did not permit women to accept or gratify their basic sexual needs, our culture does not permit women to accept or gratify their basic need to grow and fulfill their potentialities as human beings, a need which is not solely defined by their sexual role.

What does the author mean by "a problem of identity"?

• • •

The search for identity is not new . . . in American thought—though in every generation, each man who writes about it discovers it anew. In America, from the beginning, it has somehow been understood that men must thrust into the future; the pace has always been too rapid for man's identity to stand still. In every generation, many men have suffered misery, unhappiness, and uncertainty because they could not take the image of the man they wanted to be from their fathers. The search for identity of the young man who can't go home again has always been a major theme of American writers. And it has always been considered right in America, good, for men to suffer these agonies of growth, to search for and find their own identities. The farm boy went to the city, the garment-maker's son became a doctor, Abraham Lincoln taught himself to read— these were more than rags-to-riches stories. They were an integral part of the American dream. The problem for many was money, race, color, class, which barred them from choice—not what they would be if they were free to choose.

Even today a young man learns soon enough that he must decide who he wants to be. If he does not decide in junior high, in high school, in college, he must somehow come to terms with it by twenty-five or thirty, or he is lost. But this search for identity is seen as a greater problem now because more and more boys cannot find images in our culture—from their fathers or other men—to help them in their search. The old frontiers have been

Can the role of housewife and mother give women an identity as a human being, in Friedan's sense?

conquered, and the boundaries of the new are not so clearly marked. More and more young men in America today suffer an identity crisis for want of any image of man worth pursuing, for want of a purpose that truly realizes their human abilities.

But why have theorists not recognized this same identity crisis in women? In terms of the old conventions and the new feminine mystique women are not expected to grow up to find out who they are, to choose their human identity. Anatomy is woman's destiny, say the theorists of femininity; the identity of woman is determined by her biology.

But is it? More and more women are asking themselves this question. As if they were waking from a coma, they ask, "Where am I . . . what am I

If liberated, won't women encounter the same problem—the lack of anything worth pursuing—as men? Would this be desirable?

doing here?" For the first time in their history, women are becoming aware of an identity crisis in their own lives, a crisis which began many generations ago, has grown worse with each succeeding generation, and will not end until they, or their daughters, turn an unknown corner and make of themselves and their lives the new image that so many women now so desperately need.

In a sense that goes beyond any one woman's life, I think this is the crisis of women growing up—a turning point from an immaturity that has been called femininity to full human identity. I think women had to suffer this crisis of identity, which began a hundred years ago, and have to suffer it still today, simply to become fully human.

ASSIGNMENT 2
ESSAY ON SOCIAL FORCES

The autobiographical statements in this chapter cut across ethnic, racial, class, sex, and geographical lines, and reflect the American Dream of three very different young people of a generation ago. Try to define in your own terms what their aspirations were. What, for instance, was the dream of Puzo on the streets of Hell's Kitchen? or of Malcolm X after his father's death? or of Friedan in her college years? Then you can tackle the question of the specific ways that the dreams of an earlier generation of young people compare with your own and those of your friends. If possible, ask your parents or others a generation older what they hoped for in their youth; whether or not they achieved it; if they did, how, if they did not, why.

After gathering this information, write a brief essay (say, 1,500 words) contrasting the expectations that individuals have for themselves and their society today with the hopes of a generation ago. Perhaps you might want to organize your thoughts around the question: What changes in self-perception and in society have occurred since your parents were your age?

three

YOUR PEOPLE AND THE GREAT MIGRATIONS

Think for a moment about your grandparents. Imagine, if you can, the time when they were your age. (They really were, you know.) If you began to count the ways in which their world differed from the present, you would soon realize how shocking many of the changes are, or at least seem to be. No television or radio, possibly no automobiles or electricity or indoor plumbing. Certainly, no suburbs, Super Bowls, or supermarkets. And, no toothpaste in a tube or *Time* magazine, rock music, or six-packs.

But is that important? Significant aspects of human existence are timeless and transcend material and physical changes. Your grandparents, when young, dreamed dreams. They surely hoped to fulfill themselves to the extent that their society would permit. And it is precisely this crucial intersection of man and society that reveals the effects that massive historical forces have on each individual. Of course, these forces vary with the times. Our ancestors defined their expectations in terms of the political, social, and cultural environment in which they lived. Constraints that the twentieth century has gradually begun to remove circumscribed the human potential of earlier generations. Racism, religious and class oppression, and functional illiteracy were among the social forces that affected our ancestors' sense of the possible. So, many of them, refusing to accept constraints, came to the New World.

If you can discover what it was that your grandparents expected life to provide, you are on the road to a more comprehensive understanding of the options that society presented to your parents. By beginning to show you how American society has treated your family, this exercise in family history may lead you to ask why it has been so, an important step in confronting your own future.

Somewhere in the recent past your family has doubtless participated in one of the great movements of people that created this country. Someone in your family has been a part of the migration from Europe or Asia or Africa to America, the movement from East to West or from South to North, the transplantation from rural to urban living. Do you know whether your grandparents and/or great-grandparents were born in a foreign country, or whether they made any significant moves in this country?

This chapter emphasizes mobility—the uprooting of people and their resettlement in places where language, customs, and tradition were often quite different. Although the readings are set in the half-century between the Civil War and World War I, the range of experiences is timeless. They should give you some sense of those ancestors of yours who underwent this cycle of human drama, punctuated perhaps by the pain of leaving forever ancestral villages and dear friends, perhaps by a joyful sense of release from poverty and oppression.

Travel has become so easy that we sometimes forget how difficult it was for our ancestors to move from one place to another. Americans remain a mobile people: one out of every five of us moves every year. Businessmen and vacationers fly to Europe or across the country without a second thought. Millions of Americans are so accustomed to driving hundreds of miles in their automobiles over weekends that the inconvenience of a gasoline shortage takes on the proportions of a crisis. And, while surely unusual, the example of a man we know who lives in New York and works in Chicago is a sign of our times. Yet the lifetime of this country's "senior citizens" reaches back before the jet plane and automobile, when fifteen to twenty-five miles by horse-drawn wagon was an exhausting day's work. America's railroads in 1880 or 1920 may have offered better service than is available today between most cities, but getting across the ocean or across the continent was often a difficult and dangerous experience, especially for immigrants and other travelers with little money.

Yet the immigrants to the United States arrived in overwhelming numbers from around the globe. Over 35 million Europeans came to this country between 1815 and 1915, people of widely varying racial and ethnic stock who carried with them the cultural baggage of dozens of societies. The earliest arrivals were English, French, German, Irish, Scotch, and Scandinavian. Later, central, southern, and eastern European nationals predominated—Greeks, Romanians, Hungarians, Austrians, Italians, Balts, Poles, Russians, and several kinds of Slavs. Indeed, the word "immigrants" almost always brings to mind a picture of people huddled together at Ellis Island in New York harbor shortly after arriving from Italy or eastern Europe. But Europeans were not the only immigrants. The Chinese had come to the West Coast as early as the 1840s, and the Japanese began to arrive in large numbers fifty years later. Mexicans and other Spanish-speaking peoples moved across the Western borderlands. And those Englishmen who came on the *Mayflower*, or the slaves captured and brought against their will from the west coast of Africa, were just as much immigrants as those who later arrived on ocean liners.

So they came, our ancestors, searching for a better life, or merely seeking to survive. While many remained to swell the populations of the coastal cities, millions of newcomers joined in the migration to the frontierlands, or to the cities of the interior. Useful generalizations about such a range of experience are difficult to make. One rather constant phenomenon, however, was discrimination. Long-enduring examples of bias against all nonwhite peoples, including those from Africa, Asia, and Hispanic America, are now fairly well recognized. Intolerance toward Catholics and Jews, the Irish, and southern and eastern Europeans has persisted well into the twentieth century. Legislation that discriminated against specific national groups was passed as early as the 1880s; in subsequent decades an often rabid

xenophobia underscored American political life. The culmination of this fear was the passage of a restrictive immigration law in 1924, which limited annual immigration to 2 percent of each national group present in the country in 1890, a clearly discriminatory act against east Europeans and other groups that made up a small proportion of the population in 1890.

One result of racial and ethnic discrimination was the preservation of major elements of old-country cultural patterns, customs, language, and religious practices. (The image of the United States as a great melting pot where different ethnic and racial groups are melded into Americans never had much basis in fact.) This inclination toward preserving racial and ethnic self-consciousness also resulted from failure to achieve the American Dream of security and happiness. First- and second-generation immigrants for the most part entered the social structure at the bottom. The dream dimmed, but persisted. However long the hours and low the wages, the memory of the old country's serfdom was worse. Besides, sons and daughters would inherit the dream, someday. The upward climb on the ladder to success would be long and slow for most members of the ethnic groups, and slower yet for nonwhites. Their persistent attachment to racial and ethnic self-identification seems to be a reflection of this ambivalent search for the American grail.

Before you read this chapter, think a bit about your own immigrant roots. Then, as you read, try to associate these selections with the experiences of your own ancestors, their uprooting and resettling, relative assimilation and survival. Perhaps the situation of the young bride going west—her descent from an older American family, her social position that gave her obvious opportunities, and her enjoyment in her new surroundings of a latitude not allowed in later times—was very much like that of your own grandmother or great-grandmother. Optimistic expectations also fill the other essays and may well reflect your relatives' feelings. The range of hope and despair shown by the Jews of the Lower East Side of New York City and by the blacks seeking salvation in the North is common to all men at all times.

The very first selection invites you to sense the dimensions of what must be the greatest folk migration in all of human history. Your own people are in there somewhere. You might be surprised at the tale your grandparents have to tell.

WORLD MIGRATION IN MODERN TIMES
L. S. Stavrianos

The immigration of millions of people to the United States was part of a mass migration unequaled in human history. Races and cultures that had previously remained segregated over the centuries intermixed after 1500, causing a tremendous impact on world history. What do you think the major results of this mass migration were? How many effects of the greatest movement of people in all of recorded time can you see in American society today? Can you locate the probable movement of your own ancestors in this great human saga?

The European discoveries led not only to new global horizons but also to a new global distribution of races. Prior to 1500 there existed, in effect, worldwide racial segregation. The Negroids were concentrated in sub-Saharan Africa and a few Pacific islands, the Mongoloids in Central Asia, Siberia, East Asia, and the Americas, and the Caucasoids in Europe, North Africa, the Middle East, and India. By 1763 this pattern had been fundamentally altered. In Asia, the Russians were beginning their slow migration across the Urals into Siberia. In Africa the Dutch had established a permanent settlement at the Cape, where the climate was favorable and the natives were too primitive to offer effective resistance. By 1763, 111 years after their landing at Capetown, the Dutch had pushed a considerable distance northward and were beginning to cross the Orange River.

By far the greatest change in racial composition occurred in the Americas. Estimates of the Indian population before 1492 vary tremendously, from 8 million to as high as 100 million. Whatever the figure may have been, there is no disagreement about the catastrophic effect of the European intrusion. Everywhere the Indians were decimated, by varying combinations or physical losses during the process of conquest, disruption of cultural patterns, psychological trauma of subjugation, imposition of forced labor, and introduction of alcohol and of new diseases. Within a century the total indigenous population appears to have declined by 90 to 95 per cent. Most badly hit were the Indians of the Caribbean islands and of the tropical coasts, where they disappeared completely within a generation. More resilient were the natives of the upland tropical regions and of lowland tropical areas such as those of Brazil and Paraguay. Although sustaining very heavy losses, they were able to recover and to constitute the stock from which most of the present-day American Indian population is derived. Only in the twentieth century has this population approached its original numbers in tropical America, while elsewhere it still lags far behind.

The disappearing Indians were replaced by waves of immigrants from Europe and Africa. The resulting settlements were of three varieties. One consisted of the Spanish and Portuguese colonies in which Iberian settlers constituted a permanent resident aristocracy among subjugated Indians in the highlands and imported Negro slaves in the lowlands. Since there

Why do you think the initial intermixing of races was destructive rather than assimilative?

were many more men than women among the European immigrants, they commonly took Indian wives or concubines. A mestizo population grew up, which in many parts of the Americas came to outnumber both Europeans and Indians.

How are the effects of Spanish and Portuguese colonization still apparent?

A second type of settlement developed in the West Indies, where the Europeans—English and French as well as Spanish—again comprised a resident aristocracy, though with an exclusively Negro imported labor force. At first the planters employed indentured servants from Europe to work their tobacco, indigo, and cotton plantations. But with the shift to sugar in the mid-seventeenth century, much more labor was needed, and slaves were brought over from Africa. In the British Barbados, for example, there were only a few hundred Negroes in 1640, but by 1685 they numbered 46,000 as against 20,000 whites. The French islands, likewise, had 44,000 Negroes and 18,000 whites by 1700.

The third type of settlement in the Americas was to be found along the Atlantic seaboard. There the native Indians were too sparse or too intractable to serve as an adequate labor supply, and, apart from the southern colonies, the crops did not warrant importing Negro labor. Under these circumstances the English and French settlers cleared the land themselves, lived by their own labors as farmers, fishermen, or traders, and developed communities that were exclusively European in composition.

In conclusion, the mass migrations from Europe and Africa changed the Americas from purely Mongoloid continents to the most racially mixed regions of the globe. Negro immigration continued to the mid-nineteenth century, reaching a total of about fifteen million slaves, while European immigration steadily increased, reaching a high point at the beginning of the twentieth century when nearly one million arrived each year. The net result is that the New World today is peopled by a majority of whites, with substantial minorities of Negroes, Indians, mestizos, and mulattoes, in that order.

The new global racial pattern that resulted from these depopulations and migrations has become so familiar that it is now taken for granted, and its extraordinary significance generally overlooked. What happened in this period to 1763 is that the Europeans staked out claims to vast new regions, and in the following century they peopled those territories—not only the Americas, but also Siberia and Australia. As they expanded territorially so they made possible their own numerical expansion, and they exploited some of the richest resources of the planet. These European Caucasoids came in the eighteenth to the twentieth century to dominate both the areas they populated and much more besides. Taking advantage of the relatively sparse population in the New World, they literally Europeanized North and South America. This could not be done in Asia and Africa, where the indigenous populations were too numerous and highly developed. But in the Americas, and even more in Australia, the Europeans bodily transplanted their civilization in all its aspects—ethnic, economic, and cultural.

How did these migrations change the course of New World history?

The Industrial Revolution was in large degree responsible for this Europeanization. We have seen that increased productivity together with the advances of medical science had led to a sharp increase in Europe's population in the nineteenth century. This created a population pressure that found an outlet in overseas migration. Railways and steamships were available to transport masses of people across oceans and continents, and persecution of one sort or another further stimulated emigration, the chief example of this being the flight of 1 1/2 million Jews from Russia to the United States in the fifteen years preceding World War I. These various

The immigrant ships of the late nineteenth century were much larger than, for example, the slave ships that sailed at the beginning of that century. They carried nearly 10 million people from 1880–1900 alone. Were your ancestors part of this wave of migration?

factors combined to produce a mass migration unequaled in human history. With every decade the tide of population movement increased in volume. In the 1820's a total of 145,000 left Europe, in the 1850's about 2,600,000, and between 1900 and 1910 the crest was reached with 9 million emigrants, or almost 1 million per year.

Before 1885 most of the emigrants came from northern and western Europe; after that date the majority were from southern and eastern Europe. By and large, the British emigrants went to the Dominions and to the United States, the Italians to the United States and Latin America, the Spaniards and Portuguese to Latin America, and the Germans to the United States and, in smaller numbers, to Argentina and Brazil. From the perspective of world history, the significance of this extraordinary migration is that it was all directed to the New World and Oceania, with the exception of the large flow to Asiatic Russia and the trickle to South Africa. The result has been the almost complete ethnic Europeanization of North America and Australia. The Indian population in South America managed to survive but was left a minority. In other words, the colonial offshoots of the pre-1763 period now, during the course of the nineteenth century, became new Europes alongside the old.

The Americas and Australia were Europeanized economically as well as ethnically. Before 1763 the European settlements in these continents were confined largely to the coasts. But during the following century the interiors of the continents were traversed. The Industrial Revolution made this overland penetration possible by providing the necessary machines and techniques. The wilderness could not have been tamed without the roads leading inward from the coast, the canals connecting riverways, the railroads and telegraphs spanning continents, the steamers plying rivers and coastal waterways, the agricultural machines capable of cutting the prairie sod, and the repeating rifle that subdued the native peoples. These mechanical aids for the conquest of continental expanses were as essential to Latin Americans and Australians as to American frontiersmen. For example, an Argentinian writing in 1878 observed that "the military power of the [Indian] barbarians is wholly destroyed, because the Remington has taught them that an army battalion can cross the whole pampa, leaving the land strewn with the bodies of those who dared to oppose it."

Summarize the ways in which the Industrial Revolution aided this mass migration.

Principal Sources of European Emigration, 1846–1932

Great Britain and Ireland	18,000,000
Russia	14,250,000*
Italy	10,100,000
Austria-Hungary	5,200,000
Germany	4,900,000
Spain	4,700,000
Portugal	1,800,000
Sweden	1,200,000
Norway	850,000
Poland	640,000†
France	520,000
Denmark	390,000
Finland	370,000
Switzerland	330,000
Holland	220,000
Belgium	190,000
TOTAL	63,660,000

* Consists of 2,250,000 who went overseas, 7,000,000 who migrated to Asiatic Russia by 1914, 3,000,000 who migrated to the Urals, Siberia, and the Far East from 1927 to 1939 and 2,000,000 who migrated to Central Asia from 1927 to 1939. Since 1939, Russian emigration, free and forced, into the trans-Ural areas, has been the greatest single population movement in the world.

† 1920–1932 only.

Source: A. M. Carr-Saunders, *World Population* (Oxford: Clarendon, 1936), pp. 49, 56; and W. S. and E. S. Woytinsky, *World Population and Production* (New York, Twentieth Century Fund, 1953), pp. 69, 93.

The peopling and economic development of the new continents led automatically to the transplanting of European culture as well. It is true that the culture changed in transit. It was adapted as well as adopted. Canada and Australia and the United States today are not identical to Great Britain, nor is Latin America an exact reproduction of the Iberian Peninsula. But the fact remains that the languages are essentially the same, even though Englishmen are intrigued by American slang and Frenchmen by the archaic French-Canadian patois. The religions also are the same, despite the campfire revival meetings and the Mormons. The literatures, the schools, the newspapers, the forms of government—all have roots extending back to England and Spain and France and other European countries.

What specific European influences on the major institutions of American society can you name?

There are, of course, certain cultural strains in the Americas and in Australia that are not European. The Negro element in the New World has retained a certain residue of its African background. The surviving native peoples, especially the Indians in Latin America, are responsible for a hybrid culture. Nor should one forget the impact of the wilderness, leaving its indelible imprint on the European immigrants and on their institutions. All these forces explain why New York, Melbourne, and Toronto are very different from London, and why Buenos Aires, Brasilia, and Mexico City differ from Madrid.

What kinds of modifying influences might the author be thinking of?

Yet from a global viewpoint the similarities loom larger than the differences. The Arab peoples, in the course of their expansion from their homeland in the Middle East, spread westward across North Africa to the Atlantic Ocean. Today the culture of Morocco is far more different from that of the Arabian Peninsula than the culture of the United States is from that of Britain, or the culture of Brazil from that of Portugal. Yet Morocco is considered, and certainly considers itself, to be a part of the Arab world. In the same sense, the Americas and Australia today are a part of the European world.

Jews Without Money
MICHAEL GOLD

Arriving safely in America was only the first step in an extensive process of adjustment for the immigrant. There was usually a long wait at the port of debarkation, embarrassing questions to answer, forms to fill out, a complicated bureaucracy to get past. Then there was a job to find, housing to locate, a new language to learn. The land was strange, and the customs different. In facing this alien and sometimes hostile environment, most immigrants sought out others from their own country, perhaps even from their own village. In the Eastern port cities they formed ghettos that were often isolated from the rest of the city yet dependent on its larger political and economic structures. The new land and the new customs put unusual pressure on the immigrant families and often drove a wedge between husband and wife, parents and children.

In what follows, Michael Gold details a remarkable range of immigrant expectation and reality in New York City at the turn of the century. The tension, pathos, and despair that beset his own family, Jews from eastern Europe, are typical of the reactions of many other immigrants. Did your ancestors come to this country with the same illusions as Gold's? How did they react to the steady erosion of these dreams? Would you have had the courage to persevere?

SAM KRAVITZ, THAT THIEF

"Why did I choose to come to America?" asked my father of himself gravely, as he twisted and untwisted his mustache in the darkness. "I will tell you why: it was because of envy of my dirty thief of a cousin, that Sam Kravitz, may his nose be eaten by the pox.

"All this time, while I was disgracing my family, Sam had gone to America, and was making his fortune. Letters came from him, and were read throughout our village. Sam, in two short years, already owned his own factory for making suspenders. He sent us his picture. It was marveled at by everyone. Our Sam no longer wore a fur cap, a long Jewish coat and peasant boots. No. He wore a fine gentleman's suit, a white collar like a doctor, store shoes and a beautiful round fun-hat called a derby.

"He suddenly looked so fat and rich, this beggarly cobbler's son! I tell you, my liver burned with envy when I heard my father and mother praise my cousin Sam. I knew I was better than him in every way, and it hurt me. I said to my father, 'Give me money. Let me go at once to America to redeem myself. I will make more money than Sam, I am smarter than he is. You will see!'

What were your ancestors' reasons for coming to America?

71

"My mother did not want me to go. But my father was weary of my many misfortunes, and he gave me the money for the trip. So I came to America. It was the greatest mistake in my life.

Have you ever heard anyone express regrets for emigrating?

•   •   •

"I am not discouraged, children. I will make a great deal of money some day. I am a serious married man now and no greenhorn. But then I was still a foolish boy, and though I left Roumania with great plans in my head, in my heart a foolish voice was saying: 'America is a land of fun.'

"How full I was of all the *Baba* stories that were told in my village about America! In America, we believed, people dug under the streets and found gold anywhere. In America, the poorest ragpicker lived better than a Roumanian millionaire. In America, people did little work, but had fun all day.

"I had seen two pictures of America. They were shown in the window of a store that sold Singer Sewing Machines in our village. One picture had in it the tallest building I had ever seen. It was called a skyscraper. At the bottom of it walked the proud Americans. The men wore derby hats and had fine mustaches and gold watch chains. The women wore silks and satins, and had proud faces like queens. Not a single poor man or woman was there; every one was rich.

"The other picture was of Niagara Falls. You have seen the picture on postcards; with Indians and cowboys on horses, who look at a rainbow shining over the water.

Why were people so willing to believe these images?

"I tell you, I wanted to get to America as fast as I could, so that I might look at the skyscrapers and at the Niagara Falls rainbow, and wear a derby hat.

"In my family were about seventy-five relatives. All came to see me leave Roumania. There was much crying. But I was happy, because I thought I was going to a land of fun.

"The last thing my mother did, was to give me my cousin's address in New York, and say: 'Go to Sam. He will help you in the strange land.'

"But I made up my mind I would die first rather than ask Sam for help.

"Well, for eleven days our boat rocked on the ocean. I was sick, but I wrote out a play called 'The Robbers' of Schiller and dreamed of America.

"They gave us dry herring and potatoes to eat. The food was like dung and the boat stank like a big water closet. But I was happy.

"I joked all the way. One night all of us young immigrants held a singing party. One young Roumanian had an accordion. We became good friends, because both of us were the happiest people on the boat.

"He was coming to a rich uncle, a cigarmaker who owned a big business, he said. When he learned I had no relatives in America, he asked me to live at his uncle's with him. I agreed, because I liked this boy.

"*Nu*, how shall I tell how glad we were when after eleven days on the empty ocean we saw the buildings of New York?

"It looked so nice and happy, this city standing on end like a child's toys and blocks. It looked like a land of fun, a game waiting for me to play.

"And in Ellis Island, where they kept us overnight, I slept on a spring bed that had no mattress, pillow or blankets. I was such a greenhorn that I had never seen a spring before. I thought it was wonderful, and bounced up and down on it for fun.

"Some one there taught me my first American words. All night my

He describes the atmosphere of Ellis Island as "fun." Have you ever heard a different version?

72

Lack of space and inadequate facilities were common conditions aboard immigrant ships. Since ships often stopped at many ports on the way, people from widely different backgrounds had to adjust to one another's habits under these trying circumstances. What do you know of your family's experiences in reaching this country?

friend Yossel and I bounced up and down on the springs and repeated the new funny words to each other.

"Potato! he would yell at me. Tomato! I would answer, and laugh. Match! he would say. All right! I would answer. Match! all right! go to hell! potato! until every one was angry at us, the way we kept them awake with our laughing and yelling.

"In the morning his uncle came for us and took us home in a horsecar.

"I tell you my eyes were busy on that ride through the streets. I was looking for the American fun.

"*Nu*, I will not mention how bad I felt when I saw the cigarmaker uncle's home. It was just a big dirty dark room in the back of the cigar store where he made and sold cigars. He, his wife and four children lived in that one room.

"He was not glad to have me there, but he spread newspapers on the floor, and Yossel and I slept on them.

"What does it matter, I thought, this is not America. To-morrow morning I will go out in the streets, and see the real American fun.

Why did he refuse to accept the reality before him?

"The next morning Yossel and I took a long walk. That we might not be lost, we fixed in our minds the big gold tooth of a dentist that hung near the cigar shop.

73

"We walked and walked. I will not tell you what we saw, because you see it every day. We saw the East Side. To me it was a strange sight. I could not help wondering, where are all the people running? What is happening? And why are they so serious? When does the fun start?

"We came to Allen Street, under the elevated. To show you what a greenhorn I was, I fell in love with the elevated train. I had never seen anything like it in Roumania.

"I was such a greenhorn I believed the elevated train traveled all over America, to Niagara Falls and other places. We rode up and down on it all day. I paid the fare.

"I had some money left. I also bought two fine derby hats from a pushcart; one for Yossel, and one for me. They were a little big, but how proud we felt in these American fun-hats.

"No one wears such hats in Roumania. Both of us had pictures taken in the American fun-hats to send to our parents.

"This foolishness went on for two weeks. Then all my money was gone. So the cigarmaker told me I should find a job and move out from his home. So I found a job for seven dollars a month in a grocery store. I lived over the store, I rose at five o'clock, and went to bed at twelve in the night. My feet became large and red with standing all day. The grocerman, may the worms find him, gave me nothing to eat but dry bread, old cheese, pickles and other stale groceries. I soon became sick and left that job.

"For a week I sat in Hester Park without a bite of food. And I looked around me, but was not unhappy. Because I tell you, I was such a greenhorn, that I still thought fun would start and I was waiting for it.

"One night, after sleeping on the bench, I was very hungry in the morning and decided to look up my rich cousin, Sam Kravitz. I hated to do this, but was weak with fasting. So I came into my cousin's shop. To hide my shame I laughed out loud.

"'Look, Sam I am here,' I laughed. 'I have just come off the boat, and am ready to make my fortune.'

"So my cousin Sam gave me a job in his factory. He paid me twenty-five cents a day.

"He had three other men working for him. He worked himself. He looked sick and sharp and poor and not at all like the picture of him in the fun-hat he had sent to Roumania.

"*Nu*, so your father worked. I got over my greenhorn idea that there was nothing but fun in America. I learned to work like every one else. I grew thin as my cousin.

"Soon I came to understand it was not a land of fun. It was a Land of Hurry-Up. There was no gold to be dug in the streets here. Derbies were not fun-hats for holidays. They were work-hats. *Nu*, so I worked! With my hands, my liver and sides! I worked!

"My cousin Sam had fallen into a good trade. With his machines he manufactured the cotton ends of suspenders. These ends are made of cotton, and are very important to a suspender. It is these ends that fasten to the buttons, and hold up the pants. This is important to the pants, as you know.

"Yes, it was a good trade, and a necessary one. There was much money to be made, I saw that at once.

"But my cousin Sam was not a good business man. He had no head for

Did your relatives settle in a large city? Did they ever give you their impressions?

Why were immigrants generally so easily exploited?

Where did the idea of "gold in the streets" come from?

This woman is one of "1,000 marriageable girls" brought over on one ship from eastern Europe in the late nineteenth century. Marriage was thought of as both a religious obligation and a rational decision in eastern European Jewish culture, so that arranged marriages were common. Why has this idea largely been replaced among second- and third-generation Jewish-Americans?

figures and his face was like vinegar. None of his customers liked him.

"Gradually, he let me go out and find business for him. I was very good for this. Most of the big suspender shops were owned by Roumanians who had known my father. They greeted me like a relative. I drank wine with them, and passed jokes. So they gave me their orders for suspender ends.

"So one day, seeing how I built up the business, Sam said: 'You shall be my partner. We are making a great deal of money. Leave the machine, Herman. I will take care of the inside shop work. You go out every day, and joke with our customers and bring in the orders.'

"So I was partners with my cousin Sam. So I was very happy. I earned as much as thirty dollars a week; I was at last a success.

"So a matchmaker came, and said I ought to marry. So he brought me to your momma and I saw at once that she was a kind and hard-working woman. So I decided to marry her and have children.

"So this was done.

"It was then I made the greatest mistake of my life.

"Always I had wanted to see that big water with the rainbow and Indians called Niagara Falls.

"So I took your momma there when we married. I spent a month's wages on the trip. I showed America to your momma. We enjoyed ourselves.

"In a week we came back. I went to the shop the next morning to work again. I could not find the shop. It had vanished. I could not find Sam. He had stolen the shop.

"I searched and searched for Sam and the shop. My heart was swollen like a sponge with hate. I was ready to kill my cousin Sam.

"So one day I found him and the shop. I shouted at him, 'Thief, what have you done?' He laughed. He showed me a paper from a lawyer proving that the shop was his. All my work had been for nothing. It had only made Sam rich.

Could this kind of exploitation happen today?

75

"What could I do? So in my hate I hit him with my fist, and made his nose bleed. He ran into the street yelling for a policeman. I ran after him with a stick, and beat him some more. But what good could it do? The shop was really his, and I was left a pauper."

• • •

BANANAS

My proud father. He raved, cursed, worried, he held long passionate conversations with my mother.

"Must I peddle bananas, Katie? I can't do it; the disgrace would kill me!"

"Don't do it," my mother would say gently. "We can live without it."

"But where will I find work?" he would cry. "The city is locked against me! I am a man in a trap!"

"Something will happen. God has not forgotten us," said my mother.

"I will kill myself! I can't stand it! I will take the gas pipe to my nose! I refuse to be a peddler!"

"Hush, the children will hear you," said my mother.

I could hear them thrashing it out at night in the bedroom. They talked about it at the supper table, or sat by the stove in the gloomy winter afternoons, talking, talking. My father was obsessed with the thought of bananas. They became a symbol to him of defeat, of utter hopelessness. And when my mother assured him he need not become a peddler, he would

What was the "trap"?

Having survived the sea voyage in crowded, unsanitary ships, immigrants who settled in cities often faced a similar situation in their living quarters. The one-room flats that families generally occupied (left) were microcosms of the ghetto streets (right) where they were located—both teemed with too much life, both harbored conditions inimical to that life. What perils might these people have faced, and, in spite of such dangers, what would have kept them there?

turn on her and argue that it was the one way out. He was in a curious fever of mixed emotions.

Two weeks [later]. . . he was in the street with a pushcart, peddling the accursed bananas.

He came back the first night, and gave my mother a dollar bill and some silver. His face was gray; he looked older by ten years; a man who had touched bottom. My mother tried to comfort him, but for days he was silent as one who has been crushed by a calamity. Hope died in him; months passed, a year passed, he was still peddling bananas.

I remember meeting him one evening with his pushcart. I had managed to sell all my papers and was coming home in the snow. It was that strange, portentous hour in downtown New York when the workers are pouring homeward in the twilight. I marched among thousands of tired men and women whom the factory whistles had unyoked. They flowed in rivers through the clothing factory districts, then down along the avenues to the East Side.

I met my father near Cooper Union. I recognized him, a hunched, frozen figure in an old overcoat standing by a banana cart. He looked so lonely, the tears came to my eyes. Then he saw me, and his face lit with his sad, beautiful smile—Charlie Chaplin's smile.

"Ach, it's Mikey," he said. "So you have sold your papers! Come and eat a banana."

He offered me one. I refused it. I was eleven years old, but poisoned with a morbid proletarian sense of responsibility. I felt it crucial that my

From what you have read so far, what kind of man was the author's father? Why would this job depress him so?

father *sell* his bananas, not give them away. He thought I was shy, and coaxed and joked with me, and made me eat the banana. It smelled of wet straw and snow.

"You haven't sold many bananas to-day, pop," I said anxiously.

He shrugged his shoulders.

"What can I do? No one seems to want them."

It was true. The work crowds pushed home morosely over the pavements. The rusty sky darkened over New York buildings, the tall street lamps were lit, innumerable trucks, street cars and elevated trains clattered by. Nobody and nothing in the great city stopped for my father's bananas.

"I ought to yell," said my father dolefully. "I ought to make a big noise like other peddlers, but it makes my throat sore. Anyway, I'm ashamed of yelling, it makes me feel like a fool."

I had eaten one of his bananas. My sick conscience told me that I ought to pay for it somehow. I must remain here and help my father.

"I'll yell for you, pop," I volunteered.

"Ach, no," he said, "go home; you have worked enough to-day. Just tell momma I'll be late."

But I yelled and yelled. My father, standing by, spoke occasional words of praise, and said I was a wonderful yeller.   Nobody else paid attention. The workers drifted past us wearily, endlessly; a defeated army wrapped in dreams of home. Elevated trains crashed; the Cooper Union clock burned above us; the sky grew black, the wind poured, the slush burned through our shoes. There were thousands of strange, silent figures pouring over the sidewalks in snow. None of them stopped to buy bananas. I yelled and yelled, nobody listened.

My father tried to stop me at last. "*Nu*," he said smiling to console me, "that was wonderful yelling, Mikey. But it's plain we are unlucky to-day! Let's go home."

I was frantic, and almost in tears. I insisted on keeping up my desperate yells. But at last my father persuaded me to leave with him. It was after nightfall. We covered the bananas with an oilcloth and started for the pushcart stable. Down Second Avenue we plodded side by side. For many blocks my father was thoughtful. Then he shook his head and sighed:

"So you see how it is, Mikey. Even at banana peddling I am a failure. What can be wrong? The bananas are good, your yelling was good, the prices are good. Yes, it is plain; I am a man without luck."

Textbooks usually note that immigrant labor was hard. In what sense is that true here?

•   •   •

"Ach, Gott, what a rich country America is! What an easy place to make one's fortune! Look at all the rich Jews! Why has it been so easy for them, so hard for me? I am just a poor little Jew without money."

"Poppa, lots of Jews have no money," I said to comfort him.

"I know it, my son," he said, "but don't be one of them. It's better to be dead in this country than not to have money. Promise me you'll be rich when you grow up, Mikey!"

"Yes, poppa."

"Ach," he said fondly, "this is my one hope now! This is all that makes me happy! I am a greenhorn, but you are an American! You will have it easier than I; you will have luck in America!"

"Yes, poppa," I said, trying to smile with him. But I felt older than he; I could not share his naïve optimism; my heart sank as I remembered the past and thought of the future.

Do you agree?

At the age of twelve I carried in my mind a morbid load of responsibility.

I had been a precocious pupil in the public school, winning honors not by study, but by a kind of intuition. I graduated a year sooner than most boys. At the exercises I was valedictory orator.

My parents were proud, of course. They wanted me to go on to high school, like other "smart" boys. They still believed I would be a doctor.

But I was morbid enough to be wiser than my parents. Even then I could sense that education is a luxury reserved for the well-to-do. I refused to go to high school. More than half the boys in my graduating class were going to work; I chose to be one of them.

It was where I belonged. I figured it out on paper for my parents. Four years of high school, then six years of college before one could be a doctor. Ten years of study in all, with thousands of dollars needed for books, tuition, and the rest.

There were four of us in my family. My mother seemed unable to work. Would my father's banana peddling keep us alive during those ten years while I was studying?

Of course not. I was obstinate and bitter; my parents wept, and tried to persuade me, but I refused to go to high school.

Miss Barry, the English teacher, tried to persuade me, too. She was fond of me. She stared at me out of wistful blue eyes, with her old maid's earnestness, and said:

"It would be a pity for you to go into a factory. I have never seen better English compositions than yours, Michael."

"I must work, Miss Barry," I said. I started to leave. She took my hand. I could smell the fresh spring lilacs in the brass bowl on her desk.

"Wait," she said earnestly, "I want you to promise me to study at night. I will give you a list of the required high school reading; you can make up your Regents' counts that way. Will you do it?"

"Yes, Miss Barry," I lied to her sullenly.

I was trying to be hard. For years my ego had been fed by every one's praise of my precocity. I had always loved books; I was mad about books; I wanted passionately to go to high school and college. Since I couldn't, I meant to despise all that nonsense.

"It will be difficult to study at night," said Miss Barry in her trembly voice, "but Abraham Lincoln did it, and other great Americans."

"Yes, Miss Barry," I muttered.

She presented me with a parting gift. It was a volume of Emerson's Essays, with her name and my name and the date written on the flyleaf.

I thanked her for the book, and threw it under the bed when I got home. I never read a page in it, or in any book for the next five years. I hated books; they were lies, they had nothing to do with life and work.

It was not easy to find my first job. I hunted for months, in a New York summer of furnace skies and fogs of humidity. I bought the *World* each morning, and ran through the want ads:

Agents Wanted—Addressers Wanted—Barbers Wanted—Bushelmen Wanted— Butchers Wanted—Boys Wanted—

That fateful ad page bringing news of life and death each morning to hundreds of thousands. How often have I read it with gloomy heart. Even to-day the sight of it brings back the ache and hopelessness of my youth.

There was a swarm of boys pushing and yapping like homeless curs at the

What kind of educational opportunities did your grandparents or parents have?

Was self-education a real option? What kind of obstacles would he face if he tried?

door of each job. I competed with them. We scrambled, flunkeyed and stood at servile attention under the boss's eye, little slaves on the block.

No one can go through the shame and humiliation of the job-hunt without being marked for life. I hated my first experience at it, and have hated every other since. There can be no freedom in the world while men must beg for jobs.

I rose at six-thirty each morning, and was out tramping the streets at seven. There were always hundreds of jobs, but thousands of boys clutching after them. The city was swarming with these boys, aimless, bewildered and as hungry for work as I was.

I found a job as errand boy in a silk house. But it was temporary. The very first morning the shipping clerk, a refined Nordic, suddenly realized I was a Jew. He politely fired me. They wanted no Jews. In this city of a million Jews, there was much anti-Semitism among business firms. Many of the ads would read:Gentile Only. Even Jewish business houses discriminated against Jews. How often did I slink out of factory or office where a foreman said Jews were not wanted. How often was I made to remember I belonged to the accursed race, the race whose chief misfortune it is to have produced a Christ.

At last I found a job. It was in a factory where incandescent gas mantles were made, a dark loft under the elevated trains on the Bowery near Chatham Square.

This was a spectral place, a chamber of hell, hot and poisoned by hundreds of gas flames. It was suffocating with the stink of chemicals.

I began to sweat immediately. What was worse, I could not breathe. The place terrified me. The boss came up and told me to take off my coat.

Have you ever experienced this?

Have you or members of your family ever felt prejudice?

He was a grim little man, thick as a cask about the middle, and dressed in a gaudy pink silk shirt. He chewed a cigar. His face was morbid and hard like a Jewish gangster's.

"Monkey Face," he called, "show this new kid what to do."

An overgrown Italian boy approached, in pants and undershirt streaked with sweat. His slit nose, ape muzzle, and tiny malicious eyes had earned him his appropriate nickname.

"Come here, kid," he said. I followed him down the loft. There were thirty unfortunate human beings at work. Men sat at a long table testing mantles. Their faces were death masks, fixed and white. Great blue spectacles shielded their eyes.

Little Jewish and Italian girls dipped racks of mantles in chemical tanks. Boys stood before a series of ovens in which sixty gas jets blazed. They passed in the racks for the chemicals to burn off. Every one dripped with sweat; every one was haggard, as though in pain.

"Where did yuh work last?" growled Monkey Face.

"It's my first job. I'm just out of school."

"Yeh?" he snickered. "Just out of school, huh? Well, yuh struck a good job, kid; it'll put hair on your chest. Here, take dis."

I took the iron rack he gave me, and dropped it at once. It scorched my hand. Monkey Face laughed at the joke.

"You son-of-a-bitch!" I said, "it's hot."

He pushed his apish face close to mine.

"Yuh little kike, I'll bite your nose off if yuh get fresh wit' me! I'm your boss around here."

He went away. I worked. Racks of mantles were brought me, and I

Child labor was common in your grandparents' or great-grandparents' generation. Cigars, requiring unskilled drudgery for their manufacture, were often produced by family groups (like the one on the facing page) in their tenement flats. Even outside larger urban areas, children, like this young spinner in a Carolina cotton mill, were hired to run dangerous machinery for up to sixteen hours a shift. What effect might child labor have had on the family as a social unit? How is the family affected today when few young people need to work?

burned them off. Hell flamed and stank around me. At noon the boss blew a whistle. We sat on benches for our half-hour lunch. I could not eat for nausea. I wanted air, air, but there was no time for air.

There was no time for anything but work in that evil hell-hole. I sweated there for six months. Monkey Face tortured me. I lost fifteen pounds in weight. I raged in nightmares in my sleep. I forgot my college dreams; I forgot everything, but the gas mantles.

My mother saw how thin I was becoming. She forced me to quit that job. I was too stupefied to have done this myself. Then I read the Want Ads for another month. I found a job in a dark Second Avenue rat-hole, a little printing shop. Here I worked for another five months until I injured my hand in a press.

Another spell of job-hunting. Then a brief interval in a matzoth bakery. Job in an express company. Job in a mail order house. Job in a dry goods store.

Jobs, jobs. I drifted from one to the other, without plan, without hope. I was one of the many. I was caught like my father in poverty's trap. I was nothing, bound for nowhere.

Is it easier to escape the trap of poverty now?

At times I seriously thought of cutting my throat. At other times I dreamed of running away to the far west. Sex began to torture me. I developed a crazy religious streak. I prayed on the tenement roof in moonlight to the Jewish Messiah who would redeem the world. . . . I spent my nights in a tough poolroom. I needed desperate stimulants; I was ready for anything. At the age of fifteen I began drinking and whoring . . .

And I worked. And my father and mother grew sadder and older. It went on for years. I don't want to remember it all; the years of my adolescence. Yet I was only one among a million others.

A man on an East Side soap-box, one night, proclaimed that out of the despair, melancholy and helpless rage of millions, a world movement had been born to abolish poverty.

Why did radicalism have such appeal?

I listened to him.

O workers' Revolution, you brought hope to me, a lonely, suicidal boy. You are the true Messiah. You will destroy the East Side when you come, and build there a garden for the human spirit.

O Revolution, that forced me to think, to struggle and to live.

O great Beginning!

A BRIDE GOES WEST

Nannie T. Alderson and Helena Huntington Smith

Even before the vast immigrant masses of Europe reached the Eastern port cities, Americans were on the move. They traveled on horseback or in covered wagons, by canal boats, and even on foot. In the Civil War era and afterward, the construction of railroads provided new opportunity, attracting land speculators, farmers, ranchers, prospectors, and thousands of others—all lured by adventure and the hope of a fortune. Some traveled in comparative luxury, others with nothing more than the clothes on their back. But almost everyone underestimated the hardships of the trip. Thousands died, thousands more turned back discouraged and defeated, yet millions moved west despite the difficulties.

In the following selection, a woman who grew up in Virginia, visited Kansas when she was sixteen, and then married and moved to the high country of Montana recalls some of her hopes and experiences. How did her dreams differ from those of the immigrant women who came with their families to a new land? Perhaps your grandmother can recall some of the thoughts, dreams, and experiences of her youth for you, or perhaps someone in your family who has undertaken a long overland journey and lived through the trauma of resettling can recount some memories.

The year I was sixteen a new world opened up before me. My father's sister, Elizabeth Tiffany, had married a Mr. Symms and had pioneered in Kansas in the Fifties. On one of her periodic visits to Virginia she stopped to see me, because I wanted to know my father's people.* The result was an invitation to visit her in Atchison, Kansas, from September to June.

What an experience that was! Kansas then was the West. I felt that the very air there was easier to breathe. In Union [West Virginia] you had to have your pedigree with you to be accepted anywhere, but in Atchison it didn't matter a bit who your ancestors were or what you did for a living; if you were nice you were nice. What impressed me most was the fact that a girl could work in an office or a store, yet that wouldn't keep her from being invited to the nicest homes or marrying one of the nicest boys. This freedom to work seemed to me a wonderful thing. I wanted to do something useful myself, as I felt keenly my dependence on my stepfather. But Auntie wouldn't let me; she knew my mother would never consent.

How does this differ from the immigrant's experience of work?

* Her father was killed in the Civil War.—Ed.

83

So many little foolish conventions that we were brought up on at home didn't apply in Atchison. There was much less formality there; when people went visiting they took their darning or their knitting with them in the friendly old-fashioned way—but when I tried it after returning to West Virginia, mother was shocked. In Union on Sunday we were never allowed to open the piano nor to visit anybody except relatives; in Kansas we all did as we pleased about these matters, and when I remonstrated with my cousin for playing a piece of popular music, she was able to retort: "I don't think it's any more wrong than it is for you to sit on the porch and talk to boys on a Sunday afternoon!"

I had to admit that she was right. But the boys all worked, and Sunday was the only day they could come.

Why were there such differences in Southern and Western society?

On this visit I first met my husband. One evening in June, 1877 I was invited to take supper and spend the night with a Baptist preacher's family named Alderson, who were West Virginians like ourselves. There were several brothers in the home, and three or four girls had been invited. After a jolly supper one of the boys excused himself from the parlor and went out on the porch to smoke a cigar.

In a minute he was back, saying excitedly: "Mother, Walt's home!"

This announcement produced a great effect. "Walt," I learned, was a brother who had run away to Texas when he was twelve or thirteen years old, and they hadn't seen him for nine years.

They made him come inside—a cowboy in sombrero and chaps. We girls were not impressed; we thought he was funny-looking. I remember that he was rather silent and ill at ease, and soon excused himself, saying he was going to bed. In the morning the brother brought the startling news that "Walt" had not slept in bed, but had gotten up in the night, taken a quilt, and lain down on the floor of the bedroom. This strange visitor, they said, had come up with a herd of cattle to Dodge City, the wild, tough cowtown which was then a northern terminus of the great cattle trail from Texas. He had left the house very early, before any of us were up, and I didn't see him again, except once at a crystal wedding party, before going back to Virginia.

Are there any similarities between runaways today and then? Are they as common?

Much later I found out what lay behind his sudden appearance that night in his strange cowboy dress. To begin with, his birthplace was only twenty miles from mine, at Alderson, West Virginia. But he was five years older than I and his father, an anti-slavery preacher, had moved out in the rush to settle Kansas before I was born. There he built one of the first Baptist churches in the state. There were six sons and a daughter in the family, and Walter was next to the youngest.

His parents were conscientious, high-minded people who thought their first duty was to the church, not to their children and home. There was a good deal of strictness about certain matters, such as the observance of Sunday, but Walter was always wild and irrepressible. The people in Atchison used to tell a story of his riding home on a horse afternoons, behind his father; Mr. Alderson, Senior, kept a bookstore in town during the week, and Walter was ordered to come to the store after school, so as not to get into mischief playing with bad boys. For years afterwards Atchison used to smile over the picture they made; the dignified white-bearded preacher with his stove-pipe hat, and the imp of a boy perched behind him, facing the horse's tail, making all kinds of faces and comical gestures as they journeyed along the street, while the preacher bowed gravely from side to side, acknowledging what he took to be smiles of greeting to himself.

Mrs. Alderson was too busy with her church work to give much attention

Why Kansas? What was happening that caused a rush of settlement?

The great long drives of cattle from Texas to Kansas started in 1866 when the Missouri Pacific Railroad, linking the West with Eastern markets, was completed. The era lasted only twenty years but produced one of America's most enduring legends—the cowboy. What has the cowboy come to symbolize, and why is the Western such a popular art form?

to his bringing up, so much of the time he was left in the charge of his older brothers, who were allowed to punish him. He resented this, and at thirteen he ran away to Texas. Two other boys ran away with him; their fathers went after them and brought them home, but Mr. Alderson, Senior, was very wise. He said: "No, since that is what he wants, let him go and learn for himself."

Would your parents have been this tolerant? Would you?

Texas in the late Sixties was wild and rough, the very place to appeal to rebellious spirits. I have often wished that I remembered more of Mr. Alderson's experiences there. I know that when he first went down there he got a job washing dishes for his keep. Later his boots gave out, and his first piece of luck was finding five dollars, with which he bought new ones. At one time he drove a stage coach during the night; I can't recall where, only that the little town at one end of his run was called Sweet Home. That has always seemed to me a lovely name. He told me that every morning at sunup, near the end of his long night's drive, a mocking bird would be singing in a certain liveoak tree when he went by. He came to look for it, and if the bird wasn't there, the day would be spoiled for him.

He had always been good with horses, so he drifted naturally into becoming a cowboy, and went up the trail to Kansas. He spoke of it as a hard school, with poor food and much exposure to the weather. I believe he had been up to Dodge City before, but on this trip, when he got up there with the herd, it came to him all of a sudden that he would go home and see his people.

Does he fit the movie image of a cowboy?

I spent a year at home in West Virginia after our first meeting; then, when I was seventeen, I went back to Atchison to stay with my aunt again, remaining this time for four years.

I did not see Mr. Alderson at once on my second visit. Although he had stayed in Atchison, he didn't live at home, but had rooms downtown, where he went around with a fast horse-racing crowd. It may sound strange today to speak of horse-racing in Kansas, but the western part of the state at that time was not far from its wide-open frontier days, and the sporting element still held its own.

I should probably never have seen him again if his father had not taken ill. There were no nurses then; neighbors helped each other, and Auntie and I took turns at looking after the old gentleman. On a night when I was sitting up, Walter came home. He owned a half interest in a race mare which he took on the circuit, and he had been in Kansas City racing this horse when his father grew worse, and they telegraphed him to come.

He was tall—just half an inch under six feet—blue-eyed, and of a fine appearance. Later, when he came to Virginia for our wedding, my mother, who loved beauty in man, woman or child, said to me: "Why didn't you tell me he's good-looking?" I replied that I'd preferred to let her find that out for herself.

Is this "tall" by current standards?

For many nights after his arrival in Atchison we sat up together by the old gentleman's bedside, or talked quietly in the next room. In those talks he told me much about his early life, and one thing he said I have always remembered; that he had never known any pleasure in his home until I was in it. I believe that was one thing that gave him such a strong feeling for home afterwards. He told me, too, that he had made up his mind never to marry, but that I had changed it. He was already planning to go out and start a cattle ranch in Montana, and he asked me if I would be afraid to share that kind of life with him. I told him I wasn't afraid, and we became engaged soon after his father died.

My aunt and the relatives in Atchison did not approve the match at first. This was not because he was taking me to the unsettled West; they all thought the ranching business had a wealthy future, so that was looked upon as a good thing. No, they disapproved because of his wild reputation. But I had perfect confidence in him, believing then, as I do now, that it's not what a man has done before marriage that counts, it is what he does after.

I wanted to see my grandmother again before going so far away, so I went home to West Virginia and spent the next year there, getting ready to be married. How often I blessed Auntie in Atchison who had taught me to sew, and had also instilled what little smattering of common sense I had. I made all my trousseau myself. Thanks to Auntie I did have sense enough to make my underthings plain according to the standards of the day—so they had some pretense at suitability to the life I was planning to lead. When I had first arrived in Atchison my petticoats were like mother's—a mass of lace, and frills upon frills. Auntie explained that this made too much ironing for one servant, and she taught me to make simpler ones. So now I made my trousseau petticoats with just a single deep ruffle tucked solid to hold the starch, and a band of lace whipped to the ruffle. Mother thought them dreadfully plain, but when I had to iron them I thought them elaborate enough.

How long were your parents or grandparents engaged?

I made my own wedding dress of white embroidered mull, and I earned the money to buy my wedding veil. This was how it happened. My grandfather had had a body servant, Alec, who was freed at the end of the war with the other slaves. He went North and prospered, becoming steward of a hotel in the White Mountains. In all those years, however, he never lost his loyal devotion to our family, and in 1882 he visited Union, bringing with him his wife, a smart young colored woman of whom he was very proud. She needed a new dress while in Union, and he was humiliated because none of the dressmakers, who of course were white, would make one for her. He told me about it one day, almost with tears in his eyes.

What does this tell you about race relations then?

The clothes women wore during the late nineteenth and early twentieth centuries reflected both their socioeconomic class and region. The black sharecroppers from the South pictured above are obviously dressed to meet the rigors of field work. Women workers in the North also dressed simply, but in more tailored outfits since freedom of movement was not as essential in office work or clothing manufacture, two fields that employed women in large numbers. Are socioeconomic and regional factors as important today in determining dress?

I said: "Why, Alec, I'll make your wife's dress, gladly. And what's more, I'll let you pay me for it."

He said: "Miss Nannie, would you do that?" I never have seen a man so touchingly grateful. So I made the dress, and earned my wedding veil.

While I was at home making these preparations, Mr. Alderson was in Montana hunting a site for a ranch. His partner was Mr. John Zook of St. Joe, Missouri, a young man who shared his interest in horses and the out-of-doors. The two of them had owned this race mare together, and when they decided to go into ranching, the arrangement was that Mr. Zook was to provide the capital while my husband furnished the experience. The Northern Pacific was built as far as Miles City, Montana, and Mr. Alderson arrived on one of the first trains to come through from the East.

Would a cattle ranch be organized this way today?

He stopped at a road ranch up Tongue River which was run by some people named Lays. That year the buffalo were still so thick that Mrs. Lays had only to say: "Mr. Alderson, we're out of meat"; and he would go out and find a herd and kill a calf, all just as easily as a man would butcher a yearling steer in his own pasture. Yet when I came out, one year later, there was nothing left of those great bison herds, which had covered the continent, but carcasses. I saw them on my first drive out to the ranch, and they were lying thick all over the flat above our house, in all stages of decay. So wasteful were the hunters, they had not even removed the tongues, though the latter were choice meat.

Why were buffalo herds killed off?

The summer after I came out Mr. Alderson killed the last buffalo ever seen in our part of Montana. A man staying with us was out fishing when

Americans have always seemed willing to uproot themselves in pursuit of a dream, though successive generations have done so by different means. The completion of the transcontinental railroads opened the West to your great-grandparents' generation. Your grandparents or even your parents may have moved along highways from a rural to an urban area in open trucks like the one pictured above. Relocation from city to suburb by giant moving van is most common today. By what means has your family moved?

No. 3605. Indian Chiefs and U. S. Officials.
1 Two Strike.   6 Kicking Bear.   12 W. F. Cody, (Buffalo Bill)
2 Crow Dog.   7 Good Voice.   13 Maj. J. M. Burk.
3 Short Bull.   8 Thunder Hawk.   14 J. C. Craiger.
4 High Hawk.   9 Rocky Bear.   15 J. McDonald.
5 Two Lance.   10 Young man afraid   16 J. G. Worth
         of his horse.
      11 American Horse.
Taken at Pine Ridge Jan. 16. '91. Photo and copyright
      by Grabill, 1891, Deadwood, S. D.

In 1891, just a few days after the Wounded Knee massacre that signaled the end of Indian resistance to the policy of forced relocation, these surviving Sioux Indians posed before their tents on the Pine Ridge, South Dakota, reservation. Their removal further and further west and their concentration on increasingly smaller parcels of land largely destroyed that group's culture. Compare the Indian experience of uprooting with that of immigrant groups in this respect.

he saw this lonesome old bull wandering over the hills and gullies above our house—the first live buffalo seen in many months. He came home and reported it, saying: "Walt, why don't you go get him?" And next morning Mr. Alderson did go get him.

That afternoon he suggested that we take the spring wagon and go up to where the old bull had fallen. There he lay in the green brush at the bottom of a draw—the last of many millions—with the bushes propping him up so that he looked quite lifelike. I had brought my scissors, and I snipped a sackfull of the coarse, curly hair from his mane to stuff a pillow with.

I am afraid that the conservation of buffalo, or of any other wild game, simply never occurred to the Westerner of those days.

Why not?

The site Mr. Alderson chose for a ranch was near the mouth of Lame Deer Creek where it runs into the Rosebud, some sixty miles above the place where the Rosebud joins the Yellowstone. Crook had fought the Indians on the Rosebud only six years before, and Custer had marched up it, to cross over the divide and be slaughtered with all his command at the battle of the Little Big Horn. I had read about all this when it happened, and had seen a picture of Custer with his long yellow hair in one of our Southern papers, when I was just a young girl. I had been terribly and painfully impressed,

What did Custer's last stand mean for her?

90

never dreaming that I should some day live so near the battlefield, even visit it, and walk on ground that had been stained by his blood.

With the ranch selected and the cattle bought, Mr. Zook sold the race horse in Kansas and went out to the ranch to take over, while Mr. Alderson spent his share of the proceeds on coming East. We were married at my mother's house in Union, on April 4, 1883.

For weeks and weeks it had rained, as it can rain only in the West Virginia mountains, but that morning the sun came out, and I was awakened by my niece's voice exclaiming: "Why, the sun is shining on Aunt Nannie's wedding day!"

The servants' faces were all wreathed in smiles.

The ceremony was at ten, and in the afternoon Mr. Alderson and I went across the mountains by stage to Alderson, where we were to be entertained by his relatives before we took the train. As we went down into the valley toward Alderson we saw the sun setting in a great mass of gold and purple clouds; before we were through dinner it was raining again, and we heard it on the train that night. Mother wrote me afterwards that it rained for weeks.

On our way west we paid farewell visits to civilization at Chicago and St. Paul. Farther on the train stopped for an hour at Mandan, South Dakota, to enable the passengers to see a wonderful collection of mounted animals. The great heads and horns of the beasts of the prairie made a deep impression on me, since I was so soon to be living among them.

I went with romantic ideas of being a helpmeet to a man in a new country, but I was sadly ill-equipped when it came to carrying them out. Before I left Union a dear old lady had taught me how to make hot rolls, but except for that one accomplishment I knew no more of cooking than I did of Greek. Hot rolls, plus a vague understanding that petticoats ought to be plain, were my whole equipment for conquering the West.

How did railroads help close the frontier? Do you think travel by train was always as pleasant as the author describes?

What kind of role did women play in settling the West?

Letters from Negro Migrants*

Among the paradoxes that abound in history is the equivocal effect of war. World War I, occasion of hideous carnage on the battlefields of Europe, provided unprecedented opportunity for black people in America. Brutalized by Jim Crow segregationist rule throughout the South, blacks sought salvation in Northern cities, where a combination of full war production and labor shortages meant steady work at decent pay. One indication of this mass movement is revealed in census records, which show staggering net population losses of blacks in the Deep South between 1910 and 1920: 130,000 from Mississippi, 70,000 from Alabama, 74,000 from South Carolina, 75,000 from Georgia. Where did they go? To New York City and Philadelphia, to Cleveland and the other industrial cities of Ohio, to Chicago, Detroit, and St. Louis. This was the beginning of a major demographic movement that has continued into the 1970s, a movement with profound implications in twentieth-century American history. Although the statistical data are sterile, the letters that follow, written to *The Defender*, a Chicago black newspaper, indicate the full range of human emotions accompanying this extraordinary uprooting.

WHO CAME

What was happening in 1917 to open up industrial jobs in the North for blacks?

Dallas, Tex., April 23, 1917.

Dear Sir: Having been informed through the Chicago Defender paper that I can secure information from you. I am a constant reader of the Defender and am contemplating on leaving here for some point north. Having your city in view I thought to inquire of you about conditions for work, housing, wages and everything necessary. I am now employed as a laborer in a structural shop, have worked for the firm five years.

I stored cars for Armour packing co. 3 years, I also claims to know something about candy making, am handy at most anything for an honest living. I am 31 yrs. old, have a very industrious wife, no children. If chances are available for work of any kind let me know. Any information you can give me will be highly appreciated.

* Arrangement of letters and headings is supplied by the editors.

Memphis, Tenn., May 22nd, 1917.

Sir: As you will see from the above that I am working in an office somewhat similar to the one I am addressing, but that is not the purpose with which I sat out to write.

What I would like best to know is can you secure me a position there? I will not say that I am capable of doing any kind of labor as I am not. Have had an accidental injury to my right foot; hence I am incapable of running up and down stairs, but can go up and down by taking my time. I can perform janitors duties, tend bar, or grocery store, as clerk. I am also a graduate of the Law Department, Howard University, Washington, D. C. Class of '85 but this fact has not swelled my head. I am willing to do almost any thing that I can do that there is a dollar to it. I am a man of 63 years of age. Lived here all of my life, barring 5 or 6 years spent in Washington and the East. Am a christian, Baptist by affiliation.

Have been a teacher, clerk in the government department, Law and Pension offices, for 5 years, also a watchman in the War Dept., also collector and rental agent for the late R. R. Church, Esq. Member of Canaan Baptist Church, Covington, Tenn. Now this is the indictment I plead to.

Sir, If you can place me I will be willing to pay anything in reason for the service. I have selected a place to stop with a friend of earlier days at ——, whenever I can get placed there. An early reply will be appreciated by yours respectfully.

What does this tell you about the situation of blacks in the South's economy?

Palestine, Tex., Mar. 11th, 1917.

Sirs: this is somewhat a letter of information I am a colored Boy aged 15 years old and I am talented for an artist and I am in search of some one will Cultivate my talent I have studied Cartooning therefore I am a Cartoonist and I intend to visit Chicago this summer and I want to keep in touch with your association and too from you knowledge can a Colored boy be an artist and make a white man's salary up there I will tell you more and also send a fiew samples of my work when I rec an answer from you.

Would you say he has faith in himself?

Alexandria, La., June 6, 1917.

Dear Sirs: I am writeing to you all asking a favor of you all. I am a girl of seventeen. School has just closed I have been going to school for nine months and I now feel like I aught to go to work. And I would like very very well for you all to please forward me to a good job. but there isnt a thing here for me to do, the wages here is from a dollar and a half a week. What could I earn Nothing. I have a mother and father my father do all he can for me but it is so hard. A child with any respect about her self or his self wouldnt like to see there mother and father work so hard and earn nothing I feel it my duty to help. I would like for you all to get me a good job and as I havent any money to come on please send me a pass and I would work and pay every cent of it back and get me a good quite place to stay. My father have been getting the defender for three or four months but for the last two weeks we have failed to get it. I dont know why. I am tired of down hear in this——/ I am afraid to say. Father seem to care and then again dont seem to but Mother and I am tired tired of all of this I wrote to you all because I believe you will help I need your help hopeing to here from you all very soon.

From her letter, what do you think her chances are of finding a good job?

93

New Orleans, La., June 10, 1917.

Kind Sir: I read and hear daly of the great chance that a colored parson has in Chicago of making a living with all the priveleg that the whites have and it mak me the most ankious to want to go where I may be able to make a liveing for my self. When you read this you will think it bery strange that being only my self to support that it is so hard, but it is so. everything is gone up but the poor colerd peple wages. I have made sevle afford to leave and come to Chicago where I hear that times is good for us but owing to femail wekness has made it a perfect failure. I am a widow for 9 years. I have very pore learning altho it would not make much diffrent if I would be throughly edacated for I could not get any better work to do, such as house work, washing and ironing and all such work that are injering to a woman with femail wekness and they pay so little for so hard work that it is just enough to pay room rent and a little some thing to eat. I have found a very good remady that I really feeling to belive would cure me if I only could make enough money to keep up my madison and I dont think that I will ever be able to do that down hear for the time is getting worse evry day. I am going to ask if you peple hear could aid me in geting over her in Chicago and seeking out a position of some kind. I can also do plain sewing. Please good peple dont refuse to help me out in my trouble for I am in gret need of help God will bless you. I am going to do my very best after I get over here if God spair me to get work I will pay the expance back. Do try to do the best you can for me, with many thanks for so doing I will remain as ever,

Yours truly.

Do you think she will be better or worse off in the city?

These cotton pickers faced economic hardship in the South in the war years because of widespread crop failures, brought on by a boll weevil plague and extensive flooding. Given the conditions of industrial labor described in this chapter, why did they look upon the North as a land of promise?

It has been estimated that by the end of 1918 more than 1 million blacks had left the South. Why did Southern whites react with alarm to this mass emigration?

WHY THEY CAME

Mobile, Ala., April 25, 1917.

Sir: I was reading in theat paper about the Colored race and while reading it I seen in it where cars would be here for the 15 of May which is one month from to day. Will you be so kind as to let me know where they are coming to and I will be glad to know because I am a poor woman and have a husband and five children living and three dead one single and two twin girls six months old today and my husband can hardly make bread for them in Mobile. This is my native home but it is not fit to live in just as the Chicago Defender say it says the truth and my husband only get $1.50 a day and pays $7.50 a month for house rent and can hardly feed me and his self and children. I am the mother of 8 children 25 years old and I want to get out of this dog hold because I dont know what I am raising them up for in this place and I want to get to Chicago where I know they will be raised and my husband crazy to get there because he know he can get more to raise his children and will you please let me know where the cars is going to stop to so that he can come where he can take care of me and my children. He get there a while and then he can send for me. . . .

How much per month did this leave for food for ten people?

Houston, Texas, April 20, 1917.

How does his motive differ from that of the previous writer?

Dear Sir: . . . I am 30 years old and have Good Experence in Freight Handler and Can fill Position from Truck to Agt. would like Chicago or Philadelphia But I dont Care where so long as I Go where a man is a man. . . .

95

Troy, Ala., Oct. 17, 1916.

Dear Sirs: I am enclosing a clipping of a lynching again which speaks for itself. I do wish there could be sufficient presure brought about to have federal investigation of such work. I wrote you a few days ago if you could furnish me with the addresses of some firms or co-opporations that needed common labor. So many of our people here are almost starving. The government is feeding quite a number here would go any where to better their conditions. If you can do any thing for us write me as early as posible.

How common were lynchings? What purpose did they serve?

What does this indicate about the political and legal structure of the South?

Brookhaven, Miss., April 24, 1917.

Gents: The cane growers of Louisiana have stopped the exodus from New Orleans, claiming shortage of labor which will result in a sugar famine.

Now these laborers thus employed receive only 85 cents a day and the high cost of living makes it a serious question to live.

. . . Please dont publish this letter but do what you can towards helping them to get away. If the R. R. Co. would run a low rate excursion they could leave that way. Please ans.

Memphis, Tenn., 4–23–17.

Gentlemen: I want to get in tuch with you in regard of a good location & a job   I am for race elevation every way. I want a job in a small town some where in the north where I can receive verry good wages and where I can educate my 3 little girls and demand respect of intelegence. I prefer a job as cabinet maker or any kind of furniture mfg. if possible.

Let me hear from you all at once please. State minimum wages and kind of work.

In sum, why did blacks leave the South?

WHAT THEY FOUND

Macon, Ga., May 27, 1917.

Dear Mary: . . . I got a card from Mrs. Addie S——yesterday she is well and say washington D. C. is a pretty place but wages is not good say it better forther on Cliford B——an his wife is back an give the North a bad name Old lady C——is in Cleavon an wonte to come home mighty bad so Cliford say. I got a hering from Vick C—— tell me to come on she living better than she ever did in her life Charlie J——is in Detroit he got there last weak Hattie J——lef Friday Oh I can call all has left here Leala J——is speaking of leaving soon There were more people left last week then ever 2 hundred left at once the whites an colored people had a meeting Thursday an Friday telling the people if they stay here they will treat them better an pay better. Huney they are hurted but the haven stop yet. The colored people say they are too late now George B——is on his head to go to Detroit Mrs. Anna W——is just like you left her she is urgin everybody to go on an she not getting ready May you dont no how I mis you I hate to pass your house Everybody is well as far as I no Will J——is on the gang for that same thing hapen about the eggs on Houston road. His wife tried to get him to leave here but he woulden Isiah j——is going to send for Hattie. In short Charles S——wife quit him last week he aint doin no better. . . . I received the paper you sent me an I see there or pleanty of work I can do I will let you no in my next lettr what I am going to do but I cant get my mind settle to save my life. Love to Mr. A——. . . .

On the basis of what she knows of conditions in the North and South, would you advise Mary B. to migrate?

Blacks found employment throughout the North, especially in war-related industries. Despite their contribution to the war effort, after the war they were often the victims of the last-hired, first-fired principle. Has this practice changed over the years?

Chicago, Illinois.

My dear Sister: I was agreeably surprised to hear from you and to hear from home. I am well and thankful to say I am doing well. . . . Please remember me kindly to any who ask of me. The people are rushing here by the thousands and I know if you come and rent a big house you can get all the roomers you want. You write me exactly when you are coming. I am not keeping house yet I am living with my brother and his wife. My sone is in California but will be home soon. He spends his winter in California. I can get a nice place for you to stop until you can look around and see what you want. I am quite busy. I work in Swifts packing Co. in the sausage department. My daughter and I work for the same company—We get $1.50 a day and we pack so many sausages we dont have much time to play but it is a matter of a dollar with me and I feel that God made the path and I am walking therein.

Tell your husband work is plentiful here and he wont have to loaf if he want to work. . . .

Has she improved her condition? Why would she recommend others to come?

97

Pittsburg, Pa., May 11, 1917.

My dear Pastor and wife: . . . I am in this great city & you no it cool here right now the trees are just peeping out. fruit trees are now in full bloom but its cool yet we set by big fire over night. I like the money O. K. but I like the South betterm for my Pleasure this city is too fast for me they give you big money for what you do but they charge you big things for what you get and the people are coming by cal Loads every day its just pack out the people are Begging for some whears to sta If you have a family of children & come here you can buy a house easier than you cant rent one if you rent one you have to sign up for 6 months or 12 month so you see if you dont like it you have to stay you no they pass that law becaus the People move about so much. . . .

What similarities are there to what earlier immigrants found upon arriving in the city?

Hattiesburg, Miss. Chicago, Illinois, 11/ 13/17.

Which of the migrants' hopes for coming North has the writer realized? Do you think he is typical?

Dear M——: . . . M——, old boy, I was promoted on the first of the month I was made first assistant to the head carpenter when he is out of the place I take everything in charge and was raised to $95. a month. You know I know my stuff.

Whats the news generally around H'burg? I should have been here 20 years ago. I just begin to feel like a man. It's a great deal of pleasure in knowing that you have got some privilege My children are going to the same school with the whites and I dont have to umble to no one. I have registered—Will vote the next election and there isnt any 'yes sir' and 'no sir'—its all yes and no and Sam and Bill.

Florine says hello and would like very much to see you.

All joins me in sending love to you and family. How is times there now? Answer soon, from your friend and bro.

ASSIGNMENT 3
GATHERING INFORMATION ABOUT YOUR FAMILY

The time has come for you to begin to gather the basic historical information that will allow you to write a history of your family. Since this research cannot adequately be done all at once, you should do it systematically. It will serve no purpose, really, to begin at the end of the semester, with finals coming up and the paper due in three days!

The task of the historian is to collect as much information as possible about a person, an event, or a movement; to sift the relevant from the irrelevant, organizing the surviving data; and then to interpret the evidence by writing a story that attempts to make sense out of the past. Of course the past can never be recaptured or reconstructed exactly. The information available is always incomplete and often contradictory, since witnesses remember the same event differently. In addition, each historian approaches the evidence with a particular point of view and purpose. All history is necessarily subjective, therefore, but that is why it is interesting and important.

As you look over the questionnaires and suggested topics for investigation in the back of the book, the range of inquiry may tend to overwhelm you, but remember that what is aimed at is a comprehensive picture of your family: socioeconomic profiles, family power and value structures, physical and spatial factors (dwellings, communities, uprootings and resettlements), importance placed on education and religion, and so on. Nevertheless, some of the categories may not prove useful in your investigation, and you should therefore concentrate on only those areas in which you find substantial pertinent information.

As you are collecting your facts, try to be as critical as possible: ask yourself if what you are told is credible. If corroboration seems necessary to establish something crucial, consult more than one source.

Naturally the more evidence you collect, the stronger your basis for historical description and analysis will be later. Some students may be more interested (or ambitious) than others, of course. But everyone should avoid writing a simple heroic tale of sainted ancestors. Keep in mind, too, that privacy is to be respected: you do not have to include *anything* that might be embarrassing.

Begin with yourself. You may be able to provide some information from your own memory—your parents' birthdates and the names of your grandparents, for example. Other facts may be determined by consulting the documents that are probably available in your house. Look for diaries, letters, death and marriage certificates, army discharge papers, photo albums, newspaper clippings, and family Bibles (which often contain genealogical information). Drawers, attics, and crammed closets may reveal fascinating and interesting documentation, but ask permission before you explore. Look at the checklist at the end of this section for easily available sources of information outside the home.

Most of the information you seek will probably come from oral interviews with members of your family, and here a word of caution is in order. Interviewing is a delicate art at best. While it has special benefits, interviewing one's parents and grandparents also may cause special problems. The family should be informed of the purpose of this project, so that fears of embarrassment or invasion of privacy can be allayed. Assurance must be given that no use beyond the classroom is contemplated and, if you think it necessary, a commitment can be made to prior clearance before the paper is submitted.

Talking to relatives about your family's history can be a rewarding experience, but you should use your judgment and common sense about the most effective way to approach them. The best interviewers are those who have an interest in their subject and have done a careful job of preparation before they begin to interview. You should begin by doing as much research as possible before you conduct your interviews, utilizing what you have learned from the earlier chapters of this book. The next step is to gather as much useful information as you can by asking specific questions of your parents and grandparents: place of birth, date of marriage, grandmother's maiden name, and so on. It is probably better to fill out the questionnaires yourself than to ask your relatives to do it, because forms have a tendency to stifle talk rather than to stimulate it.

As you move to the more substantive questions, it is usually best to structure your interview loosely. Reading a list of prepared questions will be stilted and formal, so use the suggested questions and topics as guides only. (Of course, being fairly unstructured in your interview does not mean being unprepared.) Try to ask open-ended questions that stimulate, rather than questions that can only be answered by yes or no or questions so broad that they inhibit a response. Thus, instead of asking, "Was the depression economically difficult for you?" try inquiring, "Where did you work and how much were you paid?" Or, instead of the nonspecific question, "Where were you during World War II?" try asking, "What was the single most significant thing that happened to you during the war?" Moreover, a simple question like "What do you remember eating for Sunday dinner when you were a child?" may yield surprising information on family structure, standard of living, the role of religion, and so on. Be ready to ask follow-up questions, and be flexible enough to alter your plan and pursue a topic that you had not considered.

Do not overlook mundane topics, since you may later be able to use the information in your analysis. Seemingly inconsequential details may be of significance—holiday traditions, for instance, or the role of music in the home. If your ancestors were born in hospitals, who paid the bill? If not, who delivered the child, and what reciprocal gestures were expected as a result? In other words, concentrate on the areas of life your relatives know best, not their opinion of world leaders, unless of course they actually knew those famous people.

Your major role as interviewer is to listen carefully—not an easy job—and to act as a guide and director of the conversation. Try not to let your own preconceived ideas influence your questions or your responses to answers, and do not assume that your parents and grandparents have the same value system that you have. Guard against overly sophisticated questions; try to keep them simple and direct.

If you have a tape recorder readily available, it may prove useful, but tape may not be the best way to record your interviews. The machine, reproducing every detail of what is said, may frighten or inhibit some people. Transcribing the tapes at a later time can also be very difficult. Some interviewers prefer to take brief notes during the interview, and then to write up a summary and impressions immediately afterward. Whatever method you choose for recording your interview, try to make the situation as natural and relaxed as possible. The length of time you can talk at one session will vary, depending on the age and personality of the person to whom you are talking, as well as on your attitude and mood. Most interviewers find that two hours is the absolute maximum for one interview session. Several short sessions may be more effective than one long session, because that gives you time in between to go over what has been accomplished, to fill in gaps, to formulate new questions. If a relative lives a long distance from you, or if all of your sources of information are far away, questions may be sent through the mail. Letters are a poor substitute for face-to-face conversations, however, and consequently the facts-by-mail approach should be supplemented by interviews the next time you return home.

Human memory is often unpredictable and unreliable, especially as people grow older. The documents, pictures, and clippings you have collected should help trigger memories and establish a time sequence. Remember that you are interested in general trends, thoughts, feelings, and overall meaning more than in establishing and confirming each fact. Being a historian is in some ways like playing detective, but beware of overplaying the role. Most families have stories or legends about the family's past that have been passed from one generation to another. It is important to try to separate fact from folklore, but legends and stories can also be important. As you proceed in a flexible and open manner, you will learn a great deal. You will also acquire a new understanding and appreciation of your own heritage.

CHECKLIST

The following checklist of possible sources of information has been compiled to aid your research:

household sources
   diaries
   letters
   certificates
     birth
     marriage
     death
     education
     honors and awards
     military service
     civic participation
   photo albums
   newspaper clippings
   family Bible
   legal documents
     mortgages
     wills
hometown sources
   library and local historical society
     local genealogies
     old city directories
     miscellaneous local histories
   family plots in cemetaries
   clerical records at city hall or the municipal building
     land deeds
     tax records
     vital statistics
     church lists
     civic organization lists

Those who are seriously interested in tracing their family history and want more information should consult Gilbert H. Doane, *Searching for Your Ancestors* (New York: Bantam, 1974), which is available in most libraries and in a paperback edition. It is filled with useful information, bibliographies, and suggestions. You may find primary sources relevant to your ancestry in the genealogical section of a large public library or historical society.

For more extensive research, two government services are especially helpful: the National Archives and the Immigration and Naturalization Service. The former distributes publications which, if your school or public library does not already have them, can be acquired by writing the National Archives, Sales Branch, Washington, D.C. 20408. Particularly useful is the free pamphlet, "Genealogical Records in the National Archives" (National Archives General Information Leaflet 5). Other free pamphlets pertinent to family history are General Information Leaflets 6, 7, 8, 9, and 10. A more detailed publication, *A Guide to Genealogical Records in the National Archives*, can be purchased for the nominal fee of 65 cents.

The National Archives also keeps demographic records. A useful reference to consult for a listing of such records is *Federal Population and Mortality Census Schedules, 1790–1890 in the National Archives and the States.* You may buy census records, including slave records, for the period up to 1890.

For specific information, write to the Central Reference Room of the National Archives in Washington.

The Immigration and Naturalization Service, 119 D St., N.E., Washington, D.C. 20408, has records on immigrants' naturalization petitions. Before writing, you should try to discover when and where your ancestors entered the United States, and the name of the ship. Ask your librarian for *The Morton Allen Directory of European Passenger Steamship Arrivals.*

BIBLIOGRAPHIC NOTE

A bibliography that would adequately cover the range of historical experience sampled in this chapter is, unfortunately, too vast to list here. Instead, we refer you to a few general works, some of which contain bibliographies that you may consult for works on your particular ethnic or racial heritage.

For a general introduction, see the controversial work by Oscar Handlin, *The Uprooted: The Epic Story of the Great Migrations That Made the American People* (2nd enl. ed., 1973), or Maldwyn Allen Jones, *American Immigration* (1960), both of which have extensive bibliographies on ethnic groups. For a picture of life in immigrant urban ghettos consult Nathan Glazer and Daniel Patrick Moynihan, *Beyond the Melting Pot* (1963), and Herbert Gans, *The Urban Villagers* (1962). See also John Higham, *Strangers in the Land* (1955) for anti-immigrant hostility. Life on the vast and lonely plains is vividly sketched in O. E. Rolvaag's novel *Giants in the Earth* (1927). On the South, the best work remains C. Vann Woodward, *Origins of the New South, 1877–1913* (1951). The effects of the movement of blacks to the North are well treated in Gilbert Osofsky, *Harlem: The Making of a Ghetto, 1890–1930* (1966), and Allan Spear, *Black Chicago: The Making of a Negro Ghetto, 1890–1920* (1967).

In addition to the bibliographies in some of these works, you may consult those in American history texts for citations relevant to your own interests.

four

THE DEPRESSION

Some events are so important that their influence cuts across class lines, affects all races and ethnic groups, and leaves no region untouched. The depression of the 1930s was such an event. No one who lived through those years in the United States could ever completely forget the bread lines, the millions of unemployed, or the forlorn and discouraged men and women who saw their mortgages foreclosed, their dreams shattered, their children hungry and afraid.

The depression was precipitated by the stock market crash in October 1929, but the actual cause of the collapse was an unhealthy economy. While the ability of the manufacturing industry to produce consumer goods had increased rapidly, mass purchasing power had remained relatively static. Most laborers, farmers, and white-collar workers, therefore, could not afford to buy the automobiles and refrigerators turned out by factories in the 1920s, because their incomes were too low. At the same time, the federal government increased the problem through economic policies that tended to encourage the very rich to oversave.

Herbert Hoover, a sensitive and humane engineer, had the misfortune of being President when the depression began. Even though he broke with the past and used the power of the federal government to stem the tide of depression, especially through loans to businesses and banks, his efforts proved to be too little and too late. Somewhat unfairly his name became synonymous with failure and despair. As a result, Hoover was defeated by Franklin Roosevelt, who took office in March 1933 with the country in a state of crisis. Many banks had failed, millions were unemployed, and in the Middle West thousands of farmers seemed ready to use violence to protest their hopeless situation.

Roosevelt had a sense of confidence that was contagious. In his inaugural address he announced, "We have nothing to fear except fear itself," which was, of course, not exactly true. But he acted swiftly and decisively, if not always consistently, to right the economy. He closed all the banks and then gradually reopened those that were sound. He rushed through Congress a series of acts ranging from attempts to aid business and agriculture to emergency banking legislation and to the legalization of the sale of beer and wine for the first time in thirteen years. Very few people who lived through the 1930s were neutral about Roosevelt. He came to be hated by many businessmen, who called him a socialist or simply "that man in the White House." Others, more radical than the President, attacked him for not going far enough in his reforms, for trying to patch up the American free enterprise system rather than replacing it with some form of socialism. More important, however, he was loved and admired by the great mass of ordinary Americans, who crowded around the radio to listen to his comforting voice in "fireside chats" that explained the complex government programs.

Many of his New Deal measures, such as the Social Security Act and the Wagner Act (aiding the cause of unionism), had far-reaching influence. None, however, solved the massive social and economic problems facing the country. The long list of agencies and administrations, popularly known by their initials—from the AAA that aided farmers to the WPA that provided jobs for the unemployed—succeeded only to the extent of restoring a measure of self-respect and hope to some hard-hit by the depression. Financially, the country remained in a slump. It was not until the 1940s, when defense spending stimulated the economy, that the nation finally emerged from its worst economic crisis.

To many, the fact that the nation could go into such a deep slough was puzzling. The early and middle twenties, in which people became fully conscious of being part of the age of the machine, seemed to auger unending economic expansion. Two years before the stock market crash, in 1927, Henry Ford produced his fifteen-millionth automobile and then promptly switched from his all-black Model T to the more colorful and modern Model A. In the same year, the world "shrank" considerably when radio-telephone service was established between New York, London, San Francisco, and Manila, and Charles Lindbergh opened the way for rapid transatlantic travel by his solo flight from New York to Paris. The year 1927 also foreshadowed the great media explosion with the establishment of the first national radio network and the release of the first feature-length film with spoken dialogue. Within a few years, millions would be listening to radio shows like "The Shadow" and "The Lone Ranger" and flocking to their neighborhood theaters to live vicariously with their movie-star heroes and heroines—Clark Gable, Greta Garbo, Gary Cooper, Bette Davis. Technology, with its many facets, seemed to be widening horizons.

This promise of prosperity through technology was deceptive, though. For one thing, although radios and electric refrigerators and flush toilets were being produced by the millions, millions of Americans outside the middle and upper classes still had to use iceboxes and outhouses and live much the same way their ancestors had. Furthermore, as already noted, the prosperity of the middle class was itself based on an economic lie. The depression punctured its inflated dreams. The great majority of Americans suffered, therefore, from the economic collapse, whether they were business executives, farmers, workingmen, housewives, or secretaries. In a sense, the depression was not as devastating for the lower classes as it was for the upper and middle classes. The sharecropper in Mississippi, the unemployed black in Chicago, probably did not notice the depression as much because his life was already depressed.

There are many ways to chart the impact of the depression on the lives of Americans. One can mention the $26 billion wiped out by the stock market crash or the millions who lost their savings when the banks failed. The total industrial production in 1932 was half of what it had been in 1929. No one knows how many men and women lost their jobs; estimates of those out of work range from 12 million to 16 million at the peak of the depression, and in some cities the unemployment rate was more than 50 percent. For those who did work, the average pay ranged from twenty to thirty cents an hour in 1932 in heavy industry. In addition, one out of every four

farmers lost his farm, and millions were evicted from their homes because they could not pay the rent. (There were 200,000 evictions in New York City alone in 1931.)

But none of these statistics really communicates the hopelessness and the despair of the depression years. In Chicago men and women fought with children over the garbage dumped by trucks. A social worker noticed that the children in one city were playing a game called Eviction. "Sometimes they play 'Relief,'" she remarked, "but 'Eviction' has more action and all of them know how to play." In Philadelphia a store owner told of one family he was keeping on credit. "Eleven children in that house," he reported. "They've got no shoes, no pants. In the house, no chairs. My God, you go in there, you cry that's all."

The search for a secure job, the fear of failure, the worry about vanished savings, lost hope and shattered dreams, and the nagging worry that it would all happen over again separated those who lived through the depression from those who were born in the 1940s and after. Parents who experienced the depression urged their children to train for a good job, to get married and settle down. But often their children, products of an age of affluence, cared little about security and sometimes rejected the material objects, the signs of success, that took on such importance for parents. Studs Terkel of Chicago, who has made an art of talking to people and arranging their thoughts into books, spoke to a young woman who remarked:

Everytime I've encountered the Depression, it has been used as a barrier and a club, it's been a counter-communication. Older people use it to explain to me that I can't understand *anything:* I didn't live through the Depression. They never say to me: "We can't understand you because we didn't live through the leisure society." All attempts at communication are totally blocked.[1]

Are your feelings the same as this woman's, or do you think it is possible to bridge the gap between the depression generation and those who came after? The following selections, most of which are autobiographical accounts and recollections of the 1930s, should help you begin to understand the experience and effects of that era. After you have read them, we will ask you to go out on your own to talk to someone who remembers the depression.

[1] Studs Terkel. *Hard Times: An Oral History of the Great Depression* (New York: Pantheon, 1970), p. 39.

BREAKDOWN:
Two Reactions to the Depression
Louis Adamic

There was no typical response to the tragedy of the depression, but almost everyone suffered. Although statistics are often used to document just how widespread that suffering was, unemployment figures do not adequately convey the despair and degradation that financial loss exacts. The following accounts tell the pathetic story of two families in differing economic and social circumstances that collapsed because of the economic disaster. Both shared in suffering that went beyond physical deprivations, yet there were some subtle differences in their reactions. As you read the following accounts, try to imagine what your own response might have been.

JIM F——

Jim F—— had worked as a truck-driver for the same concern for five years, making forty-five dollars a week. He and Mrs. F—— were a happy, respectable couple. They had four children, all of them fairly normal. In April, 1930, when he was thirty-six years old, Jim lost his job when the firm went bankrupt. For six months he had no work at all. In September he drove a truck for another concern for two weeks, making only twenty-three dollars a week. It was his last job. In December he lost all his savings— $350—in a bank failure. Then two of the children became ill. He had a hard time in borrowing money to pay the doctor and the druggist. They began to pawn things; finally, Mrs. F—— was forced to pawn her wedding ring. In September, 1931, the rent was three months in arrears. The landlord threatened eviction. Then Jim "got out of his mind," as Mrs. F—— put it to me, and joined two other men (also married men and fathers of children, living in the same apartment-house) in a robbery. They got thirty-three dollars and were arrested almost at once. The family situation was explained to the district attorney and reputable persons testified as to Jim's pre-Depression character, but in vain. Jim was sentenced to five years in Sing Sing. In October, when Jim was being tried, Mrs. F——, not knowing what else to do, appealed to organized charity for the first time and now, living in a single-room flat with her children, she managed to keep

Do you think this could happen to-day?

105

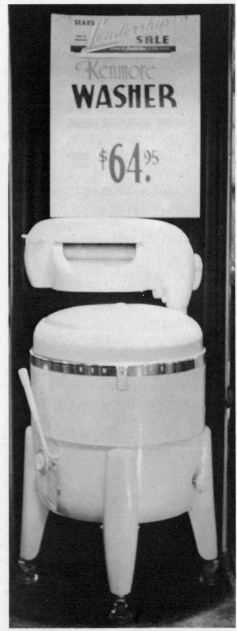

Although everyone was hit to some extent by the depression, the differences between middle-class and lower- or working-class modes of living can still be detected in photographs of the period. The difference is obvious in these pictures of how clothes might be washed in a farmer's family and in a white-collar family. Subtler differences can be detected by examining the two views of a family meal on the next page. What differences can you find? With which pattern would your parents have been more familiar?

them and herself alive on the few dollars she received as relief. She felt disgraced. None of her relatives and former friends knew where she was. Jim himself was a hopeless man in Sing Sing. He felt that when he got out of prison, even should the conditions improve, his chances of employment would be slim because of his criminal record. Mrs. F—— visited him in prison just before Christmas (the fare was paid by the charity organization). His forehead, when she saw him, was scarred and blue, because every now and then he went "crazy" and banged his head against the walls of his cell. But the worst phase of the situation was that the children were being seriously affected. Unable to restrain herself, Mrs. F—— wept a great deal, and the children bawled with her. There were nights when all five of them cried for hours. They all slept in the same room, except the oldest boy, whose bed was the tub in the windowless bathroom. All four children, two of them of school age, were underweight, suffering with frequent ailments due to poor resistance. When I visited the family one child was in bed with a cold; two other children were in the same bed—the only one—" to keep warm." There was no heat in the dwelling. Mrs. F—— said to me, "We'd all be better off dead."

Why was accepting relief looked upon as a disgrace? Is this still the case?

What did the depression do to the American Dream?

MR. D——

In 1929 Mr. D——was worth over $200,000. He was a retired business man, playing the market "a little." He had a fine home in a New York suburb. His oldest son was at Harvard. Two daughters were in private schools. Mr. and Mrs. D—— had just booked a 'round-the-world passage when the Crash came. Of a sudden the world tumbled down about their heads. Hoping to save at least a part of his fortune, Mr. D—— mortgaged his home, but he no sooner got the mortgage money than it was "swallowed up by Wall Street." He was too proud to appeal to people he knew who were still wealthy. For two years the whole family struggled to save the home. During 1931 they actually starved. They sold their expensive furniture, piece by piece. The girls had to be recalled from their schools. The son quit Harvard. But it was no use. Gradually the family broke up even before the foreclosure on the home, late in 1931. The children now were scattered all over the country. One of the girls sang in a night club in Chicago. The son was a Communist who swore he would never marry or have children under the "present system." After the foreclosure Mr. and Mrs. D—— moved into a furnished room in New York City. He could get nothing to do. His mind was being affected by his plight. Finally, Mrs. D—— appealed to the charity organization they had supported in a small way for years before the Crash.

Was the depression worse for someone like Mr. D—— or for someone like Mr. F——?

HOW THE E. FAMILY LIVES
Eli Ginzberg and Hyman Berman

The following is the story of "commonplace people" with few ambitions who seem never to have been influenced by the American Dream. They were working-class people who barely survived before the depression; after the crash, they faced an even tighter budget. The budgets included here indicate how inexpensive most things were in the 1930s, and how it was possible to survive, and for a time even live comfortably, on a small income. But for many even a small income was difficult to achieve, as this family found out. Could you live on their "ideal budget"? Why didn't a family like this collapse like those of Jim F—— and Mr. D——?

Mr. E., age thirty-six, is a mechanic in a large factory on the "west side" of Chicago. He is married to a childhood playmate now aged thirty-three, and has three children—Helen, aged seven, Robert, aged five, and Julia, aged 15 months. Mr. E. and his wife have had a common school education and are commonplace people who have no particular abilities or disabilities, but are fairly energetic and thrifty. Until recently they have managed to make a fairly comfortable living. About two years ago they had a fund of several hundred dollars saved up and were hoping to make a first payment on a home in one of the outlying neighborhoods. At that time Mr. E.'s health began to fail, and in a short time he was compelled to quit work. A local physician told him he had "consumption," and Mr. E. began to treat his cough with home remedies and patent medicines. Meantime there was no income, and in about five months every resource was exhausted; savings were spent, cheaper quarters found, superfluous furniture sold, credit at neighborhood stores exhausted, sick benefits from the lodge were withdrawn, and expenses trimmed at every point, even to dropping payments on life insurance. In short there was nothing to do but follow the suggestions of an interested neighbor and "appeal to the charities." They were then about $250 in debt. . . .

. . . An estimate of the family's original average of expenditures follows:

Is health care better provided for today? Can families still be wiped out financially by illness?

Rent (four rooms, stove heat)	$35.00
Fuel and light (coal and gas)	$7.50
Food	62.25
Clothing	24.00
Household expenses (including upkeep on furniture)	8.20
Carfare	5.00
Health	5.00
Insurance	1.15
Spending money and recreation	4.00
Savings	8.50
Average monthly total expense	$160.60

Could a family live on this today?

109

Mr. E.'s earnings at 72 cents an hour, including a little extra money he earned at overtime work, had enabled him to meet this budget very easily. During his illness, of course, the standard of living rapidly fell and no organized scheme of expenditures could be found from the household account book. During the last month before they appealed to the charities, the E.'s had pared their expenses down to absolute necessities: "We barely lived," as Mrs. E. expressed it.

Their expenditures, when classified as above, were as follows:

How many hours would Mr. E have had to work to meet his budget? Have unions made a difference in this respect?

Rent	$23.00
Fuel and light	4.50
Food	47.88
Clothing	8.00
Household expenses	3.16
Carfare	.85
Health	12.00
Insurance	0.00
Spending money and recreation	.36
Savings	0.00
Total	$99.75

Value of articles given by neighbors, friends, relatives:

Food	$10.00
Clothing	3.00
Fuel	2.00
Total	$114.75

When Mr. E. came home from the sanitarium some eight months later and went back to his work, the worker made a similar estimate to determine whether the family would be fully self-supporting, or would need further assistance. Her figures were approximately those shown in the table, but when the social worker talked over the budget problem in a friendly way with Mrs. E., the worker pointed out several changes that she proposed should be made. Among these were:

Item	Total	General Family Expense	Mr. E.	Mrs. E.	Helen	Robert	Julia
Housing	$ 35.00	$35.00					
Food	59.81		$17.77	$14.30	$10.40	$ 8.67	$ 8.67
Clothing	29.00		9.00	7.50	5.00	3.75	3.75
Fuel and light	8.50	8.50					
Household expenses	5.00	5.00					
Carfare	5.04		3.64	1.40			
Spending money and recreation	2.50		1.00	1.00	.25	.25	
Health	7.00	7.00					
Education	.90	.75			.15		
Insurance	6.25		5.00	1.25			
Savings	10.00	10.00					
Total	$169.00	$66.25	$36.41	$25.45	$15.80	$12.67	$12.42

(1) A better grade of food could be secured with perhaps a slight decrease in cost by purchasing in larger quantities rather than from day to day, and by patronizing "cash-and-carry" shops; (2) household expenses could be materially reduced by the same plan and by purchasing furniture, when needed, for cash rather than on installments; (3) the worker believed that the family should have a daily and Sunday paper or some good popular

magazine; (4) the expenditures for health had been too low previously, dental care in particular being badly needed; (5) the family had too little insurance for safety; (6) some economies should be effected in spending money; and (7) it ought to be possible to increase the savings item a little. The total budget was a little larger than formerly, but Mr. E. had had a slight increase in wages and could meet it easily. . . .

Mrs. E. confided to the worker that their income had never been large enough to meet their real needs though they had succeeded in living within it and saving a little. Neither she nor Mr. E. had "aspirations beyond their station in life," but they both thought that their present living quarters were inadequate, that they needed several new pieces of parlor furniture and some really nice clothing. They would like to go to church more often and to make friends and also to join one or two neighborhood organizations. Mr. E. in particular was anxious to join a popular fraternal order to which many of the men at the shop belonged. They felt debarred from these relations now because they could not afford suitable clothing and proper home furnishings. For her part she had always wanted to go to the opera and see what it was like, and she wanted to send her washing to the "wet wash." Mr. E. had had the promise of a foreman's job before he became ill, with an increase of pay. He and his wife had thought then that they would be able to have everything they wished. In fact they had worked out a tentative monthly budget. Mrs. E. was reluctant to show this "ideal" budget since they "weren't in the habit of counting too much on the future." The estimate was:

Would your family be satisfied with these expectations today? Would you?

Rent (5 rooms, steam heat)	$60.00
Fuel and light (gas and electricity)	5.00
Food	65.00
Clothing	32.00
Household expenses	12.00
Carfare	6.00
Health	5.00
Insurance	3.00
Organization and church dues	5.00
Spending money and recreation	15.00
Savings (including $30 monthly to buy a home)	42.00
Total	$250.00

What would a comfortable monthly budget for a family of four total today?

As the budget of the E. family indicated, little money was available for entertainment in the 1930s. Reading was a popular family pastime, as the increase in library circulation throughout the country in these years shows. The most popular at-home entertainment by far, however, was listening to the radio. Away from home, people liked to gather at a familiar meeting place to discuss the hard times. And, because movie tickets were relatively inexpensive—as little as 15 cents—an evening at the movies was a popular entertainment, especially when escapist themes were dramatized. What effect has television had on changing the way Americans spend their leisure time in the 1970s?

I'd Rather Die

Eli Ginzberg and Hyman Berman

One of the hardest things for many people to get used to in the 1930s was the idea of being poor, for somehow Americans were not supposed to be poor. If one worked hard, got good grades, one ought to be a success. The following is the account of a father and son and how they dealt with poverty and failure. Neither seems to have been radicalized by his experience of poverty, as might have been expected. In fact, both tried to adjust themselves to the system that had failed them. Perhaps it was easier to be poor when most of those around you were also poor. But there was a toll to be paid for that adjustment. As you read their story, try to determine what effect the depression had on their willingness to accept the American Dream.

I went to work for Travis and Son a few weeks after Dad died. It's an overall factory—run by Old Dave MacGonnigal and his four boys.

Dad was a pattern-maker there and worked for Old Dave over forty-five years. If things hadn't gone the way they did, I'd never known what he went through to keep us alive all those years. After Dad's death when the bottom dropped out from under the family I couldn't find a job anywhere. Finally I applied to Old Dave MacGonnigal.

". . . Well," he said to me, "you needn't think that because you've got that high school diploma you can sit around on your tail here and talk Latin. We work here, boy. I put on overalls and work like the rest. You soldier on me and I'll fire you like a shot—understand?"

Seemed to me at the time that the job was something handed down out of heaven. I was so happy and relieved I didn't even ask the old man how much he was going to pay me. Rushed on home as fast as I could go to tell Mom.

I can tell you I didn't feel that way when the end of the first week came around. I drew six dollars and fifty cents.

I don't ever remember want or any feeling of insecurity when I was little. Dad made good money in those days—say, about $50 or $60 a week. You know, a pattern-maker has a pretty important job in an overall factory. If the patterns he lays out aren't right to the fraction of an inch the cutters will ruin a lot of goods. There's a good deal of figuring to it, complicated figuring, and he can't make mistakes. Dad never learned mathematics because he hadn't a chance to go to high school. But he'd worked out a system of his own with all sorts of funny little signs and symbols. Nobody else understood it. He could take a problem of figuring up goods and have it done in a minute where some of the efficiency experts Old Dave had in from time to time would take an hour to work it. And Dad's would be nearer the right answer than the experts'. The boys in the cutting room

Why didn't a young man like this become a radical and try to change the system?

told me all about it when I came there to work. So they paid Dad a pretty good salary, though not what he was worth.

We had our own home . . . and we had a car. My two older brothers and my sister finished high school. My oldest brother, after being a salesman for a few years . . . worked his way through Columbia University. I don't guess he could have done it by work alone. But he won one scholarship after another and finally a travelling fellowship that gave him a year in Europe. . . .

The first hard times I remember came in 1933, when I was in the eighth grade. Travis and Son shut down and for six months Dad didn't draw a penny. Things must have been pinching for two or three years before that because by that time the house was mortgaged and the money spent. I don't know much about the details. Anyhow, my brother . . . couldn't help much.

Then we were really up against it. For a whole week one time we didn't have anything to eat but potatoes. Another time my brother went around to the grocery stores and got them to give him meat for his dog—only he didn't have any dog. We ate that dog meat with the potatoes. I went to school hungry and came home to a house where there wasn't any fire. The lights were cut off. They came out and cut off the water. But each time, as soon as they left, my brother went out and cut it on again with a wrench.

I remember lying in bed one night and thinking. All at once I realized something. We were poor. Lord! It was weeks before I could get over that. . . .

Why are people ashamed to be poor in America?

. . . We lost our car and house and kept moving from one house to another. Bill collectors hunted us down and came in droves. Every now and then my brother or Dad would find some sort of odd job to do, or the other brother in Chicago would send us a little something. Then we'd go wild. I mean we'd go wild over food. We'd eat until we were sick. We'd eat four times a day and between meals. We just couldn't help ourselves. The sight and smell of food sort of made us crazy, I guess.

The winter of 1934 was the hardest time of all. . . . We were completely out of coal one time when we were living away out at the edge of town. The weather was freezing bitter then, so at night my brother and I would bundle up and go about a quarter of a mile away to a big estate on the Tennessee River. We made a hole in the fence and stole some of the wood that was piled a good distance from the house. We just walked in and got it. I don't remember that we tried to be quiet about it in particular.

After awhile things got some better. My brother in Chicago got so he could send money home and my other brother got another newspaper job. Dad went back to regular work at Travis and Son, though he only got about $20 a week. . . .

I went on through high school and made good marks. In my senior year I had an average of 98 and was elected class president and was valedictorian at graduation. I expected to go to college the next fall. Now, I can't see how on earth I could have expected to. I knew that there was no money for it. But somehow or other it just seemed to me that a way would turn up.

Do good marks in school assure you of a better job or success in life?

Mother felt the same about it. She'd say, "If you want a college education badly enough you will get it. Any boy who is determined can work his way through."

That summer we had a scare. There was some sort of strike at Travis and Son. Seems that after the NRA blew up, Old Dave put the girls in the sewing room on piecework and some of them just couldn't make a living. They protested but it didn't do no good. . . . Then some organizer came and

What was the NRA?

got them to go out on a strike. The men went out too, and they ganged around the entrance blocking off part of the street.

Dad didn't know what to do. He walked the floor at home. He said that the girls were right, but he didn't believe they could win out because the mayor had said he'd back Old Dave to the limit. I remember Mama telling Dad, "Oh, Bob, please don't do anything foolish—! We've been through such a hard time. What on earth would we do if we had to face it again? I couldn't bear it!"

So Dad went to work the next morning. I had some errands to do for Mama so I went to town with him. Old Dave had called up and said he'd have policemen to carry Dad through the strikers. When we got there the policemen were ready all right. They told Dad they'd rush him through. He started out, with me tagging behind. Then he made me go back to the corner and started again. The strikers were bunched up at the door of the factory. They weren't saying a thing or making a move. Just men and women standing there watching.

I saw Dad stop again. He had an argument with the police. I heard him say pretty loud, "No, I'll go by myself or I won't go at all." He said it two or three times.

The policemen were mad. "Okay, Cap," I heard one of them say. "It's your look-after, not mine."

Dad walked on without them, but they sort of edged along some way behind.

All at once the strikers began yelling and meeowing. Dad walked on. When he was right at them, about a dozen men and women grabbed at him and started tearing his coat and shirt.

I started running down there and so did the police. . . . But right then the strikers got into a free-for-all fight among themselves. Dad had a lot of good friends among them and these friends jumped on the ones who'd grabbed him. They pulled them off and Dad walked on through and went into the factory. He never was bothered again. Old Dave and the others had to have the police to get in and out. Dad came and went without anybody trying to stop him.

So the strike petered out and the strikers were out of jobs. Some of them came to Dad and he tried to get them back on. But Old Dave said he wouldn't touch a one of them with a ten-foot pole.

One night late in July Dad didn't come home at his usual time. . . . The doctors never did know what was wrong with Dad. He was sixty, but there wasn't anything like cancer or tuberculosis. One of the doctors at the hospital told me he was really just worn out completely. I guess he was right.

Do you think the depression made people more or less willing to go on strike?

116

HARD TIMES
Studs Terkel

The depression meant different things to different people. For a wealthy young Southern belle it was a disconnected telephone that symbolized a changed role. For a farmer from South Dakota it was surpluses amid starvation and using old automobile seat covers for clothing.

The following two interviews were done by Studs Terkel, a historian and writer, who uses a tape recorder to discover the past as ordinary people remember it. His technique is as interesting as the stories he uncovers. Perhaps you too can learn something about the impact of the depression on your family and your neighborhood by asking questions and listening.

DIANA MORGAN

She was a "southern belle" in a small North Carolina town. "I was taught that no prince of royal blood was too good for me." (Laughs.) Her father had been a prosperous cotton merchant and owner of a general store. "It's the kind of town you became familiar with in Thornton Wilder's Our Town. *You knew everybody. We were the only people in town who had a library."*

Her father's recurring illness, together with the oncoming of hard times—the farmers and the townspeople unable to pay their bills—caused the loss of the store. He went into bankruptcy.

The banks failed about the time I was getting ready to go to college. My family thought of my going to Wellesley, Vassar, Smith—but we had so little money, we thought of a school in North Carolina. It wasn't so expensive.

It was in my junior year, and I came home for Christmas. . . . I found the telephone disconnected. And this was when I realized that the world was falling apart. Imagine us without a telephone! When I finished school, I couldn't avoid facing the fact that we didn't have a cook any more, we didn't have a cleaning woman any more. I'd see dust under the beds, which is something I'd never seen before. I knew the curtains weren't as clean as they used to be. Things were beginning to look a little shabby. . . .

The first thing I noticed about the Depression was that my great-grandfather's house was lost, about to be sold for taxes. Our own house

Compare Diana Morgan's reaction to the depression with that of the boy in the previous article.

117

was sold. It was considered the most attractive house in town, about a hundred and fifty years old. We even had a music library. Imagine my shock when it was sold for $5,000 in back taxes. I was born in that house.

I never felt so old in my life as I felt the first two years out of college. 'Cause I hadn't found a new life for myself, and the other one was finished.

I remember how embarrassed I was when friends from out of town came to see me, because sometimes they'd say they want a drink of water, and we didn't have any ice. (Laughs.) We didn't have an electric refrigerator and couldn't afford to buy ice. There were those frantic arrangements of running out to the drugstore to get Coca-Cola with crushed ice, and there'd be this embarrassing delay, and I can remember how hot my face was.

All this time, I wasn't thinking much about what was going on in this country. . . . I was still leading some kind of social life. Though some of us had read books and discussed them, there wasn't much awareness. . . . Oh, we deplored the fact that so many of our young men friends couldn't find suitable things to do. . . .

One day a friend of my father stopped me on the street and said, "Would you like a job? A friend of mine is director of one of those New Deal programs. She'll tell you about it."

Oh, I was so excited, I didn't know what to do—the thought of having a job. I was very nervous, but very hopeful. Miss Ward came. She looked like a Helen Hokinson woman, very forbidding, formal. She must have been all of forty-five, but to me she looked like some ancient and very frightening person from another world.

She said to me, "It's not a job for a butterfly." She could just look at me and tell that I was just totally unsuitable. I said I was young and conscientious and if I were told what I was supposed to do, I would certainly try to the best of my ability. . . . She didn't give me any encouragement at all.

When she left, I cried for about an hour. I was really a wreck. I sobbed and sobbed and thought how unfair she was. So I was very much amazed to receive a telegram the next day summoning me to a meeting in Raleigh—for the directors of women's work.

There were dozens of women there, from all over the state, of all ages. It seemed to me very chaotic. Everyone was milling around, talking about weaving projects, canning, bookbinding. . . . Everyone there seemed very knowledgeable. I really didn't know what they were talking about. And nobody really told me what I was supposed to do. It just seemed that people were busy, and I somehow gathered that I was in.

So I went back home. I went to the county relief offices at the courthouse. There were people sitting on the floor of a long hallway, mostly black people, looking very depressed, sad. Some of them had children with them, some of them were very old. Just endless rows of them, sitting there, waiting. . . .

My first impression was: Oh, those poor devils, just sitting there, and nobody even saying, "We'll get to you as soon as we can." Though I didn't know a thing about social work, what was good and what wasn't good, my first impulse was that those people should be made to feel somebody was interested in them. Without asking anybody, I just went around and said, "Have you been waiting long? We'll get to you just as soon as we can."

I got the feeling the girls in the office looked very stern, and that they had a punitive attitude: that the women just had to wait, as long as they were there and that you had to find out and be sure they were entitled to it before they got anything.

Why did so many people lose their homes during the depression? Did anyone in your family suffer such a loss?

What was the purpose of such projects?

118

I didn't know a thing about sewing, bookbinding, canning . . . the approved projects. I'd never boiled an egg or sewed a stitch. But I knew seamstresses, who used to make clothes for us when we were children. I went to see them and got them to help me. I sought help from everybody who knew how to do things.

In the meantime, I would work in the relief office and I began interviewing people . . . and found out how everybody, in order to be eligible for relief, had to have reached absolute bottom. You didn't have to have a lot of brains to realize that once they reached that stage and you put them on an allowance of a dollar a day for food—how could they ever pull out of it?

Caroline, who used to cook for us, came in. I was so shocked to see her in a position where she had to go to the agency and ask for food. I was embarrassed for her to see me when she was in that state. She was a wonderful woman, with a big heart. Here she was, elderly by now, and her health wasn't good at all. And she said, "Oh the Lord's done sent you down from heaven to save me. I've fallen on hard times. How beautiful you are. You look like an angel to me." In the typical southern Negro way of surviving, she was flattering me. I was humiliated by her putting herself in that position, and by my having to see her go through this. (Weeps softly; continues with difficulty.)

For years, I never questioned the fact that Caroline's house was papered with newspapers. She was our laundress for a while, and I remember going to her house several times. Caroline was out in the yard, just a hard patch of dirt yard. With a big iron pot, with fire under it, stirring, boiling the white clothes. . . .

She was always gracious and would invite me in. She never apologized for the way anything looked. I thought to myself at the time: How odd that Caroline uses newspapers to paper walls. I didn't have any brains at eleven or twelve or whatever to think: what kind of country is this that lets people live in houses like this and necessitates their using the Sunday paper for wallpaper. I'm shocked that I can't say to you: "When I was twelve, I was horrified when I first went into this house." I was surprised, but I wasn't horrified.

The girls at the office—when the clients had all gone—it's funny you treat them this way, and you still call them clients—when they had all gone, the girls would be very friendly with me. They would ask what I wanted to know and would show me the files. I was quite impressed with their efficiency. But when they were dealing with clients, they were much more loose. I didn't see why they had to be this way. Perhaps they were afraid the people in town would think they were too easy with the welfare people.

Because even then, people were saying that these people are no good, they didn't really want to work. Oftentimes, there were telephone calls, saying so-and-so Joe Jones got a bag of food from Welfare, he got an automobile, or his wife's working or something like that. I spent my time away from the job talking to my old friends, defending the program, saying: You don't know about the situation. They would tell me I was terribly sentimental and that I had lost my perspective. That was when I first heard the old expression: If you give them coal, they'd put it in the bathtub. They didn't even have bathtubs to put coal in. So how did anybody know that's what they'd do with coal if they had it?

We were threatened the whole time, because funds were constantly being questioned by the legislators. After I'd been there three months, the program *was* discontinued. By this time, I was absolutely hooked. I could almost weep thinking about it. I told Miss Ward, who had by now become

Is securing relief still the same?

How do you react to poverty?

Do you know what your parents thought about the idea of relief in the 1930s?

my staunch friend, that this is what I want to do with myself: I want to do something to change things.

By this time, the girls in the office—Ella Mae was the one I liked best—were perfectly willing to let me interview people, because they had more than they could do. Something like 150 cases each. In two months, I was employed as a case worker.

As I recall, when a person came into the office and applied for help, you filled out a form, asked all those humiliating questions: Does anybody work? Do you own your own house? Do you have a car? You just established the fact they had nothing. Nothing to eat, and children. So you give them one food order. You couldn't give them shoes, or money for medicine—without visiting and corroborating the fact that they were destitute.

So, of course, you get out as fast as possible to see those people before the $4 grocery order ran out. You know, the day after tomorrow, I used to drive out to make house calls. It was the first time I'd been off Main Street. I'd never been out in the rural area, and I was absolutely aghast at the conditions in the country.

I discovered, the first time in my life, in the county, there was a place called the Islands. The land was very low and if it rained, you practically had to take a boat to get over where Ezekiel Jones or whoever lived. I remember a time when I got stuck in this rented Ford, and broke down little trees, and lay them across the road to create traction, so you could get out. Now I regard that as one of my best experiences. If somebody said to you: What would you do, having been brought up the way you were, if you found yourself at seven o'clock at night, out in the wilderness, with your car stuck and the water up to your hubcaps or something like that? Wouldn't you worry? What would you do? I could get out of there: I could break down a tree or something. It helps make you free.

I would find maybe two rooms, a dilapidated wooden place, dirty, an almost paralyzed-looking mother, as if she didn't function at all. Father unshaven, drunk. Children of all ages around the house, and nothing to eat. You thought you could do just absolutely nothing. Maybe you'd write a food order. . . .

• • •

This family . . . the Rural Rehabilitation program came along, the RRA. I had the joy of certifying certain families from the relief rolls to go to the land bought by the government. To have better houses, to have equipment. And I saw this family move to a different house. Saw that woman's face come alive—the one who'd been in that stupor—her children clean, her house scrubbed—I saw this family moved from a hopeless situation. . . . The man had been a sharecropper. Apparently, he had once been a very good worker. There he was with nothing, till . . . I could go on about that. . . .

I had twelve families in this program. And Ella Mae had twelve. It was a beautiful farm, maybe two, three hundred acres. With houses, not two-room shacks. Ella Mae and I were involved in the thrilling task of selecting the families. Ella Mae would say, "I think Jess Clark would be good." And Davis, the man in charge of the program, would say, "That old, lazy bum? He's not gonna be able to do nothin'. You're just romantic." So we became personally involved in seeing these people prove their own worth. . . .

Every month the program was threatened with lack of funds. We didn't

Who applied for relief in the 1930s?

How did the depression change woman's role?

Are rehabilitation programs superior to relief programs?

120

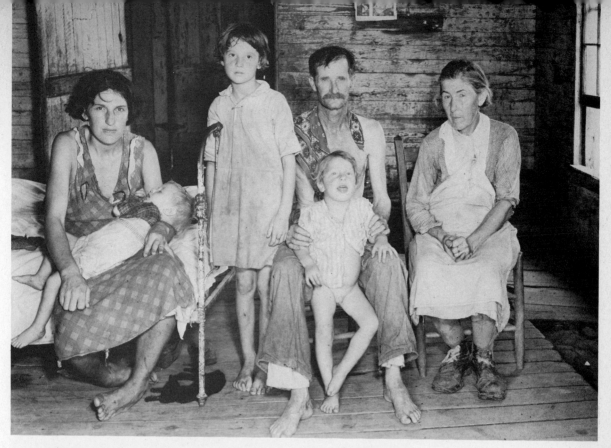

Rural areas in the South, farmed mostly by poor black and white tenants and sharecroppers, were hardest hit by the depression: for more than 1 million families, annual income was no more than $300 to $400. Many—facing conditions of miserable housing, shoddy clothing, and inadequate diet— took to the road, often settling into already crowded city slums in order to become eligible for local relief funds. Why did social workers react as they did to the migrants' plight?

know if Congress was gonna discontinue it. A lot of the public thought the money was being spent foolishly.

With the program in danger of being killed from month to month, the state administrator suggested she accept other job offers. She attended the New York School of Social Work, under federal auspices; she married; there was an absence of six months from the county.

The first thing I did when I got back, I got out of the car and rushed over to the courthouse—to know how did those people perform. Did they make it?

I talked about this one white family. There was a Negro family, nine of them living in one room. The man was not young; he was in his sixties. But he impressed me as being a strong person—who would really make it, if he had a chance. Every one of the people we had certified had done well and had begun to pay back the loans. Not one of them had been lazy and done a bad job. They were absolutely vindicated. The people were vindicated, not us.

OSCAR HELINE

For all his seventy-eight years, he has lived on this Iowa farm, which his father had cultivated almost a century ago. It is in the northwestern part of the state, near the South Dakota border. Marcus has a population of 1,263.

On this drizzly October Sunday afternoon, the main street is deserted. Not a window is open, nor a sound heard. Suddenly, rock music shatters the silence. From what appeared to be a years-long vacant store, two girls and a boy emerge. They are about thirteen, fourteen.

I ask directions. They are friendly, though somewhat bewildered. "An old man?" They are eager to help. One points north; another, south; the third, west. Each is certain "an old man" lives somewhere in the vicinity.

Along the gravel road, with a stop at each of three farmhouses: no sign, no knowledge of "an old man," nor awareness of his name. At each is a tree bearing the identical sticker: "Beware The Dog." One trots forth, pauses warily and eyes the stranger in the manner of Bull Connor and a black militant. The young farmers are friendly enough, but innocent of Oscar Heline's existence.

At the fourth farm, an elderly woman, taken away from the telecast of the Tigers–Cardinals World Series game, knows. . . . Several gravel roads back I find him.

The struggles people had to go through are almost unbelievable. A man lived all his life on a given farm, it was taken away from him. One after the other. After the foreclosure, they got a deficiency judgment. Not only did he lose the farm, but it was impossible for him to get out of debt.

He recounts the first farm depression of the Twenties: "We give the land back to the mortgage holder and then we're sued for the remainder—the deficiency judgment—which we have to pay." After the land boom of the early Twenties, the values declined constantly, until the last years of the decade. "In '28, '29, when it looked like we could see a little blue sky again, we're just getting caught up with the back interest, the Thirties Depression hit. . . ."

Why did the depression hit farmers particularly hard?

122

The farmers became desperate. It got so a neighbor wouldn't buy from a neighbor, because the farmer didn't get any of it. It went to the creditors. And it wasn't enough to satisfy them. What's the use of having a farm sale? Why do we permit them to go on? It doesn't cover the debts, it doesn't liquidate the obligation. He's out of business, and it's still hung over him. First, they'd take your farm, then they took your livestock, then your farm machinery. Even your household goods. And they'd move you off. The farmers were almost united. We had penny auction sales. Some neighbor would bid a penny and give it back to the owner.

Grain was being burned. It was cheaper than coal. Corn was being burned. A county just east of here, they burned corn in their courthouse all winter, '32, '33. You couldn't hardly buy groceries for corn. It couldn't pay the transportation. In South Dakota, the county elevator listed corn as minus three cents. *Minus* three cents a bushel. If you wanted to sell 'em a bushel of corn, you had to bring in three cents. They couldn't afford to handle it. Just think what happens when you can't get out from under. . . .

We had lots of trouble on the highway. People were determined to withhold produce from the market—livestock, cream, butter, eggs, what not. If they would dump the produce, they would force the market to a higher level. The farmers would man the highways, and cream cans were emptied in ditches and eggs dumped out. They burned the trestle bridge, so the trains wouldn't be able to haul grain. Conservatives don't like this kind of rebel attitude and aren't very sympathetic. But something had to be done.

Why couldn't farmers sell their goods if there was so much hunger in the land?

I spent most of my time in Des Moines as a lobbyist for the state cooperatives. Trying to get some legislation. I wasn't out on the highway fighting this battle. Some of the farmers probably didn't think I was friendly to their cause. They were so desperate. If you weren't out there with them, you weren't a friend, you must be a foe. I didn't know from day to day whether somebody might come along and cause harm to my family. When you have bridges burned, accidents, violence, there may have been killings, I don't know.

How is the farmer's situation different today?

There were some pretty conservative ones, wouldn't join this group. I didn't want to particularly, because it wasn't the answer. It took that kind of action, but what I mean is it took more than that to solve it. You had to do constructive things at the same time. But I never spoke harshly about those who were on the highway.

Some of the farmers with teams of horses, sometimes in trucks, tried to get through. He was trying to feed his family, trying to trade a few dozen eggs and a few pounds of cream for some groceries to feed his babies. He was desperate, too. One group tried to sell so they could live and the other group tried to keep you from selling so they could live.

The farmer is a pretty independent individual. He wants to be a conservative individual. He wants to be an honorable individual. He wants to pay his debts. But it was hard. The rank-and-file people of this state—who were brought up as conservatives, which most of us were—would never act like this. Except in desperation.

Are farmers still rugged individualists?

There were a few who had a little more credit than the others. They were willing to go on as usual. They were mostly the ones who tried to break the picket lines. They were the ones who gained at the expense of the poor. They had the money to buy when things were cheap. There are always a few who make money out of other people's poverty. This was a struggle between the haves and the have-nots.

The original bankers who came to this state, for instance. When my father would borrow $100, he'd get $80. And when it was due, he'd pay back the $100 and a premium besides that. Most of his early borrowings were on this basis. That's where we made some wealthy families in this country.

We did pass some legislation. The first thing we did was stop the power of the judges to issue deficiency judgments. The theory was: the property would come back to you someday.

The next law we passed provided for committees in every county: adjudication committees. They'd get the person's debts all together and sit down with his creditors. They gave people a chance. People got time. The land banks and insurance companies started out hard-boiled. They got the farm, they got the judgment and then found out it didn't do them any good. They had to have somebody to run it. So they'd turn around and rent it to the fella who lost it. He wasn't a good renter. The poor fella lost all his capacity for fairness, because he couldn't be fair. He had to live. All the renters would go in cahoots. So the banks and companies got smart and stopped foreclosing.

Through a federal program we got a farm loan. A committee of twenty-five of us drafted the first farm legislation of this kind thirty-five years ago. We drew it up with Henry Wallace. New money was put in the farmers' hands. The Federal Government changed the whole marketing program from burning 10-cent corn to 45-cent corn. People could now see daylight and hope. It was a whole transformation of attitude. You can just imagine . . .*(He weeps.)*

Who was Henry Wallace? What did he accomplish?

It was Wallace who saved us, put us back on our feet. He understood our problems. When we went to visit him, after he was appointed Secretary, he made it clear to us he didn't want to write the law. He wanted the farmers themselves to write it. "I will work with you," he said, "but you're the people who are suffering. It must be your program." He would always give his counsel, but he never directed us. The program came from the farmers themselves, you betcha.

Another thing happened: we had twice too many hogs because corn'd been so cheap. And we set up what people called Wallace's Folly: killing the little pigs. Another farmer and I helped develop this. We couldn't afford to feed 45-cent corn to a $3 hog. So we had to figure a way of getting rid of the surplus pigs. We went out and bought 'em and killed 'em. This is how desperate it was. It was the only way to raise the price of pigs. Most of 'em were dumped down the river.

The hard times put farmers' families closer together. My wife was working for the country Farm Bureau. We had lessons in home economics, how to make underwear out of gunny sacks, out of flour sacks. It was cooperative labor. So some good things came out of this. Sympathy toward one another was manifest. There were personal values as well as terrible hardships.

Have you ever heard anyone say he profited from the experience of the depression?

Mrs. Heline interjects: "They even took seat covers out of automobiles and re-used them for clothing or old chairs. We taught them how to make mattresses from surplus cotton. We had our freedom gardens and did much canning. We canned our own meat or cured it in some way. There was work to do and busy people are happy people.

The real boost came when we got into the Second World War. Everybody was paying on old debts and mortgages, but the land values were going

Franklin Roosevelt drew much of his support from the working class—farmers and industrial laborers. In return for their confidence, he initiated a wide-based program of relief and reform that, nevertheless, failed to lift the country out of the depression. Why, in the light of his failures, did he largely continue to receive their support?

down. It's gone up now more than ever in the history of the country. The war. . . . (A long pause.)

It does something to your country. It's what's making employment. It does something to the individual. I had a neighbor just as the war was beginning. We had a boy ready to go to service. This neighbor one day told me what we needed was a damn good war, and we'd solve our agricultural problems. And I said, "Yes, but I'd hate to pay with the price of my son." Which we did. (He weeps.) It's too much of a price to pay. . . .

What do you think about this economic justification for war?

In '28 I was chairman of the farm delegation which met with Hoover. My family had always been Republican, and I supported him. To my disappointment. I don't think the Depression was all his fault. He tried. But all his plans failed, because he didn't have the Government involved. He depended on individual organizations.

It's a strange thing. This is only thirty-five years ago—Roosevelt, Wallace. We have a new generation in business today. Successful. It's surprising how quickly they forget the assistance their fathers got from the Government. The Farm Bureau, which I helped organize in this state, didn't help us in '35. They take the same position today: we don't need the Government. I'm just as sure as I'm sitting here, we can't do it ourselves. Individuals have too many different interests. Who baled out the land banks when they were busted in the Thirties? It was the Federal Government.

How did your parents feel about Hoover? about Roosevelt?

What I remember most of those times is that poverty creates desperation, and desperation creates violence. In Plymouth County—Le Mars—just west of us, a group met one morning and decided they were going to stop the judge from issuing any more deficiency judgments. This judge had a habit of very quickly O.K.'ing foreclosure sales. These farmers couldn't stand it any more. They'd seen their neighbors sold out.

There were a few judges who would refuse to take the cases. They'd postpone it or turn it over to somebody else. But this one was pretty gruff and arrogant: "You do this, you do that, it's my court." When a bunch of farmers are going broke every day and the judge sits there very proudly and says: "This is my court . . ."; they say: "Who the hell are you?" He was just a fellow human being, same as they were.

These farmers gathered this one particular day. I suppose some of 'em decided to have a little drink, and so they developed a little courage. They decided: we'll go down and teach that judge a lesson. They marched into the courtroom, hats on, demanded to visit with him. *He* decided he would teach *them* a lesson. So he says: "Gentlemen, this is my court. Remove your hats and address the court properly."

They just laughed at him. They said, "We're not concerned whose court this is. We came here to get redress from your actions. The things you're doing, we can't stand to have done to us any more." The argument kept on, and got rougher. He wouldn't listen. He threatened them. So they drug him from his chair, pulled him down the steps of the courthouse, and shook a rope in front of his face. Then, tarred and feathered him.

The Governor called out the National Guard. And put these farmers behind barbed wire. Just imagine . . . (he weeps) . . . in this state. You don't forget these things.

Is this equally applicable today?

Is farmer protest of the 1930s in any way comparable to student protest of the 1960s?

ASSIGNMENT 4
A PROJECT IN ORAL HISTORY:
IMPACT OF THE DEPRESSION

This project in oral history has several objectives. First, you should utilize your interviewing techniques by talking to a resident of the community in which you are living. Select a person, aged fifty to sixty or older, and attempt to recover some of the history of the depression years.

You might follow a line of questioning similar to this: Do you remember the stock market crash? What did you think of Herbert Hoover? Did you or your family lose any money in the market or in bank failures? What was your attitude toward Franklin Roosevelt? Did you ever listen to him on the radio? What else did you listen to on the radio? Were you or someone in your family unemployed? Do you know anyone who worked for the CCC or WPA? What kinds of experiences did he or she have? Did you move from one house to another? What did you do for fun? Did people have more fun in those days? Were the movies important in any way? What about the importance of the automobile? What did economic hardship do to family life? Did anyone you knew lose faith in the American system? Does the fact that you lived through the depression influence your ideas and attitudes today?

Try not to let a preconceived idea of how the discussion should flow interfere with the direction the conversation will spontaneously take. Use your common sense and be flexible. Interrupt as little as possible, except when you have to jog the interviewee's memory. Your role is to listen.

Use the same techniques and questions

when you interview members of your own family on their depression experiences. Then, write a preliminary report on your findings, to be incorporated later in your research paper.

BIBLIOGRAPHIC NOTE

For a lively introduction to the depression era, see W. E. Leuchtenburg, *Franklin D. Roosevelt and the New Deal, 1932–1940* (1963). Enormous detail and texture emerges from the continuing biographical studies on Roosevelt and his times by Frank Freidel and Arthur Schlesinger, Jr. For specific information on aspects of life then, you should consult David Shannon, ed., *The Great Depression* (1960), a collection of contemporary bits and pieces, and the very graphic book by Dorothea Lange and P. S. Taylor, *An American Exodus: A Record of Human Erosion in the Thirties* (1969). Studs Terkel's *Hard Times* (1970), a selection of which has been included in this chapter, provides not only excellent firsthand accounts of life in the thirties but a model of the techniques used in oral history as well.

five

WORLD WAR II

Strange as it must seem to a generation of Americans accustomed to an overwhelming American presence throughout the world, the United States sat on the sidelines as World War II approached. Although the likelihood of a second world war increased throughout the 1930s, not many Americans appeared to notice. The armed struggle between Japan and China seemed far away to an American middle class that was preoccupied with preserving itself amid a severe economic depression. Even the ominous regime that Adolf Hitler led to power in Germany in 1933 could parade its barbarism throughout the decade without arousing much American censure. Germany abandoned the League of Nations in 1933, and by 1935, in flagrant scorn of the armaments provisions of the Treaty of Versailles, had rebuilt a vast army and air force. Then in March 1936 it flouted international opinion by forcibly reoccupying the Rhineland. Yet just six months later a team of Americans participated with athletes from around the world in the Berlin Olympics, thus tacitly acknowledging Hitler's international respectability. Popular American myopia continued from 1936 to 1939 as the German *Luftwaffe* enjoyed a dress rehearsal for World War II in the service of Francisco Franco's Fascists in the Spanish Civil War. Even the 1938 German seizure of Austria passed without effective objection. President Franklin D. Roosevelt joined most other world leaders in praising the Munich Pact, the high point of appeasement.

From the American perspective these were matters for the Europeans to settle. In effect, the United States government played the role of a minor power throughout the 1930s, neither participating in the recurring European diplomatic crises nor seeking to generate popular support for international collabora-

tion. Many American political leaders reflected the popular belief that American involvement in World War I had been a mistake, that Europeans, insufficiently grateful for American aid in the earlier war, were about to battle again and were trying to maneuver the United States into another of their seemingly endless conflicts.

On September 1, 1939, the war began in earnest when Germany invaded Poland, and England and France kept their alliance with Poland by declaring war on Germany. Americans worried and wondered; still, most thought that the United States was safe and could stay out of war. Then Hitler's *Blitzkrieg* of the spring of 1940 shattered the western front: Norway, Denmark, and the Low Countries fell; France was taken with astonishing ease; now England stood alone against the Nazi war machine. Although most Americans clearly sympathized with Britain and the Allied powers, the strong public opposition during 1940 and 1941 to full belligerency limited the role of the United States. It did send arms and supplies to England, and the navy expanded the scope of its activities in Atlantic and Caribbean waters. Yet most Americans still hoped that the United States could avoid joining the fight.

These hopes were destroyed on December 7, 1941, the day of the surprise Japanese attack on Pearl Harbor that quickly brought the United States into war against the Axis powers of Germany, Italy, and Japan. Although the careful observer of the long-deteriorating relationship between Japan and the United States might have predicted the outbreak of hostilities, the attack on Pearl Harbor shocked all Americans. To this day millions of people can recall exactly what they were doing when the news flashed over the radio. Pearl Harbor united and activated the people of this country in a way seldom experienced, before or since. Patriotism ran high as the nation prepared to defeat the Axis. All of the debates about intervention or isolation were swept away: innocent and peace-loving America had been attacked by the forces of evil.

World War II, like the depression, was a transcendent event that affected all Americans and their families. Over 400,000 Americans lost their lives in the war and more than 670,000 were wounded. For many families the war meant utter tragedy—the death in faraway places of sons, husbands, fathers, brothers, and other loved ones. Even many of the military men who survived would be haunted all their lives by the memory of the terror and slaughter and the untimely deaths of comrades and friends.

Paradoxically, many men and women found military service the high point of their lives. The terror faded with time and only the memory of adventure, comradeship, and the glory of being involved in an epic common cause remained. Strange names like Truk, Leyte, Anzio, El Alamein, and Midway assumed permanent, almost fond memories for those who were there. Catapulted out of small-town lives and mundane jobs into exotic places, many men and women in the armed services felt released from the normal restraints and responsibilities of marriage, family, and work. Despite occasional or frequent danger, many had the time of their lives, whether in the Moroccan desert or on shore patrol duty at Atlantic City, New Jersey.

An even more common shared experience—of soldier and civilian alike—was uprooting. Although Americans have historically been a mobile people, the impact of World War II on mobility was extraordinary. Military service naturally relocated millions. All men between the ages of eighteen and forty-five had to register for the draft; many others enlisted. There were 500,000 in the armed forces by 1940; 3,800,000 by 1942; and over 12 million by 1945. By the end of the war one out of every five American males between the ages of eighteen and forty-five had served in the armed forces. Many of those not in the services found work in war industries, jobs that frequently meant having to move. Statistics indicate a substantial migration away from New England and the upper Plains states; in another exodus hundreds of thousands left the South, from all along the arc stretching from West Virginia toward Mississippi and Oklahoma. Across the nation nearly 10 million people left farms

during the decade of the 1940s. Increasing numbers crowded into the major cities of New York and northern New Jersey, and into Chicago, Cleveland, Detroit, Baltimore, and Miami. In particular, people sought the sun-drenched new world of California.

Millions of these Americans moved eagerly into a war-based economy, and the nation's policymakers discovered a hedge against another major economic disaster. Gone finally was the depression of the 1930s, with full employment returning for the first time since the 1920s. The American economy, fed by public and private capital, thus entered its still-continuing dependence on the production of war or war-related materials. For unemployed workers the return to full production was a great opportunity after the lean thirties and surely sufficient reason to uproot a family. Employment in major industries, which had dropped to 23 million in the depths of the depression, ballooned to over 42 million in 1943. Unemployment, near 13 million in 1933, fell to 670,000 in 1944. Spending for national defense became a way of life for the American government. For working people, war jobs suggested the possibility that good wages and steady work would mean a decent home and a better education for their children.

Among the beneficiaries of the wartime demand for labor were black Americans. Repeating a pattern established during World War I, a mass of black Americans streamed out of the rural South to the urban North to find steady jobs at decent wages. The war did not end racial tension and violence, but it did raise hopes for justice and equal opportunity. Many of the black American servicemen sent abroad, even while relegated to units racially segregated by American military precedent, found psychological release from the oppression of racism for the first time.

Yet the opportunities that the war provided for American blacks were severely circumscribed. Jammed into the black ghettos of central cities, which rarely provided adequate housing, transportation, education, or cleanliness, many black families became trapped. At the war's end black men and women fell victim in large numbers to the "last hired, first fired" principle of black employment. And returning black servicemen found that the high democratic idealism of wartime struggle had little relevance to postwar life in the slums of Northern cities or the dusty towns of the rural South.

Racism's twisted cruelty was more overtly expressed when the government of the

United States arbitrarily incarcerated most Americans of Japanese descent. Soon after Pearl Harbor, about 125,000 Japanese-Americans (over 70 percent of them American citizens) were forcibly removed from their West Coast homes and imprisoned in concentration camps in the interior. Their property was seized with little or no compensation, and the process was upheld by the Supreme Court. No similar treatment was considered necessary either for German-Americans or Italian-Americans. The objectives of total victory justified all expedients, notwithstanding some uneasiness, and minor protests, about putting American citizens in concentration camps. As in most wars, however, the fervor of patriotic righteousness devoured its minority of dissenters.

This fervor was constantly promoted on the American homefront. Grade-school children went on scrap drives, saved tin foil, bought savings stamps, and helped in the family "victory garden," a backyard fruit-and-vegetable patch designed to free food production for the war effort and to encourage full participation in the national struggle. High-school students might join paramilitary drill teams or wrap bandages as Red Cross volunteers. Housewives went into factories in large numbers, working on assembly lines, in arsenals, or in offices. Local service clubs formed air-raid-warden squads or organized war-bond drives. In town meetings and along flag-festooned parade routes big cities and small towns proclaimed their united support for total victory.

From Hollywood came a flood of war movies, simplistic but appealing stories of heroism and virtue struggling against treachery—and winning. The many warriors of Sunset Strip—John Wayne, Alan Ladd, Randolph Scott, Brian Donleavy—reassured Americans of the nobility of their cause and the inevitability of their victory. Betty Grable, Veronica Lake, and Rita Hayworth made their own contributions to morale.

For the American middle class the sense of national unity effectively compensated for wartime hardship, not the least of which was strict rationing of a broad variety of foods and consumer goods. Horsemeat appeared on some dinner tables. Leg paint replaced nylon stockings. Yellow-colored margarine pretended to be butter. Automobile production stopped, tires and gasoline were in limited supply. Yet the army of middle-class consumers hardly uttered a protest. Organized labor abandoned its precious right to strike. The harmony of common purpose pervaded the land.

Yet the phenomenon of united war effort should not obscure the diversity of experience, the enormously complex impact that World War II had on American society. In particular, the social history of families reflected substantial changes. The uprooting and resettlement of so many families obviously shattered long-settled patterns of residence. Millions of fathers were taken from the home. Social flux affected marriages, the birth rate, divorces. The number of marriages rose sharply during wartime, many of them entered into in haste under the pressures of imminent separation. The nation's population increased by 6.5 million during the war years. Yet in 1946, the year after the war ended, divorces soared to 610,000, the highest level in American history to that point.

Thus the American nuclear family, traditional backbone of the social structure, underwent significant alteration. Opportunity and good fortune on the road to middle-class happiness beckoned many. Others were permanently affected by the sights and sounds of distant places and returned home with new ideas. The war left irreparable scars on those many families whose lost sons would remain forever young in the frozen uniformed photos on the mantlepiece. The war experiences of Americans, all along the human range from joy to tragedy, remain fresh for the generation before yours.

THE AMERICAN CENTURY
Henry Luce

For most Americans, World War II began with the attack on Pearl Harbor, and the purpose of the war was simply to defeat the enemy. But to some of its leaders, the war had larger meaning. In the following article, written just after the United States entered the war, Henry Luce, then publisher and owner of Time-Life, defined the war in terms of an American mission—creating an American century. To what extent do you think this sense of America's destiny and responsibility toward the world exists today? Do you know many people now who share Luce's perceptions and beliefs? Are they younger or older people? Is there a generational difference in your own family on questions of foreign affairs?

We Americans are unhappy. We are not happy about America. We are not happy about ourselves in relation to America. We are nervous—or gloomy—or apathetic.

· · ·

There is one fundamental issue which faces America as it faces no other nation. It is an issue peculiar to America and peculiar to America in the 20th Century—now. It is deeper even than the immediate issue of War. If America meets it correctly, then, despite hosts of dangers and difficulties, we can look forward and move forward to a future worthy of men, with peace in our hearts.

If we dodge the issue, we shall flounder for ten or 20 or 30 bitter years in a chartless and meaningless series of disasters.

The purpose of this article is to state that issue, and its solution, as candidly and as completely as possible.

· · ·

. . . We are *not* in a war to defend American territory. We are in a war to defend and even to promote, encourage and incite so-called democratic principles throughout the world.

· · ·

The big, important point to be made here is simply that the complete opportunity of leadership is *ours*. Like most great creative opportunities, it is an opportunity enveloped in stupendous difficulties and dangers. If we

What circumstances led Luce to this conclusion? Do you agree?

What does "leadership" mean in this context?

132

World War II stirred the patriotic fervor of many Americans—a sentiment that endured long after the war ended. What has happened to cause some contemporary Americans to distrust this sentiment?

don't want it, if we refuse to take it, the responsibility of refusal is also ours, and ours alone.

• • •

In the field of national policy, the fundamental trouble with America has been, and is, that whereas their nation became in the 20th Century the most powerful and the most vital nation in the world, nevertheless Americans were unable to accommodate themselves spiritually and practically to that fact. Hence they have failed to play their part as a world power—a failure which has had disastrous consequences for themselves and for all mankind. And the cure is this: to accept wholeheartedly our duty and our opportunity as the most powerful and vital nation in the world and in consequence to exert upon the world the full impact of our influence, for such purposes as we see fit and by such means as we see fit.

What are the implications of the last sentence?

133

Two Experiences in the Combat Zone

CHARLES E. KELLY and JAMES J. FAHEY

Have you ever talked to soldiers about their wartime experiences? Some will tell you a great deal, but for others the horror was too great, the memories too personal. The war changed many people who fought in it. It uprooted them from their hometown and neighborhood and introduced them to new lands and customs. For some, the army provided a chance for adventure and the close comradeship that comes with shared danger. (After the war, veterans' organizations became their social clubs.) For many the war meant that they would never be the same again.

As you read the following selections, think about the way that World War II influenced your family and your community. Was any member of your family in the war? What effect has that experience had on his or her attitudes toward war and peace and patriotism?

KELLY: HEROISM IN WAR

Leaving the Salerno beach fifty feet behind me, I pumped my knees up and down in a sort of dog trot, moving straight ahead. That first rush took me past a dead G.I., lying peacefully, as if asleep, with his head on his pack, his rifle by his side. I pulled my eyes away and told myself, *Don't let that worry you.*

Then came a big drainage ditch with G.I.'s lying down inside of it. "Come on! It ain't deep! Jump!" I jumped, only to find the water and slime up to my eyes. The bottom was oozy; my feet sank into it, and I was weighted down by ammunition. I let go of my automatic rifle, but as soon as I dropped it, I felt lonely and lost, and ducked my head under to find it. Groping around, I got my hand on it. There was a small tree handy and, using one of its branches, I pulled myself out of the muck, and so to the other side.

There is no rhyme or reason to how the mind of a soldier in battle works. There I was charging into Italy, passing dead men and coming close to drowning in a ditch, and, after cleaning my rifle as best I could, all I could think about was whether or not the photographs in my wallet had been ruined.

I took them out, tried to wipe them off on the grass, and waved them back and forth to stir up a little air to dry them.

Machine-gun bullets were boring into the ground in front of me and, at intervals, when the blup-blup of their impact came too close together, I hit

Do you think this preoccupation with insignificant details serves a purpose in combat?

134

the dirt. Those machine guns blazed away at us and mopped up our staff sergeant. He went down with bullets in his head.

I kept right on moving forward, and the next time I looked around to check my position, I was alone. The orders I'd heard back on shipboard had gone out of my mind. All I remembered was hearing somebody say, "When you get on the beach, keep moving forward."

Hopping over a wall and following a little path, I jumped over another wall into a clump of thorn bushes. Machine-gun bullets were streaking up and down the path I had just left, so I lay down in those bushes and played dead until the fire slackened. Finally I found a break through the thorns and, at the end of the break, a row of our men dug in. They were from two of our outfits, all mixed up together.

Once more, I started looking for my outfit. After a while I got tired of going along doubled up and stooping over, so I stood up and started walking. I decided I was thirsty, and stopped at a farmhouse well to get a drink. There were grapes and peaches around, and I stuffed some of them into me. I passed deserted farms and houses until they all ran together in my mind and I couldn't tell one from the other. Finally I figured I had walked about eight hours, and must be about twelve miles inland. Turning around, I saw a highway, and started to walk along it heading back in the direction from which I had come. Then, in the distance, German medium Mark IV tanks hove in sight. I dived into a ditch, squinted along my BAR—Browning automatic rifle—and began to fire as they came close, but the slugs from my gun made no impression on them. I was aiming at the tanks' slit openings, but there is so much noise and racket inside one of those things that the Heinies probably didn't hear me. They rumbled and clanked by, and I kept on walking down the highway, coming at last to a little creek, where I drank, took off my shoes and bathed my feet. My toes were stuck together from the sea water I'd waded through back at the Salerno beach. I washed my socks to get the salt out of them and put the same socks back on, keeping my extra ones in reserve.

How does this differ from the war movies?

I put in about fifteen minutes trying to remember the things I was supposed to have had firmly fixed in my head when we landed on the beach. Finally I remembered what our detail was supposed to do. I could see the mountain Lieutenant O'Leary had told us about. He had called it Mountain Forty-two and we were supposed to take it. So I started toward it.

After climbing for a while, I came to a winery and found the first battalion of our regiment dug in there and all around it in the open fields. I wanted to ask them where my outfit was, but their trigger fingers were too itchy; they were shooting at sounds and dimly seen movements, and it wasn't any time to be dropping in unannounced to tear a social herring with them. So I dug in behind a bush and went to sleep.

It would have been nice to fill my canteen with water before I started again, but my canteen had picked up a bullet hole somewhere along the way. I hadn't known about that bullet before, although it must have given quite a jerk when it ripped through. I tried to rub the sleep from my eyes and walk down the highway. Both sides had infiltrated into and behind each other, so that you had to be on the alert each minute and watch every moving thing on each side of you.

German bullets were zipping around like high-velocity bees, but I finally found my outfit dug in, in spattered, shallow holes. They greeted me with, "Where the hell have you been?"

When I reported to Lieutenant O'Leary, he said, "I was sure they'd got you."

By the time American troops landed at Salerno, the locale of Commando Kelly's story, the Italians had surrendered. American soldiers, expecting nothing more than a pleasant walk up the Italian coast, met stiff German resistance instead. Does the experience of shared danger in battle tend to produce exaggerated patriotism?

Every once in a while a shell landed near us, but they didn't do any real damage.

After a time we started down the road, and ran into a little Italian boy, who said, "Germans. Germans. Germans." My pal, La Bue, spoke to him in Italian, but the kid was frightened and didn't make much sense.

While La Bue was bickering with him, Lieutenant O'Leary shouted, "Here come some Heinie scout cars! Get off the road!"

We dived for cover and the scout cars opened fire. Bullets and fragments of shells bounced from our rifles, and two of us were hit. All of a sudden, one of our boys got his bazooka on his shoulder and let go with a tremendous, crashing "Boom!" and immediately afterward one of our men jumped up on a wall beside the road, leaped like a frog to the top of one of those panzer wagons and dropped his hand grenade into it. That particular scout car stopped then and there. The others speeded up, trying to get past us, when a company of our antitankers we hadn't seen up to that time went into action with its 57-mm. cannon. It was chancy stuff, for if that 57-mm. had missed its target, it would have gotten us. But as it was, everything worked out nice and clean and efficient. The bazooka kept on booming, and, quicker than it seemed possible, that whole small reconnaissance detachment was knocked out.

The place was a shambles. Scout cars were going up in flames. Tires were burning with a rubbery stink, and bodies were burning too. One German leaped out and started to run. When we went after him, he put his revolver to his head and killed himself. We had thought that only the Japs did that, and for a moment I was surprised and shocked.

Then a deep-rooted G.I. habit asserted itself. A moment before, hell had been popping on that stretch of road. Now, two seconds later, all we

thought of was souvenirs. Milky Holland found a German Lüger. Looking back at it, I can remember no feeling about the German dead except curiosity. We were impersonal about them; to us they were just bundles of rags.

How do you explain this impersonality?

About two hours afterward, things were so quiet that some of us sneaked off into the near-by town, but we weren't relaxed and casual, and we took our rifles and sidearms with us. The townspeople were out waving at us and offering us water, wine and fruit. La Bue, a kid named Survilo and I had a yen to see the inside of an Italian jail. A woman had told us it was where they kept the Fascist sympathizers. The leading Fascist citizen of the town was in there, mad as blazes and yelling his head off behind the bars. La Bue listened to him for a while, then got mad himself and tried to reach through the bars and tickle him with the end of a bayonet. The Fascist really sounded off then.

When we came out, we saw some pretty Italian girls. La Bue made a date with one of them—the procedure following the same line as if we had been back in Pittsburgh's North Side. He asked her if she could get a couple of friends for us. Smiling, she said she could, and, feeling that we had accomplished something important, we went back to our bivouac.

Have you ever heard anyone say war was the best time of his life? Why did he feel this way?

But, just as they sometimes do in the North Side of Pittsburgh, our plans laid an egg. Platoon Sgt. Zerk Robertson pointed to a town named Altavilla, five or six miles away, and said, "See that town over there? That's where I'm going, and I want some volunteers to go with me. I'm taking the second platoon and some sixty-millimeter mortars." La Bue looked at me, and I looked at him, and we thought of our dates, but there wasn't anything we could do about it, and presently we were walking out along the highway.

137

Was fighting in the Pacific more bitter because of the hardships induced by the rugged terrain? Was racism a factor as well?

FAHEY: FEAR IN THE SOUTH PACIFIC

July 15, 1943: We returned from our prowl up the Slot in search of Jap ships but nothing happened. I guess the Japs are licking their wounds. . . .

. . . Fighting the Japs is like fighting a wild animal. The troops said that the Japs are as tough and fierce as they come; the Jap is not afraid to die, it is an honor to die for the Emperor, he is their God.

A lot of the fighting is done at night and you can smell the Japs 25 yards away. The jungle is very hot and humid and drains the strength quickly. The jungle is also very thick; you could be right next to a Jap and yet you could not see him. The Japs also have Jap women with them. The Japs watch from coconut trees in the daytime and then when it becomes dark they sneak into your foxhole and cut your throat or throw in a hand grenade. A 200 lb. soldier was pulled from his foxhole and killed in short time. You also hear all sorts of noises made by the animals and you think it is the Japs. This is too much for some men and they crack up.

They say the Japs also have some Imperial Marines who are 6 ft. 4″ tall. The Japs are experts at jungle fighting and they know all the tricks. You would hardly believe the tricks they use. In the darkness for instance, they like to throw dirt in your eyes and then attack you. Many of our troops get killed learning their tricks. The Japs take all kinds of chances, they love to die. Our troops are advancing slowly, it is a very savage campaign. Very few Japs surrender, they die fighting, even when the situation is hopeless.

How do you explain the more ideological, almost hysterical bias toward the enemy in this article?

What patriotic attitudes might this war experience produce?

State of the Nation
John Dos Passos

The war meant movement—both the movement of troops to training camps and the migration of war workers and their families to industrial and port cities. Perhaps your family participated in this wartime migration. In the section that follows, John Dos Passos describes some of the tensions and difficulties caused by wartime migration into a Southern city. Was the war the real cause of this tension, or were there deeper causes? Does war lead to progress and prosperity, or does it cause the opposite? Are there any traces of social and economic change brought about in your own community as a result of war?

The bus rumbles down the sunny empty highway through the rusty valleys and the bare rainwashed fields and the scraggly woods and the hills the color of oakleaves that are the landscape of winter in the southeast states. Inside, the air is dense with packed bodies and stale cigarette smoke. There's a smell of babies and an occasional sick flavor from the exhaust. The seats are all full. Somewhere in the back a baby is squalling. A line of men and women stands swaying in the aisle. Behind me two men are talking about jobs in singsong voices pitched deep in their chests.

'What's it like down there?' one is asking the other.

'Ain't too bad if you kin stand that bunch of loudmouthed foremen . . . If you look crosseyed at one of them guards he'll reach out and yank off your badge and you're through and that's all there is to it.'

'Well, I've worked in about all of 'em.'

'Say, ain't I seen you somewheres before?'

'I dunno. Might have been on this bus. I been on this bus a thousand times.'

• • •

A TOWN OUTGROWS ITSELF

We are in the city now. The bus is swinging out of the traffic of the crowded main street round the low gray building of the bus station, and comes to a stop in the middle of a milling crowd: soldiers, sailors, stout women with bundled up babies, lanky backwoodsmen with hats tipped over their brows and a cheek full of chewingtobacco, hatless young men in lightcolored sport shirts open at the neck, countrymen with creased red necks and well-washed overalls, cigarsmoking stocky men in business suits in pastel

In terms of age, sex, and social class, what groups are represented in this cross section of war-industry workers?

139

shades, girls in bright dresses with carefully curled hair piled up on their heads and highheeled shoes and bloodred fingernails, withered nutbrown old people with glasses, carrying ruptured suitcases, broadshouldered men in oilstained khaki with shiny brown helmets on their heads, negroes in flappy jackets and pegtop pants and little felt hats with turned-up brims, teenage boys in jockey caps, here and there a flustered negro woman dragging behind her a string of white-eyed children. Gradually the passengers are groping their way down the steep steps out of the bus and melting into the crowd.

Out on the streets every other man seems to be in work clothes. There are girls in twos and threes in slacks and overalls. Waiting for the light at a crossing a pinkfaced youth who's dangling a welder's helmet on a strap from the crook of his arm turns laughing to the man who hailed him. 'I jes' got tired an' quit.' Ragged families from the hills and the piney woods stroll staring straight ahead of them along the sidewalks towing flocks of little kids with flaxen hair and dirty faces. In front of a window full of brightcolored rayon socks in erratic designs a young man with glasses meets two girls in slacks. 'We missed you yesterday,' they say. 'I was sick. I didn't go in. Anyway, I've got me a new job . . . more money.'

The mouldering old Gulf seaport with its ancient dusty elegance of tall shuttered windows under mansard roofs and iron lace overgrown with vines, and scaling colonnades shaded by great trees, looks trampled and battered like a city that's been taken by storm. Sidewalks are crowded. Gutters are stacked with litter that drifts back and forth in the brisk spring wind. Garbage cans are overflowing. Frame houses on treeshaded streets bulge with men in shirtsleeves who spill out onto the porches and trampled grassplots and stand in knots at the streetcorners. There's still talk of lodginghouses where they rent 'hot beds.' (Men work in three shifts. Why shouldn't they sleep in three shifts?) Cues wait outside of movies and lunchrooms. The trailer army has filled all the open lots with its regular ranks. In cluttered backyards people camp out in tents and chickenhouses and shelters tacked together out of packingcases.

How did the war affect the character of the city?

In the outskirts in every direction you find acres and acres raw with new building, open fields skinned to the bare clay, elevations gashed with muddy roads and gnawed out by the powershovels and the bulldozers. There long lines of small houses, some decently planned on the 'American standard' model and some mere boxes with a square brick chimney on the center, miles of dormitories, great squares of temporary structures are knocked together from day to day by a mob of construction workers in a smell of paint and freshsawed pine lumber and tobacco juice and sweat. Along the river for miles has risen a confusion of new yards from which men, women, and boys ebb and flow three times a day. Here and there are whole city blocks piled with wreckage and junk as if ancient cranky warehouses and superannuated stores had caved in out of their own rottenness under the impact of the violence of the new effort. Over it all the Gulf mist, heavy with smoke of soft coal, hangs in streaks, and glittering the training planes endlessly circle above the airfields.

Was your city a war-industry city? Are there any evidences of wartime buildings left?

RIFFRAFF

To be doing something towards winning the war, to be making some money, to learn a trade, men and women have been pouring into the city for more than a year now; tenants from dusty shacks set on stilts above the bare eroded earth in the midst of the cotton and the scraggly corn, small

Some 27 million people moved during the war, mostly to urban areas, to be near factories turning out war goods. To meet the severe housing shortage that developed, trailer camps like this one in Nashville sprang up. How might native townspeople have reacted to this influx of newcomers?

farmers and trappers from halfcultivated patches in the piney woods, millhands from the industrial towns in the northern part of the state, garage men, fillingstation attendants, storekeepers, drugclerks from crossroads settlements, longshore fishermen and oystermen, negroes off plantations who've never seen any town but the county seat on Saturday afternoon, white families who've lived all their lives off tobacco and 'white meat' and cornpone in cranky cabins forgotten in the hills.

For them everything's new and wonderful. They can make more spot cash in a month than they saw before in half a year. They can buy radios, they can go to the pictures, they can go to beerparlors, bowl, shoot craps, bet on the ponies. Everywhere they rub elbows with foreigners from every state in the Union. Housekeeping in a trailer with electric light and running water is a dazzling luxury to a woman who's lived all her life in a cabin with half-inch chinks between the splintered boards of the floor. There are street cars and busses to take you anywhere you want to go. At night the streets are bright with electric light. Girls can go to beautyparlors, get their nails manicured, buy readymade dresses. In the backwoods a girl who's reached puberty feels she's a woman. She's never worried much about restraining her feelings when she had any. Is it any wonder that they can't stay home at dusk when the streets fill up with hungry boys in uniform?

What longer-range effects did the war have by changing society this way?

'It's quite dreadful,' says the man with his collar around backwards, in answer to my question. He is a thinfaced rustylooking man in black with darkringed dark eyes who sits rocking in a rocking chair as he talks. 'We are quite exercised about the problems these newcomers raise for the city . . . Juvenile delinquency, illegitimate babies, venereal disease . . . they are what we call the riffraff. I've seen them in their homes when I was travelling about the state inspecting C.C.C. camps for the government.

141

Casual love affairs or marriages entered into hastily before soldiers left for overseas duty were common during the war. Crowded housing conditions, pregnancies, and forced separations often further strained relations. What other factors might have contributed to the high postwar divorce rate?

They live in an astonishing state of degradation, they have no ambition. They put in a few measly crops, hoe their corn a little, but they have no habits of regular work. Most of them would rather freeze than chop a little wood. Most of the time they just sit around taking snuff and smoking. You see little children four and five years old smoking stubs of cigars. It's *Tobacco Road* and what was that other book? . . . *Grapes of Wrath*. People say those books are overdrawn, but they are not . . . They aren't exaggerated a bit. No wonder there's absenteeism . . . They've never worked regularly in their lives . . . They live in a daze. Nothing affects them, they don't want anything. These awful trailer camps and filthy tent colonies, they seem dreadful to us, but they like it like that. They think it's fine. They don't know any different.'

What is this man really reacting to?

'Don't you think malnutrition might have something to do with their state of mind?' He was strangely inattentive to my question. A smell of frying fish had begun to fill the bare front room of the rectory. Somewhere out back a little bell had tinkled. The man with his collar around backwards began to stir uneasily in his chair. 'I'm afraid I'm keeping you from your supper,' I said, getting to my feet. 'Yes,' he said hastily. I thanked him and said goodbye. As I was going out the door he added, 'Of course the people who come to my church, whom you were asking about, are foremen, skilled mechanics, good union men, they are a much better element. These other people are riffraff.'

Waiting for the bus at the streetcorner in front of one of the better trailer camps that has clean white gravel spread over the ground, and neat wooden platforms beside each shiny trailer for use as a front stoop, I get to talking to a young man in a leather jacket. He's just worked four hours overtime because the other fellow didn't get there to relieve him at his machine. He's tired. You can tell by his breath that he's just had a couple or three beers. He's beefing because of the state regulations limiting the sale of whiskey and cutting out juke boxes in beer parlors. When a man's tired, he says, he needs relaxation. Works better next day. What's the use of dancing if you can't have a drink? What's the use of drinking if you can't dance? If this sort of thing keeps up he's going to pick up and move some place where things are wide open. Meanwhile several busses so jammed with soldiers from the airfield there's no more room, have passed us by. Hell, he groans, might as well go get him another beer, and he trots back into the silent 'Dine and Dance' joint across the street.

● ● ●

'And now they've unloaded the race problem on us,' mumbled the Mediator. 'We were gettin' along all right until they stirred that up on us. We were givin' the colored folks the best break we could.'

'Ain't never no trouble,' said the roofer, 'unless somebody stirs it up.'

'Washington kicked off and the politicians down here are runnin' with the ball . . . White supremacy's a gold mine for 'em.'

'As if we didn't have enough troubles organizin' this pile of raw muleskinners into decent union men and citizens,' cried out the man in the stetson hat, 'without having these longhaired wiseacres come down from Washington to stir up the race question . . . You know as well as I do that there isn't a white man in the South who isn't willing to die for the principle of segregation.' He paused. All the men in the room silently nodded their heads. 'Hell, we were jogglin' along all right before they sprung that on us. Sure, we have colored men in the unions in the building trades; the bricklayers even had colored officers in some of their locals.'

'It's a thing you just have to go easy on,' spoke up the Mediator. 'Most white mechanics down here 'ud rather have a colored helper than a white helper, but when a colored man gets a notch up above them, they don't like it . . . Ain't a white man in the South'll stand for it. We tried that once in reconstruction days . . . I know of two of those niggers that fair practices board ordered upgraded who are dead niggers today. A piece of iron just fell on 'em.'

'If they'd only just concentrate on givin' the negro a square deal within his own sphere most of the liberalminded people in the South would go along.'

'There are small towns out here where all the young white men have gone to the army or war industry, and where the old men are all deputy sheriffs with guns slapped on their hips.' The Mediator was talking in his slow drawling voice. 'The people in those little towns are scared. If some day a drunken nigger made a pass at a white woman all hell 'ud break loose. Now there ain't nothin' going to happen, we know there ain't nothin' goin' to happen, but, mister, you tell your friends up North that this ain't no time to rock the boat.'

'We've got our friends in the industrial unions to thank for that,' said the young man in the stetson hat, spitting out his words savagely. 'They came down here when we had the whole coast organized solid and put in their oar. They beat us at an election in this one yard . . . they got the negroes to vote for 'em, but they couldn't get 'em to join their union. What kind of labor politics is that? They've only got nine hundred members to this day, out of thousands. That's not majority rule . . . That doesn't sound like democracy to me.'

A few days before in a mining town in the northern part of the state I'd had lunch with a young college man from North Carolina, who had given me in a slow serious voice the industrial union side of the race question.

What do you think of the argument that segregation and equal economic opportunity can coexist?

They knew it was a difficult matter, he'd said, but they had decided to face it squarely. At first the employers down here had hired negro labor to break the white unions, but now that the negroes were joining up the employers were trying to hire all white men. On the whole the negroes had stuck to their locals through hard times better than the whites. In locals where they'd faced the issue squarely . . . equal rights for all . . . there had been very little trouble, even in locals made up of country boys from the farms. He told me of one local right in the black belt where they had tried it without having any real trouble, but the strain on the organizer, who was a Southern boy, had been terrific. He'd gone to a hospital with a nervous breakdown. I laughed. He didn't. It wasn't easy, he went on unsmilingly, but prejudice was something that tended to die away if nobody stirred it up. The cure was firmness and courage—meet it head on.

I told him about a meeting I'd drifted into in the basement of a colored church in a war industry town in the North. It was a meeting to protest against the separate dormitory the government was erecting for colored people. Quietlooking elderly negroes were sitting on cane chairs round an oldfashioned coal stove listening to the booming oratory of a preacher from the city. In a voice stirring as a roll of drums he invoked the Four Freedoms and asked how this country could fight for democracy in the rest of the world while there was still discrimination and segregation for thirteen million of our citizens at home. A lawyer had talked about the Constitution and said that now was the time for negroes to rise up and insist that they would no longer be treated as secondclass citizens. If they were called upon to send their sons and brothers to die for their country they had the right to demand equal rights everywhere throughout the broad land. Very much stirred, the listeners had whispered fervent amens at every pause. A young labor organizer had gotten up and said that such injustices made him ashamed to be a white man.

I was asking whether, perhaps, if only as a matter of tactics, it would not be better to work for fair play, equal wages, equal living conditions, first. Wasn't trying to break up segregation that way an infringement of the liberty of white men who didn't want to mix with negroes? After all, white men had rights, too.

'We have found,' the young man said quietly, 'that to get fair play for poor whites we've got to fight for equal rights for poor negroes. Of course we have to use tact, a great deal of tact. But in the unions, at least, the question has to be met head on.'

Does this argument seem valid today?

If poor whites actually benefit from black advancement, why do they seem to resent it so much?

TWENTYFIVE YEARS BEHIND THE TIMES

And all the while, by every bus and train the new people, white and black, pour into the city. As fast as a new block of housing is finished, it's jampacked. As soon as a new bus is put into service, it's weighed down with passengers. The schools are too full of children. The restaurants are too full of eaters. If you try to go to see a doctor, you find the waitingroom full and a long line of people straggling down the hall. There's no room in the hospitals for the women who are going to have babies. 'So far we've been lucky,' the health officers say with terror in their voices, 'not to have had an epidemic. But we've got our fingers crossed.'

Lines of men wait outside of every conceivable office. If you get to see the mayor in the City Hall, you find him, a certain desperation under his bland exterior, desperately calling up Washington to try to pry loose some sewer pipe. The housing project has attended to the plumbing within its domain. The army has attended to these matters within its camps, but nobody has thought of how the new projects are to be linked up with the watermains and sewers of the city.

If you go to see the personnel director of one of the big yards—he used to be a football coach—you find him fuming because he can't get the old team spirit into his employees. 'What can you do when workingmen are making such big wages they don't give a damn?'

If you ask a labor man why management and labor can't get together to take some action about absenteeism and labor turnover, he snaps back at you: 'Management down here won't talk to labor. The men running these yards are twentyfive years behind the times.'

'I try to tell the president of one of these concerns,' says the Government Man, 'that he ought to set up a modern labor relations department and he just gives me a kind of oily grin and says, "Oh go 'long—you get it all out of a book."'

The Government Man's office is under continual siege. Today two very pretty girls in overalls with magnificent hairdos and long sharp red polished nails have been waiting all morning to tell their story. Meanwhile, they tell it to a sympathetic telephone girl. They are welders. They want a release from this company so that they can go somewhere else where they can get more money. The mean old company won't see it their way. Can't the government do something about it? A group of farmboys is complaining that the local police won't let them run their cars without getting local plates. They can't get local plates until they get paid at the end of the week. Without their cars they can't get to work. Can't the government do something about it? In the hall some very black negroes are hunched in a group leaning against the white marble sheathing of the wall of the officebuilding. They are appealing to Caesar. At the personnel office they've been told that if they quit their jobs they'll have to leave town. They want Uncle Sam to say if it's true. No, it's not true, not yet.

'It's incredible,' says the Government Man when his office is finally clear. 'Labor turnover in this town has reached twentyfive percent a quarter. That means every man Jack of 'em changed his job in a year. It's rugged individualism, all right. What they do is come into town and get some training, then when they've qualified for the lowest rate of skilled work they go and get 'em a job somewhere else. They can say they've had experience and can get in at a higher rate. After they've worked there a while, they move to some other outfit and get taken on in a higher category still, and they don't know a damn thing about the work because they spend all their time on the bus travelling around. It's the same thing with the foremen and executives. Before any one of them has a chance to learn his work he's snatched off somewhere else. I can't keep anybody in my office. Don't know anything about organizing industry, but they all get big jobs in management. It's upgrading for fair. It's very nice, but nobody stays any place long enough to learn his job. It's a nightmare.'

And still . . . the office is in a tall building. We both happen to look out the window at the same time. Across a welter of sunblackened roofs we can see in the slanting afternoon sunlight the rows of great cranes and the staging and the cradled hulls and beyond, in the brown strip of river, packed rows of new tankers, some splotched with yellow and red, some shining with the light gray of their last coat of paint. In spite of turmoil and confusion, ships are getting built, ships, ships, ships.

Do economic booms create as many problems as they solve?

What effect did the war have on the social position of women in the short run and in the long run?

What effect would this high turnover have on labor unions? on the quality of workmanship? on prices?

145

Both Germany and Japan fatally miscalculated this country's ability to quickly and effectively mobilize the homefront for the production of war goods. Every American's aid was enlisted. Children went on scrap drives to collect rubber and metals—resources in short supply due to Japanese control of Pacific sources. Women—adopting the government-inspired image of "Rosie the Riveter"—cut their hair, donned overalls, and went to work in factories, thereby freeing men for the battlefront. Everyone invested his savings in war bonds because there were few consumer goods for purchase. Did a member of your family participate in the home-front effort? How?

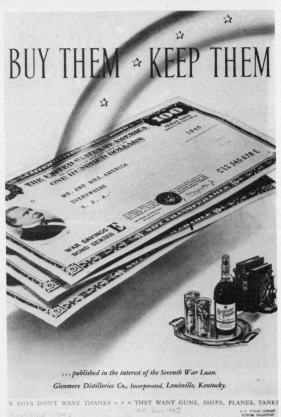

BUY THEM ☆ KEEP THEM

...published in the interest of the Seventh War Loan.

Glenmore Distilleries Co., Incorporated, Louisville, Kentucky.

A Choice of Weapons
Gordon Parks

The United States Armed Forces were segregated during World War II. At that time black soldiers had to face subtle and direct prejudice everywhere they went. There were many racial incidents and one major race riot in Detroit in these years. The following is an account of some of the problems faced by one black man, Gordon Parks. He writes of his bitter experiences as a press corps member assigned to an all-black air force unit during the war. What did black men and women learn from the war? How did their experiences contribute to the civil rights movement of the 1950s and 1960s? Would you have had as much patience as Gordon Parks demonstrated?

The hot air smelled of gasoline and planes when I arrived at Selfridge Field the next morning. Though it was early the sprawling air base was alive with men and all kinds of machines, from jeeps to P-40 fighter ships. A sergeant met me at the gate in a command car; and, as we halted at company headquarters, a squadron of fighter ships thundered up into the hot sky. I stood marveling at the climbing ships, finding pleasure in the fact that black boys were inside them. And, thinking back to Richard Wright's *Native Son,* I recalled the Negro boy's remark when he witnessed a similar sight: "Look at those white boys fly," he had said in a special sort of awe. Now I was thinking the same thing about these black boys as they flashed above the earth like giant birds.

Why was aviation so long a domain of whites only?

• • •

We spent our weekends in Detroit. And Paradise Valley, a Negro section of the city, opened its arms wide to the nattily uniformed pilots and officers. They were already heroes to these people who had never seen black boys with wings on their chests before. There was no shortage of women; they came from miles around—"in furs, Fords and Cadillacs," Tony used to crow in delight. The problem was to pick wisely from the multitude. Tony was cocky, proud and brazen with good humor; and he was like a one-eyed dog in a sausage factory after two weeks at the base. A very unpretty woman approached him one night at a bar, but Tony, his sights fixed on something more choice, ignored her. Hours later, when we were leaving the bar loaded and broke, the woman passed us and got into a beautiful new Cadillac. Tony stopped in his tracks. Then, walking up to the woman, he tipped his hat, "Baby," he said, "you look like King Kong, but this car and those furs you've got on are a natural gas. Move over, honey. Let Tony

147

baby drive this thing back to camp." She smiled, moved over and we journeyed out to Selfridge in style.

As the training went into fall, the men's attitude began to change. The fun was about over now. And the talk of women and the joking gave way to more serious things. Racial tensions began to have an effect on their actions and thinking. There were several incidents of white enlisted men on the base not saluting Negro officers. And black soldiers in combat were writing back about being segregated in barracks and mess halls in the war zones. The Negro newspapers were filled with stories about the black men being turned from the factory gates when war plants cried desperately for more help. The Pittsburgh *Courier* carried a long piece about Negro soldiers being assigned to menial labor. And there was a front-page article about an army band playing "God Bless America" when the white soldiers boarded the troopships; then, when Negroes went up the gangplank, the band switched to "The Darktown Strutters' Ball."

And one Sunday night a race riot erupted in Detroit. Fighting spread all over the city; twenty-five Negroes and nine whites were killed and hundreds of both races were injured. The black man was beginning to meet humiliation with violence. White supremacy had become as much an enemy as "blood" and "race" doctrines of the Nazis. Vindictiveness was slowly spreading through the air base. One could feel it in the air, in the mess halls, the barracks and the ready huts.

Once, after I returned from a trip to Washington, I found a note Tony had left for me. It read:

> Dear Gordon,
>
> Sorry to miss you but I'm on my way to Steubenville with Judy Edwards' body. As you probably heard, poor Judy spun in and I had to take his body all the way to Detroit because "there are no facilities" for handling Negro dead up there at Oscoda. It's about three hundred miles from Oscoda to Detroit, and in a goddamn Army ambulance you can imagine how long it took us to get there. Even as I write this to you, my feelings keep swinging from a murderous rage to frustration. How could anybody do anything like this?
>
> His body was lying wrapped in a tarpaulin in the back of the ambulance; and I had trouble accepting the fact that he was dead, for every time I looked back there, the body seemed to move. I now wonder if the doctors at the hospital had examined him, since this would have required them to touch him too. By the time night had fallen I felt so badly that all I could say was "Judy, I'm sorry. . . . I'm sorry. . . ." We have all suffered some brutal indignities from the whites in this country but this was the final indignity of all. All during the trip I was in an emotional state, alternately talking to the driver and quietly crying for Judy, for his family, for the country and for myself. I felt shame and revulsion for having to wear the uniform I had on. The driver seemed to be caught up in the same mood. We were two of the loneliest soldiers in the world.
>
> I won't tell his folks about this trip because it will just hurt them more. At least to them he was a hero and I'll make sure that when I arrive in Steubenville everyone knows it. The whole dirty business will come into even sharper focus when they lower him into the grave. He'll get an honor guard (a white one), the rifle fire and all the trappings. See you when I get back.
>
> Tony

I stuffed the letter into my pocket and walked over to the airstrip. The night was clear and cold and the stars seemed lower than usual. The fighter ships lined up on the quiet field were ghostly. I walked along beside them, noted the names stenciled in white block letters on the cockpits: Gleed, Pruitt, Tresville, Knox, Bright, Walker and many others. How many of these names will be on little white crosses this time next year? I wondered. At least the 332nd would go into battle with pilots who had

How does the Dos Passos article support this claim?

What were these "race" doctrines? Why didn't American whites perceive the parallel?

What ironies in the black man's position in this country does this letter bring out?

Despite changes, have you heard any Vietnam War veterans express similar bitterness?

When blacks did participate in air units, they were usually assigned the job of protecting the bomber planes that brought destruction like this to many German and Italian cities. Over eighty black pilots won the Distinguished Flying Cross for their service during the war. Have history books given adequate coverage to black accomplishments of this sort?

faced the enemy before. This would be more of a chance than the 99th Squadron was allowed; for, unlike the white pilots, they had gone into their first battle without one seasoned pilot to lead them. The costly pattern of segregation had arranged a lonely death for some of these men—even over enemy territory. Hitler's Luftwaffe must have laughed when they screamed into the formations of those *schwarz* boys—knowing there wasn't an experienced fighter amongst them.

What argument against segregation is exposed here?

• • •

A little after mid-December an order came from the Pentagon halting all furloughs. We knew what this meant. Any day now we would be going overseas. A new tempo hit the base; the men rushed about, restless, patting one another's backs, awaiting moving orders. They came one morning about a week before Christmas. That afternoon Colonel Davis called me to headquarters. "We're about to pull out," he said, "and your traveling papers are not in order."

"What's wrong with them?" I asked.

"You'll have to take that up with Washington. I'd advise you to fly there. We'll probably be leaving before they can get word back here to you."

I packed the battle gear that had been issued to me that morning, took a

149

bus to Detroit, then a plane to Washington; I arrived there late that evening. Stryker had left the OWI [Office of War Information] by now and had gone to work in New York for the Standard Oil Co. In fact, just about everyone I knew there had gone; the rest were preparing to leave. Besides, it was a weekend and no officials were around. I didn't know where to turn. The one man I did reach had developed a strange case of laryngitis, and was unable to talk, he said. Finally in desperation I tried to reach Elmer Davis, head of the OWI, but he was away on a trip. I fretted through Saturday and Sunday. Then the first thing Monday morning I went to see Ted Poston, a friend of mine in the OWI press section. He had heard the rumors. And Ted put things in their true perspective: "There's some Southern gentlemen and conservative Republicans on Capitol Hill who don't like the idea of giving this kind of publicity to Negro soldiers."

Why did they fear publicity?

I was shocked—and so was Ted—but there wasn't much we could do about it. The next day I reached Elmer Davis by telephone and told him my story. He listened attentively. When I finished he said, "Don't worry, Gordon, I'll be in touch with the Pentagon this afternoon. You report there tomorrow. I'm sure everything will be all right."

That night, on the Howard University campus, I met Captain Lee Rayford and Lieutenant Walter Lawson, two pilots from the 99th Fighter Squadron. They had returned to the States after completing their required number of missions. Captain Rayford was the holder of the Purple Heart, the Distinguished Flying Cross, the Croix de Guerre, the Air Medal, and the Yugoslav Red Star. He had been shot up over Austria by a Messerschmitt 109. Both of them could have remained Stateside as instructors. Instead they had volunteered to go back to the war zone. We ate dinner together, and since they had to go to the Pentagon the next day we agreed to meet and go together.

We had no sooner boarded the bus and seated ourselves behind the driver than his voice came at us, metallic and demanding. "If you fellas wanta ride into Virginyuh, you gotta go to the rear." We looked at one another questioningly, deciding in our silence not to move. The driver stood up and faced us, a scrawny disheveled man with tobacco-stained teeth and a hawk nose. The armpits of his uniform were discolored from sweat. "You all heard what I said. This bus ain't goin' nowhere till you all go to the back where you belong."

Was the driver's action legal?

"We intend going to Virginia in the seats we're in," Lee said with finality.

"Okay, if you ain't back there in one minute I'm callin' the MP's and havin' you put off."

"You'd better start calling right now," Lee replied.

Two white Air Force captains and a major were seated across the aisle from us and I noticed that they stirred uncomfortably. Several other whites were scattered in the near-empty bus and an elderly Negro woman sat at the rear. I watched her through the rear-view mirror. She had half risen from her seat; there was courage, dignity and anger in every line of her small body. Her look demanded that we stay there, and I was determined not to disappoint her. The bus had become dead quiet while the driver stood glowering at us.

"Fellows." One of the young white captains was speaking now. "We know how you feel about this," he said, his voice cloaked in false camaraderie, "but the major has an appointment at the Pentagon in a half hour. He wonders if you would mind moving back so that we can be on our way?"

My two friends were outranked. But there were no bars on my shoulders. The American eagle on my officer's cap was as large and significant as his or the major's. I took a good look at the old woman in the rear. She was standing now, gripping the seat ahead of her. Then, borrowing the captain's icy politeness, I stood and addressed the major. "Sir," I said, "as you can see, these men are fighter pilots. They have completed their missions but they have volunteered for more duty at the front. Would you like to order your fellow officers to the rear? They have no intention of moving otherwise." My anger was rising, so I sat back down.

The bus driver stood watching us until the major finally spoke to him. "Drive on," he said. "Can't you tell when you're licked?" The driver cursed under his breath, threw himself into the seat and slammed in the gears and we lurched off toward Virginia. "Hallelujah!" the Negro woman shouted from the rear. "Hallelujah!" Her voice rang with pathos and triumph. "Thank God we don't have to sit in the back of our P-38's," Lawson sighed as we got off the bus.

What aspects of the civil rights movement of the 1960s does this incident fore-shadow?

• • •

Our plane took off in a blinding rainstorm—and it landed in another one at Norfolk, Virginia. A taxi took me to the ferry landing where I would cross over into Newport News. I sat there in the waiting room for an hour on top of my battle gear among a boisterous group of white enlisted men. Four Negro soldiers were huddled in a nearby corner. Two of them were propped against each other sleeping. Most of the white boys seemed to be making a festivity of these last hours. But there was a sort of emptiness attached to their laughing and drinking. Obviously they were headed for some departure point. It's all to hide the fear, I thought. Their faces were so young.

We filed out when the ferry whistled. It was still raining and we stood near the edge of the dock watching the boat fasten into the slip. Through the wetness I noticed a sign reading COLORED PASSENGERS and another one reading WHITES ONLY. The four black soldiers moved automatically to the colored side, and so did I. How ironic, I thought; such nonsense would not stop until we were in enemy territory.

After all the outgoing passengers were off and the trucks and cars had rumbled past, we started forward. Then I saw a Negro girl step from the ferry. She had been standing in the section marked for cars; now she was in the direct line of the white enlisted men, who stampeded to the boat screaming at the tops of their voices. I saw the girl fall beneath them into the mud and water. The four Negro soldiers also saw her go down. The five of us rushed to her rescue. She was knocked down several times before we could get to her and pull her out of the scrambling mob.

"You lousy white bastards!" one of the Negro soldiers yelled. "If I only had a gun!" Tears were in his eyes, hysteria in his voice. A long knife was glistening in his hands.

"Soldier!" I shouted above the noise, letting him get a look at my officer's cap. "Put that knife away!"

He glared at me fiercely for a second. "But you saw what they did!"

"Yes, I saw, but we're outnumbered ten to one! You can't fight all of them. Get on the boat!" He looked at me sullenly for another moment, then moved off. We cleaned the mud from the girl's coat and she walked away without a word. Only proud anger glistened on her black face. Then the four of us joined the soldier I had ordered away. He was standing still tense beneath the sign reading "colored passengers."

"Sorry, soldier," I said. "We wouldn't have had a chance against a mob like that. You realize that, don't you?"

151

"If I gotta die, I'd just as soon do it where I got real cause to." His tone was resolute. I had to answer. I was tempted to hand him the bit about the future and all that, but the future was too uncertain. The yelling was even louder now on the other side of the boat. "Sons-of-bitches," he muttered under his breath.

"Good luck," I said to them as we parted on the other shore. "So long," they said—except the one I had spoken to—then they moved off into the darkness and rain again. I turned away, feeling I had somehow let him down.

"Colored move to the rear!" The voice met me again when I got on the bus with some of the white enlisted men. Sick of trouble, I made my way to the back and sat down; I was the only Negro aboard. Some of the whites were standing, but I had four empty seats around me. "Gordy! My God, it's Gordy!" a voice rang out above the noise. And suddenly a soldier was rushing back toward me. "Bud!" I shouted, getting to my feet only to be knocked back to my seat by his bear hug. It was Bud Hallender, a husky man I had played basketball with back in St. Paul. Now he was down beside me, slapping my back and wringing my hands.

"You all cain't ride back there with that nigra! Move back up front where you belong!" Bud ignored the command; now he was telling the others I was the co-captain of his basketball team, his friend.

"You all hear me? You cain't ride back there with that nigra!"

"Go screw yourself!" Bud shouted back. "Drive on or we'll throw you off this goddamned crate and drive it ourselves!" Laughter rocked the bus. The driver plopped down into his seat without another word and drove off toward the heart of town. And Bud and I talked excitedly of a time and place where things had been different. Finally, at the terminal we wished each other a jovial goodbye.

• • •

Tony and I went out for some fresh air the next night. "It's hard to believe but we've had trouble right here on this base," he said as we walked along, "so we'd better stay in this area."

"What kind of trouble?"

"The same old jazz. One of our ground crewmen was beaten up by some white paratroopers night before last. Then they've tried to segregate us at the base's movie house. Everyone's in a hell of a mood." We became suddenly quiet as we circled the area.

A shot sounded nearby and the two of us stopped in our tracks. Then there was another shot. Someone seemed to be returning the fire. "We'd better get in. Sounds like trouble," Tony said. Our barracks had already gone dark when we entered it. Several men were at the windows with guns looking out cautiously into the night. When all was quiet again, the lights went back on and the gambling and the letter writing and the drinking started again. New orders came the following morning. We would take to the boat two days earlier than had been proposed. I was happy about this. There seemed to be less danger at sea than on this troubled base.

Colonel Davis sent for me just before noon. I hurried anxiously to his office. No more trouble, I hoped; it was too close to sailing time. But when he looked up at me his face was calm. It was, after all, some routine matter he would speak about, I thought.

"I'm sorry. Your papers are not in order. A final call from the Pentagon has come through. You will not be able to embark with us."

"This is ridiculous," I said. "Can't you do anything? Someone in

Does violent confrontation have a legitimate place in solving racial problems?

What does this incident show about the solidity of white opinion on racial issues in the 1940s?

This all-black infantry battalion represents only a small fraction of the half-million blacks who saw overseas service in World War II. How did wartime experiences at home and abroad help fuel the civil rights struggles of the 1960s?

Washington is trying to prevent coverage of your group overseas, Colonel. This is the first Negro fighter group. It's history. It has to be covered. Can't you protest in some way, Colonel?"

"There's nothing, absolutely nothing I can do. The orders are from the Pentagon. They cannot be rescinded. I'm terribly sorry."

I had lost. And suddenly anesthetized to the colonel and all that was around him, I turned and started out. "You are aware that you are sworn to the strictest of secrecy about what you have seen or learned here," he was saying as he followed me to the door. "You realize the dangers of any slip."

"Yes, I understand, Colonel."

"It is even possible to detain you until we are overseas under such conditions. But I am sure you won't discuss our movements with anyone."

"I won't. Don't worry. I want to forget the whole thing as quickly as possible." I rushed back toward the barracks, angry and disgusted. I couldn't bring myself to say goodbye to the pilots again. I packed quickly and waited for the command car the colonel had ordered for me.

The pilots were readying themselves for the boat when the car arrived; and I slipped through the rear door without even a backward glance. At

What do you know about black fighting groups in World War II? in other wars?

153

five o'clock the next morning, after wiring Sally, I boarded a plane for Washington. I would change planes there and go on to New York, where I would wait for my wife and children. The thought of even stopping in this city irked me. I wouldn't live there again if they gave me the White House rent free, I thought as the plane roared down the runway.

We began circling over Washington at dawn; and far below I could see the landing field, lying like small strips of cardboard under a wispy patch of cloud. Further out in the distance the monuments of the city shone milk-white in the winter sunlight and the water in the mall sparkled like an oblong jewel between the sculptured trees; there was the Capitol standing quiet and strong on one end and the Lincoln Memorial set on the high quarter of the opposite slope. What a beautiful sight to be wed to such human ugliness, I thought. And as we dropped lower I could see the tops of the stores, theaters and restaurants whose doors were still closed to me.

What irony of symbolism is he pointing out here?

I thought back to the fighter pilots. They would soon be far out to sea, sailing toward war and death, ignoring at least temporarily, their differences with the land they were leaving to defend. This was the price for a questionable equality.

154

LIFE IN THE CAMPS

The locking up of Japanese-Americans in concentration camps during World War II was in many ways a logical extension of the anti-Oriental racism that had existed on the West Coast since the arrival of the first Chinese immigrants in the 1840s. Japanese laborers began to arrive in California in the decade following the Exclusion Act of 1882, which barred further Chinese immigration. Despite their record of good citizenship and hard work in menial tasks, the first generation of Japanese-Americans endured similar discrimination: the "Gentlemen's Agreement" of 1907 ended Japanese immigration. Many of the Nisei, the second generation of Japanese-Americans, born and brought up in the United States in the period between the two world wars, became substantial businesspeople and property owners. Nevertheless, in the wake of Japan's attack on Pearl Harbor in December 1941, an outpouring of bigotry and fear persuaded officials in California and Washington to "relocate" the Nisei. Ultimately ten "relocation camps" were established in remote areas, from California to Arkansas. Losing their homes and businesses, the Nisei and their children, charged with no crimes and denied legal recourse, became prisoners of war in their own country. The following letters reflect life in the camps.

. . . Left Fresno at 8:55 this morning and reached the Assembly Center at about 9:10 A.M. We first stopped at the registrar's office to be checked and registered. Our bags and pockets were searched, to my surprise. For what? I don't know. Luckily we all passed. I mean nothing was taken from us. Then our baggage was inspected from corner to corner. What a feeling I had when they went through our personal belongings. . . .

When I first entered our room, I became sick to my stomach. There were seven beds in the room and no furniture nor any partitions to separate the males and the females of the family. I just sat on the bed, staring at the bare wall. For a while I couldn't speak nor smile. Well, after getting over with my shock, I started to get the baggage in. . . .

Then we wanted to know where our rest rooms were. This was too much for me. There is no privacy. I just can't explain how it is, but it's worse than a country privy. After it's been used a couple of times, there is a whole stack of flies. Once you open the door the flies can be seen buzzing

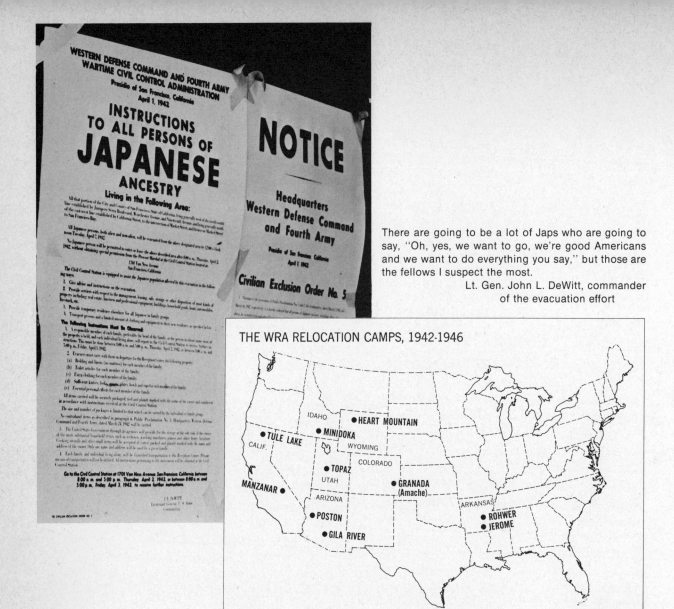

There are going to be a lot of Japs who are going to say, ''Oh, yes, we want to go, we're good Americans and we want to do everything you say,'' but those are the fellows I suspect the most.

Lt. Gen. John L. DeWitt, commander of the evacuation effort

THE WRA RELOCATION CAMPS, 1942-1946

What we hate to recall is not so much the hardships that the war and Evacuation brought to us but the vast sense of alienation we suffered when we were like the man without a country.

Kats Kunitsugu, "Evacuation—the Pain Remains," *Pacific Citizen*, Dec. 20–27, 1968

What would your reaction have been?

around; it is like a nest of bees. We just couldn't go in there, so we excavated. The hospital being facilitated with flush toilets, we sneaked in. Then we tried the showers, which are not so bad except that there is no privacy. Well that's that for the day's happening.

As to what I think of camp life; I think it's hell. That's the only word I could think of to describe it.

● ● ●

Every Nisei . . . was extremely annoyed when he was reminded by some visiting Caucasian that he had been placed in the assembly center "for his own protection." Also, without exception, everyone was highly indignant at the practice of focusing floodlights from twelve watchtowers on camp every night from twilight to dawn. When informed by the administration that the searchlights had been installed to protect us from outsiders who might leap over the fence to injure us, his usual retort was: "Why should the lights be focused on the barracks and not on the outer fence as a logical procedure?" Similarly, there was keen resentment against the barbed-wire fence surrounding camp and many a time I watched a novice throwing rocks at it to discover if the wires were actually charged.

No systematic study was made of the attitudes of little children but the narrating of a few stray incidents might be of some aid in identifying them. One afternoon in late June, I heard a great commotion behind my barrack and on investigation perceived a group of twelve boys about six to ten years of age shouldering wooden guns and attacking a "Japanese fort" while lustily singing "Anchors Aweigh." . . . Similarly, in the blackout of May 24, little children raced down our street yelling at the top of their lungs: "Turn off your lights! The Japs are coming!"

A Nisei mother once told me with tears in her eyes of her six-year-old son who insisted on her "taking him back to America." The little boy had been taken to Japan about two years ago but was so unhappy there that she was compelled to return to California with him. Soon afterwards they were evacuated to Santa Anita, and the little boy in the absence of his Caucasian playmates was convinced that he was still in Japan and kept on entreating his mother to "take him back to America." To reassure him that he was in America she took him to the information center in her district and pointed to the American flag but he could not be consoled because Charlie and Jimmie, his Caucasian playmates, were not there with him in camp.

It is also interesting to note that whenever little children sang songs these were not Japanese folksongs but typically American songs like "God Bless America," "My Country 'Tis of Thee," "My Old Kentucky Home," "Row, Row, Row Your Boat," "Jesus Loves Me," and other songs known to every American child. The "Americanness" of the Sansei may serve to identify the character of their Nisei parents.

When 1,500 work orders were sent out by the Personnel Office to U.S. citizens above the age of sixteen a day before the camouflage project was opened, approximately 800 were reported to have refused to work. Some excused themselves by claiming that they were allergic to the dye on burlap strips or to the lint which fell off from them, but at least half of that number was said to have refused on principle. They felt that they were really "prisoners of war" and that the U.S. government had no right to appeal to them to aid in the war effort on a patriotic note. The battle cry during the camouflage strike of June 16–17 seemed to be: Give us the treatment accorded other American citizens and we will gladly cooperate in completing the number of nets requested by the U.S. Army. . . .

What do you think of the term "relocation" as a description of the experience recounted here?

If your parents were members of an ethnic group at war with the United States, did they fear any repercussions? Did they question why only Japanese-Americans were being removed?

What unjust aspect of the internment is the author indicating here?

Like the chapter on the depression of the 1930s, this chapter on World War II was chosen because of our assumption that the war was an event of such major consequence that it touched the lives of nearly everyone. Yet, as the readings attempt to illustrate, the effects of the war on people were not as uniform as might be expected. At the same time that soldiers were dying on distant Pacific islands, men unemployed through most of the thirties found steady work.

Your assignment is to interview members of your family about their experiences in the war, at home and abroad. For many people this may well dredge up feelings of pain and terror; you must therefore be sensitive in deciding what is an appropriate line of questioning. Try to discover the ways in which the war affected your family and how existence in the early 1940s contrasted with life in the 1930s. Your investigation should come to some conclusion on the changes that the war brought in terms of economic and social conditions, place of residence, political convictions, opportunities gained, and hardships suffered. Then, after completing your interviews, write a brief preliminary report on your findings, to be incorporated later into your research paper.

BIBLIOGRAPHIC NOTE

The literature on World War II military campaigns and specific battles is enormous. You should be able to find accounts of any particular wartime military episode that is related to your family's experiences. Two of the best accounts of soldiers' experiences in combat are *The Story of G. I. Joe* (1945) by Ernie Pyle, a wartime correspondent, and *The Naked and the Dead* (1948) by Norman Mailer, the brilliant American novelist.

The history of the homefront is still inadequately written. But see Richard Polenberg's collection, *America at War: The Home Front, 1941–1945* (1968) and his *War and Society: The United States 1941–1945* (1972). Fun to read is Richard R. Lingeman, *Don't You Know There's a War On?* (1970). Several excellent works have recently appeared on the Japanese-American internment camps, including Roger Daniels, *Concentration Camps USA* (1972).

six

YOUR TIMES

Ready for an unanswerable question? What is the relationship between you and the major forces that shape the world in which you live? This chapter asks you to begin to define your own situation in relation to the total scheme of American society and culture.

You certainly are living in an extraordinary period of American history. In your lifetime the United States has undergone enormous change. Some of the things that you regard as commonplace today—the drug scene, the women's movement, racial confrontation, radicalism, sexual permissiveness, epidemic violence, moonwalks—scarcely existed in the public mind in the early 1960s. Richard Nixon, defeated for the presidency in 1960 and in the California gubernatorial race two years later, was "finished" politically. Only farmers wore overalls. Men's hair was cut short, regularly. Only a few dozen American "advisors" were in Saigon. Criticism of the American "way of life" was largely rhetorical, as in the handsome young President Kennedy's early sixties' pledge "to get America moving again." The Peace Corps and the civil rights movement were two visible outlets for what seemed to be boundless American optimism and idealism. Americans were confident that material progress would meld with social justice.

Things did not work out that way, despite unprecedented changes that have made the United States of the 1970s in so many ways a different society from the one that emerged from World War II in 1945. Over that quarter-century the speed of change has accelerated, to the point where many people have come to associate change, not with progress and a better life, but with fear and anxiety over the possible destruction of civil-

ization. Whether you interpret change as good or bad—or some change as worthwhile and some as disastrous—it is impossible to deny that the years since the end of World War II have brought unprecedented developments in science and technology, altering your life and that of every American significantly.

Since the day you were born, almost every industrial index has told the same story: MORE. More television sets, more refrigerators, more computers, more miles of highways for more automobiles. Taller buildings. Larger airplanes. Better toilet tissue. Consider the simple pleasure of listening to music in your home: the idea of placing a thick 78-rpm disc on a "record player" seems positively medieval when contrasted with the technological sophistication of the sound systems of the 1970s. Yet the old American assumption that change = progress is for the first time in serious question. More of everything obviously also means more energy expended from finite sources, and more water and air pollution as well. What in your judgment is an acceptable societal price for material progress?

Even if ecological questions are ignored, the "progress" that technological change is supposed to have ushered in is subject to serious questioning. General prosperity and increasing affluence in the years after World War II caused many people to assume that the problems of poverty were at last being solved, and that inequality was being reduced. Even the publication of Michael Harrington's best-selling *The Other America* and the rediscovery of poverty in the 1960s did not dispel the stubborn misconception that the separation between rich and poor was gradually disappearing. The facts are quite different and suggest no significant shift in the income of rich and poor. The very rich have managed to preserve their wealth, and the upper middle class has improved its position; but the middle class floats on a sea of debt despite five-figure incomes, and the lower middle class and lower class find it difficult to hold their own. While hard and true statistics are difficult to establish, the hoary axiom that "the rich get richer and the poor get poorer" may well be accurate. Michael Harrington has even argued that the Internal Revenue Code is now used to redistribute income from the poor to the rich. Whatever the validity of this heretical opinion, the fact remains that in 1970, 2 percent of the people owned 43 percent of the wealth of the country. That ratio has not altered significantly in the last fifty years.

The changes of the past half-century have been essentially in the physical and material props of life, as you have come to understand through a comparison between your world and that of your grandparents and parents.

Now consider your own situation at this moment of historical time. How free are you to control your own destiny? To what extent can you (or anyone else) set out, with reasonable expectations, to achieve considerable wealth and power? How do you define those forces that seem to inhibit your freedom to become exactly what you want to become?

The material in this chapter seeks to provide you with a basis for defining your relationship with the society in which you live. As you look at these signs of our times, try to analyze them in terms of trends that may have some effect on your own life today or sometime in the future. What leaves you optimistic, and what depresses you? What suggests freedom and enlightenment, and where do you find increasing regimentation and plasticity? Do you agree with some politicians who find the present stimulating and challenging? Or are the critics who predict strife, technological depersonalization, and authoritarianism more accurate? Why do you believe what you do?

The assembly line has come to symbolize the depersonalization of work: workers feel little pride in their labor because they see their contribution to the end product as insignificant. Do you think your education will protect you from encountering this problem, or do white-collar workers face the same dilemma?

For the vast majority of people, work takes up a greater part of life than anything else. The contemporary notion that work should be intellectually stimulating as well as materially rewarding is apparently in conflict with many of the demands of business and technological efficiency, demands which even before one embarks on a career make themselves felt, for education is strongly influenced by the kinds and quality of work available. The following section presents a collage of work and one's educational preparation for it in today's world. As you go through this section, try to define your own ideal of work—and ask yourself how likely you are to achieve it.

UNHAPPY WORKERS

How happy are most Americans in their work? Not very, reports Studs Terkel, author of a book on attitudes toward work.

Of the 85 million white- and blue-collar workers in this country, most of them hold jobs which make them sick—so contends Terkel.

Workers suffer from headaches, backaches, ulcers, alcoholism, drug addiction, and even nervous breakdowns, all because they find their work unsatisfying and consider it "another form of violence."

After three years of research, Terkel reports that most of the people he interviewed found their work monotonous or painful.

Examples—an executive: "My day starts at 5 A.M. I've had an ulcer since I was 18."

A farm worker: "There were times when I felt I couldn't take it any more. It was 105 in the shade and I'd see endless rows of lettuce and feel my back hurting . . ."

Assembly line worker: "I stand in one spot, about a two or three feet area, all night. The only time a person stops is when the line stops."

Bus driver: "Most of the drivers, they'll suffer from hemorrhoids, kidney trouble and such as that. I have a case of ulcers . . ."

Model: "I feel like someone's clothes hanger. One day someone will say I'm great. In the next studio they'll say I'm terrible. It changes from minute to minute; acceptance, rejection."

Although occupational discontent is widespread, Terkel explains that workers fear most the loss of their jobs, of not being needed, of being easily replaced, of being held in small value by the system, of being compelled to retire.

What they crave is meaningful work, work which will accord them respect, recognition, pride in a job well done.

When such satisfactions are placed beyond their grasp, their frustration mounts and they retaliate with sabotage, absenteeism, and substandard production.

What are your parents' greatest concerns about the work they do? Do you think your generation will escape these concerns?

What kind of work do you expect to do? What do you think the chances are for finding it meaningful?

A College Student Makes a Big Decision

GERALD N. ROSENBERG

Back at the Fieldston School in Riverdale, my friends and I used to sit around the lunch table and wonder out loud what college life would be like. We were unsure and a bit scared. Perhaps our biggest fear was that we would be forced to make a decision on what to do for the rest of our lives.

Above all, we did not want to be trapped. We wanted to do a lot of sampling before making a career commitment.

We were not the only ones who were frightened by the idea of important decisions. Very few of the college students we met knew what they wanted to do. Often, they seemed to dread the idea of graduation, of being thrust into a situation in which they knew important decisions were unavoidable.

I entered Dartmouth in the fall of 1972, fully expecting to spend four care-free years in the beautiful hills of New Hampshire.

I knew that by my senior year my parents would expect me to make a career decision, but I was confident that I could postpone making this decision, and please my parents at the same time, by going to graduate school.

By last spring, however, I realized that I had been tricked.

Late in March I received a memorandum reminding me that I had three weeks to submit my program for the next four years.

It was all in accordance with the Dartmouth Plan. Under this program, designed to offer "maximum freedom of choice," a student needs credit for 11 quarter terms—three in the freshman year—to graduate. Of the remaining eight quarters, three must be at Dartmouth, including one required summer term, and the rest can be spent at other recognized institutions.

My dream of care-free college had been shattered. Under the guise of "maximum freedom," I was being asked to plan my college career.

Did I want to graduate in three years or in five? Did I want to enter any one of the 26 foreign study programs, ranging from Scotland to Sierra Leone and from Toulouse to Tonga?

I could tutor in inner-city schools in Jersey City or Oakland, or I could work at an Indian Job Corps center in Montana. I discovered that there was a 12-college exchange system with other Eastern schools. I could become a public affairs interne or join an Outward Bound wilderness program.

The more I looked around, the more options I discovered.

Confusion on Confusion

With all these options to choose from, I also had to make sure that I could complete the requirements for a major. Certain courses are offered only once every two or three years and to complete a major, these courses are often required. I would have to be on campus when they were offered. But I did not know what I was going to major in!

Also confusing me was the fact that, once submitted, my plan was supposed to remain unchanged. Although there were procedures by which changes could be made, the idea of changing a plan seemed to be discouraged. I felt as if I was planning my life on paper rather than being allowed to live it.

Bewildered, I trudged off to the trusty computer, hoping that modern technology could make my decisions. After telling the computer that I wanted to spend the spring of 1974 as a public affairs interne, the summer of 1974 at Dartmouth and the spring of 1975 in Strasbourg, France, I eagerly waited.

The computer, however, informed me that, given my specifications, there were approximately 80 different acceptable plans and that it would not bother to print them. Aghast, I typed in three more specifications and the computer

Are you locked into a particular college program? Do you think the system needs changing?

disgorged about 25 acceptable plans. Technology had failed me.

With one week left to complete my plan, I became frantic, I talked to deans, professors, friends and parents. Most knew exactly how they would use the plan but could offer little advice on how I should use it. In desperation, I realized that I would have to sit down and make some hard decisions.

The plan that I finally submitted last April—on Friday the 13th—is very tentative. It allows me to graduate in the spring of 1975, at the end of my third year of college.

My plan called for a vacation last summer, study at Dartmouth last fall and this winter, public service work in Washington this spring (hopefully as a Public Service Interne), study at Dartmouth this summer and fall and next winter, and finally, study in Strasbourg, France, in the spring of 1975.

As interesting as the plan may sound, I am still irked by the idea that someone expects me to know what I will want to do two or three years from now.

Perhaps I am still scared to commit myself for such a long period of time. But the fact is that I feel better now for having been required to sort myself out.

Over the past decade, colleges have given their students more responsibility, not only in the area of academic studies but also with respect to their social lives. Coed dorms like this one are a feature of many campuses. Some have argued that this kind of freedom is a necessary preparation for adult life, while others maintain that it places additional burdens on those going through a difficult time of life. What is your opinion?

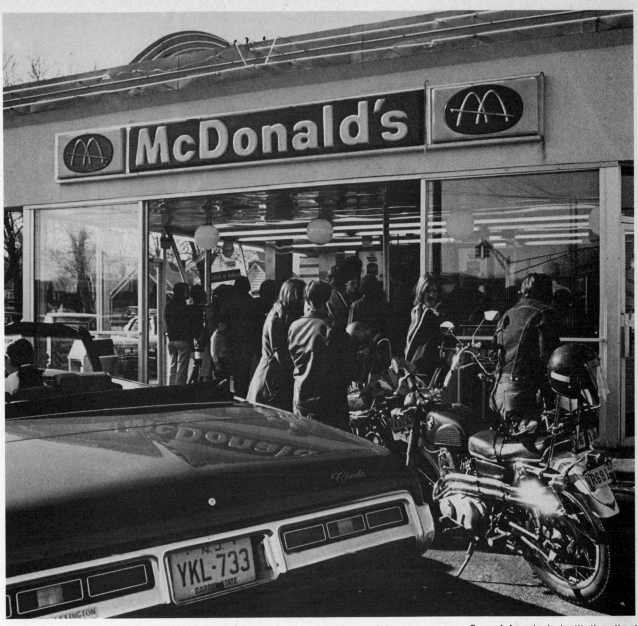

One of America's institutionalized pleasure palaces is the fast-food place. Where are they likely to be located, whom do they attract, and why do these people come? Are they a symbol of the good life or the opposite to you?

PLEASURE

The meaning of the concept of pleasure is utterly subjective, in form and in substance. Social and economic trends as well as advertising do change our concepts of what is pleasurable, whether it be home appliances or dope in the streets. As you look at the following section, ask yourself how the diverse types of pleasure displayed here relate to your idea of what the good life is—or should be.

The Football Phenomenon and Its Place on Campus

IVER PETERSON

Millions of armchair quarterbacks saw some good college football during the annual New Years' Day bowl-game binge, but they probably did not see the best. After all, the University of Oklahoma's Sooners trounced both Cotton Bowl teams—Nebraska and Texas—during the regular season, and tied Southern California, which lost to Ohio State in the Rose Bowl.

The reason for their absence, as college sports fans know, is that the Big Red team from Norman, Okla., is under a two-year ban from playing televised bowl games. The ban was imposed by the National Collegiate Athletic Association and Oklahoma's Big Eight Conference after the Sooners fielded two players with doctored high school transcripts.

The illegally altered class standings, which made the two players appear eligible for the football scholarships that the University of Oklahoma had pressed upon them, pointed up an important element in the controversy over big time college sports. The intense demand for blue-chip athletes and a winning team has apparently presented too much of a temptation to coaches and players to go beyond the strictly limited inducements for prospective players permitted by the N.C.A.A.—free tuition, room and board, some laundry and book money, and some transportation expenses.

Other Offers Reported

And the college sports scene is rife with reports that many other inducements, including money, cars, clothes and a job, are offered under the table.

"I used to think everything I heard was exaggerated," Darrell Royal, coach of the Texas Longhorns and athletic director of the University of Texas, told the Chronicle of Higher Education, "but we've had too many people come here that told us what people have offered them. You're out there trying to sell yourself and your school, and the guy ain't hearing a word you're saying. All he's wondering about is when you're going to start talking money."

To its credit, the University of Oklahoma, like other important sports colleges, acted quickly if not entirely openly to correct these abuses when they were discovered, and the attitude among officials there seems to be that the growing venality of college sports can be contained by good faith and constant vigilance.

But the question that skeptics have long been asking is not just how major colleges should contain the greed and excesses of college sports, but what business does an institution of higher learning have in producing and promoting multimillion-dollar public spectacles in the first place.

A stranger at the University of Oklahoma who poses that question comes away with the realization that probably came to the men who ran the country's public colleges and universities a long time ago. It is that, in more ways than just sports, there is a vast gap between the ideals of higher education and the realities of life at a large, state-supported public university.

Realities in America

. . . Dr. Sharp [president of the University of Oklahoma] and others in his position know that these realities are that American public education has drawn its support from the public by providing what the public needs and wants. Land grant colleges were founded to produce agriculturalists and technicians when intensive farming began after the Civil War; after 1957, campuses produced scientists in response to Sputnik, and today the emphasis is on cheap, informal and easily accessible two-year community colleges. And on sports.

Last season, for example, more than 400 million fans watched nearly 3,000 college football games. About 30 mil-

What do athletics have to do with academic pursuits?

How important are sports, especially football, on your campus?

168

lion of the fans paid an estimated $150 million—not including bowl games—to attend in person. The television networks spent another $13.5 million for broadcast rights, and will pay more next season.

And as Wade Walker, the University of Oklahoma's athletic director, points out, sports—and especially football—is a lot more than a game. Being a real fan almost means believing in a particular way of life. . . .

More Than a Game

. . . William Maehl, professor of history at the university and president of the Faculty Senate, described the importance of football to Oklahoma in a way that might be applied to many other states, or indeed, to much of the country.

"This is a young state," he said. "It has no real traditions, and football provides a kind of focus of values that is much more important to people here than it would be, perhaps, to people in an Eastern state."

Mr. Walker, the Oklahoma athletic director, sees it clearly:

"If you only had one toy when you were a youngster, but it was a good toy, you could still go out in the neighborhood and stick your chest out and say, 'that's mine!'

"Well, this is a rural state, and our football gives John Doe Q. Public, wherever he lives, something to identify with—it gives him something to stick out his chest about, and say, 'Boy, I'm a Sooner! I'm part of the Big Red!' It gives him something wholesome."

There is nothing abstract in Mr. Walker's view of the connection between sports and American ideals. "We're teachers," he said of himself and his coaching staff. "We teach a philosophy, we teach a skill, and we danged sure also teach a little bit of religion. And we teach discipline—this is one of the last areas where true discipline is taught, where love for the American flag and respect for the American President is taught, through discipline."

Mr. Walker spends most of his time, he said, promoting support for the

Sooners by making this kind of appeal and urging fans to "get a piece of the action, be a part of the Big Red." And they respond.

External Pressures

Fan loyalty has its pitfalls, however, and officials at big time sports schools have learned that they have to tread gingerly between promoting the enthusiasm of loyal supporters and resisting the demands that seem to accompany the support.

When Chuck Fairbanks ended the 1966-'67 season at Oklahoma with a 6-3-1 record—a disaster for a team that is used to being top or near the top in the country—"Chuck Chuck" stickers appeared on the bumpers of Oklahoma cars, and the coach did leave, to take over the New England Patriots in the National Football League.

Then, when the Big Eight and N.C.A.A. probation was announced, along with a prohibition against the Sooners appearing on television for two seasons, Gov. David Hall of Oklahoma won political points by appealing for a lifting of the TV ban and by threatening to go to court when the appeal failed. The episode made some friends for Governor Hall, but it angered and embarrassed members of the university.

Dr. Sharp, the university's president, said his administration had to resist "constant external pressures to use [football] for political or commercial purposes." He added, "We resist these pressures because we feel that they are an intrusion into the academic purpose of the university."

. . . Relations with the Legislature "understandably are eased" when the Sooners have a good season, Dr. Sharp said, but he insisted that success on the gridiron was not all that important in terms of money. . . .

"But remember, I haven't been through a losing season," he added, "and I would have to go through a losing season before I could make a final judgment on that."

He made it sound like something he would just as soon avoid having to do.

Do you agree with these justifications for sports in college?

In what ways are political pressures on a university dangerous?

169

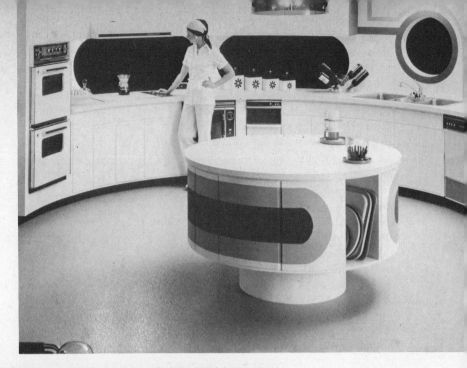

For many Americans happiness is gauged by material well-being. By this standard, ownership of the ultra-modern electronic kitchen on the right would qualify a person as relatively well-off and happy. Many members of your own generation have rejected the logic of this equation. Can you suggest why? How essential is material well-being to happiness?

Do these two scenes—a crowd at a rock festival and a row of suburban houses—suggest the existence of a generation gap in the American pursuit of pleasure? If so, what is the nature of the gap? If not, what similarities do you see?

Forty percent of all adults in the nation attended a church or synagogue during a typical week of 1973, according to the annual Gallup Poll on religious service attendance, the same percentage recorded in 1971 and 1972.

However, the Gallup organization reported yesterday, over-all church and synagogue attendance has declined nine percentage points since 1958.

The poll attributed the drop "almost entirely" to falling church attendance among Roman Catholics. In 1973, it said, the percentage of Catholics who attended church in a typical week was 55 per cent, compared with 71 per cent in 1964.

Protestant church attendance, according to the poll, reflected virtually no change over the same period. In 1973, 37 per cent of the nation's Protestants attended service in an average week, compared with 38 per cent in 1964.

Synagogue attendance also showed little change over the last 10 years, with 19 per cent attending service in a typical week in 1973 compared with 17 per cent a decade earlier.

To estimate the average attendance during 1973, the Gallup Poll took representative samples of the adult population in selected weeks to account for seasonal fluctuations.

A total of 6,154 persons, 18 and older, were interviewed personally in more than 300 scientifically selected sampling localities.

The following question was asked:

"Did you yourself happen to attend church or synagogue in the last seven days?"

The statistics were projected to approximately 55 million adults who attended a church or synagogue in a typical week.

Findings from previous years were consistent with the current poll: women are more frequent churchgoers than men, the South and Middle West had the best record for attendance, and young adults, 18 to 29 years old, were less likely to attend church in 1973 than older adults.

Comparison percentages of Roman Catholic and Protestant church attendance follow:

	Catholic	Protestant
1964	71%	38%
1965	67	38
1966	68	38
1967	66	39
1968	65	38
1969	63	37
1970	60	38
1971	57	37
1972	56	37
1973	55	37

The premise behind this wayside prayer station is that the religious impulse is still present in the contemporary world but needs another form of expression. Do you find any evidence that your generation is looking for a new way to practice religion?

One small step for man, one
giant leap for mankind?

DANGERS AND CHALLENGES

Is our age a time for hope or despair? That is the question posed in this
section. To answer you will have to decide what problems are solvable
and what promising trends of the present can be continued as the years
go by. In coming to some conclusions about the present, you will have
traveled some distance in situating yourself in the future.

E.P.A. Finds Biggest Rivers Among the Dirtiest

WASHINGTON, Jan. 17 (UPI)—Some of the nation's biggest rivers—including parts of the Ohio, Mississippi and Missouri—are also the dirtiest, according to a new study by the Environmental Protection Agency.

The agency said that the major problem appeared to be nutrients, such as phosphorus and nitrogen, which can overfertilize waters and thereby cause heavy growth of vegetation and the shutting off of oxygen supplies.

E.P.A. said the cleanest rivers among 22 it studied were the upper Missouri, Columbia, Snake, Willamette, upper Mississippi, Yukon, Tennessee, Susquehanna and the lower Colorado.

The worst third in the survey were the lower Red, Hudson, lower Ohio, lower Mississippi, lower Arkansas, middle Ohio, the Mississippi near Minneapolis, the lower Missouri, upper Arkansas and middle Missouri.

In between were the Rio Grande, Alabama, upper Ohio, upper Red, Brazos, Potomac, upper Colorado, middle Mississippi and Sacramento.

Pollutants that have been the subject of the most control, such as sewage and bacteria, showed over-all improvements in the river study, the agency said. But pollutants such as phosphorus and nitrogen, which can enter the rivers naturally from erosion of the land or from commercial and industrial sources such as detergents, are on the increase.

Up to 84 per cent of the stretches of rivers studied showed increased phosphorus levels during the 1968 to 1972 period compared with the previous five years, the report said. Nitrogen nutrients increased in up to 74 percent of the stretches of water covered by the survey.

Is pollution a concern in your community? What has been done about it?

Do you believe in the notion that technology created the problem of pollution and will solve it as well? Or do you think the solution lies in a fundamental change in people's attitudes?

Is crime a big-city phenomenon or is it more pervasive? Has a member of your family, or have you, been victimized by crime recently?

Do recent political events destroy or affirm your confidence in the American form of government?

PROBLEMS OF GREATEST CONCERN

Crime	63%
Drugs	28%
High cost of living, inflation	20%
Transportation, 35 cent fare	19%
Housing	13%
Problems of the aged	11%
Schools	11%
Unemployment	9%
Quality of city services	9%
Corruption in government	9%
Pollution	9%
Welfare abuse	7%
The courts	7%
Garbage collection	7%
Energy shortages	7%
Health care	6%
Deteriorating neighborhoods	5%
Traffic	4%
Racial discrimination	3%

What are your most fundamental social concerns?

Woman's role has evolved considerably in your own lifetime. In the 1960s militant feminists took to the streets to make their concerns known to the general public. In this decade women have concentrated on making concrete economic gains. Careers have become more important to them, especially in fields like sports and the professions previously dominated by men. What risks does society face in the redefinition of woman's role? What are the risks in maintaining the status quo?

POPULATION CHANGE AND DISTRIBUTION, 1970

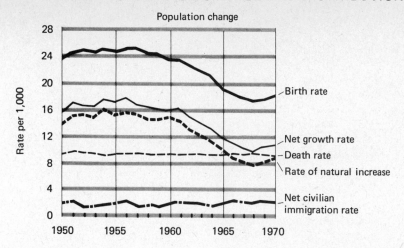

Population change

Rate per 1,000

28
24
20
16
12
8
4
0

1950   1955   1960   1965   1970

- Birth rate
- Net growth rate
- Death rate
- Rate of natural increase
- Net civilian immigration rate

What does this chart imply about population changes as a problem? What conclusions do you draw from differences in population distribution among males and females at some levels? About the proportion of the population under thirty-five?

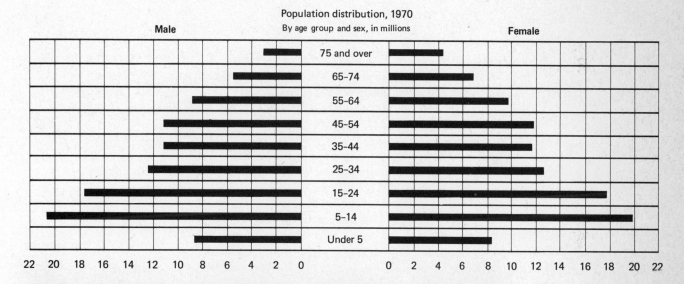

Population distribution, 1970
By age group and sex, in millions

Male   Female

75 and over
65–74
55–64
45–54
35–44
25–34
15–24
5–14
Under 5

22 20 18 16 14 12 10 8 6 4 2 0   0 2 4 6 8 10 12 14 16 18 20 22

Does the American nuclear family have a future as well as a history?

177

ABOUT THE AUTHORS

Jim Watts is Associate Professor of History at the City College of New York, where he has taught since 1965. Because of an ongoing interest in experimental modes of teaching history, he has participated in the production of history courses over radio and television and has made historical films. He was awarded a National Endowment for the Humanities Younger Humanist Fellowship for the 1973–1974 academic year to develop cross-disciplinary approaches to historical studies.

Allen F. Davis is Professor of History at Temple University, where he has taught since 1968. He is the author of two works—*Spearheads for Reform: The Social Settlements and the Progressive Movement* and *American Heroine: The Life and Legend of Jane Addams*—the latter, winner of the 1974 Christopher Award. In addition, he has coedited several books and is currently serving as Executive Secretary for the American Studies Association.

A NOTE ON THE TYPE

The text of this book has been set in linofilm in a type face called Helvetica—perhaps the most widely accepted and generally acclaimed sans-serif face of all time. Designed by M. Miedinger in the 1950s in Switzerland and named for its country of origin, Helvetica was first introduced in America in 1963.

The readings were set in linofilm. The type face is Primer, originally designed for Linotype by Rudolph Ruzicka, who was earlier responsible for the design of Fairfield and Fairfield Medium, Linotype faces whose virtues have for some time now been accorded wide recognition.

The complete range of sizes of Primer was first made available in 1954, although the pilot size of 12 point was ready as early as 1951. The design of the face makes general reference to Linotype Century (long a serviceable type, totally lacking in manner or frills of any kind) but brilliantly corrects the characterless quality of that face.

The book was composed by Black Dot, Crystal Lake, Illinois; printed and bound by Halliday Lithograph Corp., West Hanover, Mass.

appendix

MATERIALS FOR RESEARCH AND WRITING

The materials in this section should be used only as they are useful to you. First read the two examples of writing, noting as you do the kinds of evidence that the two writers needed for their very different kinds of excursions into family history. Then, look over the suggested topics for your own research and the detailed questionnaires as well. Do not think that you must fill in every space, answer every question, retrieve every bit of requested information. Instead, after reading all the material through, select what seems most pertinent to your investigations. As you uncover documents and conduct your oral interviews, return to this section to refresh your memory. Questions and possible areas of information that you rejected or overlooked the first time through may seem on second glance necessary to your work.

Tomatoes
Ruth Tirrell

This brief essay, while it focuses on a family's involvement with fruits and vegetables over several generations, also provides some illuminating insights into the American past. Notice how easily this family swoops back in four generations to the era of John Adams, who was President from 1796 to 1801. Contrast this generation span with that of your own family. In addition, consider the implications of gardening on this scale: where did they find time for such work and why wasn't the produce simply purchased at the corner market? How does your family obtain and prepare food today? How does this differ from the customs of your ancestors? Food can tell you a great deal about a family and a culture.

My mother, who is well along in her tenth decade, still starts tomato seedlings on a sunny window sill each spring (but lets me set them in the ground). Tomatoes, to her, are the No. 1 crop. By careful choice of varieties—one is an early, quick-growing hybrid—we get four months of fresh fruit in suburban Boston.

In my mother's childhood, however, tomatoes were hardly worth the bother, often not ripening until September on the Rhode Island farm of her great-grandmother. And in the latter's childhood—she was born before the eighteenth century ended—most people still regarded the "love apple" as poison. Thomas Jefferson was experimenting with the tomato in Virginia. All her life, she was skeptical of the tomato's value. Under her eye, my mother first planted seeds of peas and beans, not tomatoes.

In the continuity of their gardening, however, matriarch and great-granddaughter, between them, have spanned the eras from John Adams to Richard Nixon. Their lives overlapped for thirteen years.

When Grover Cleveland began his Presidency and my mother was a child, many crops grown on the farm were the same as in colonial days. The "three sisters" of the Indians—squash (or pumpkin), beans and corn—flourished in harmony together. Corn was of three kinds: field corn for the stock; sweet yellow corn to eat on the cob; and white flint corn for the johnnycake meal that Rhode Islanders claim tastes far better than the white corn meal of the South. (It does.) The flat johnnycakes, cooked slowly on a griddle, were served three times a day at the farm. Yeast bread, never.

Corn may have been a small cash crop. Otherwise, all food produced was for the family's benefit, including city relatives like my mother who came to the farm on vacation, when 25 or more people often sat down to the table.

Beans were "string" then, not "snap." Speckled shell beans and corn, fresh or dried, made the Indian dish succotash. Salads were cucumbers and a coarse, curly loose-leaf lettuce, dressed with sugar and vinegar homemade from apples. The lettuce thrived in summer heat and didn't have to be planted. Mature plants self-sowed the next spring.

A staple in summer was beet greens, cooked with bacon and served with vinegar. Beet roots were grown as fodder, and sowings made from mid-April on, and had to be thinned.

Turnip thinnings, which make the favorite cooked greens of the South, were thrown to the hens. Turnips were an important winter vegetable and kept well in a special cellar. Likewise potatoes, onions and cabbage.

Squashes were stored in the attic near the chimney. Carrots, like beets, were for cattle, but parsnips for people. They stayed in the ground and were dug during thaws. The first fresh food of spring was wild dandelions, then rhubarb and asparagus.

Fertilizer was manure—horse, cow, sheep, pig and fowl. Litter was spread on the fields, residues ploughed in, nothing wasted. In most respects, this was an "organic" farm (like all farms once), before the term was coined. But poison—probably paris green—was used on potato bugs. Many pests, including the Japanese beetle and the Mexican bean beetle, hadn't arrived.

Many good things, too, were missing. Vegetables of Italian origin, for instance. No broccoli, no arúgola nor zucchini. The only summer squash was the bright yellow, warty crookneck (which my mother still prefers for its "nutty" texture and flavor). It was a sprawling vine then instead of a compact bush like modern summer varieties.

Unknown—perhaps even by name—were the exotic crops, eggplant and pepper, which once took months of growth in hot weather. The hybrids of today, developed to grow fast in short summers, must still be started inside here in the Northeast.

But looking back, my mother thinks that harvests of fruits were richer and more varied then. The farm had a big strawberry bed and a raspberry plantation, red, yellow and black kinds. Dozens of currant bushes—red, black and white—would be a rare sight now. (As host for the blister rust disease that attacks the white or five-needled pine, currants are now banned from many areas.)

Currants and raspberries—which ripen simultaneously—were often combined in pies and preserves for a marvelous sweet-acid taste better than either alone. Currant clusters, sprinkled with powdered sugar, served as dessert.

Apples of many kinds were a mainstay. A child's favorite was the pretty Snow apple (or Fameuse) with purest flesh and striped purplish-red skin. The Rhode Island Greening stayed fresh until spring packed in barrels of leaves in a cool shed. Apple slices were dried on racks in the sun for winter pies. Apple butter was made outside, too, in a huge cauldron on a cairn of stones. In summer, the cauldron held giant geraniums.

White-fleshed peaches with rosy hearts grew in the poultry yards. The hens fertilized the trees and cleaned up the fallen fruit. The superior fruit seemed to cling to the trees until ripe.

Wild fruits were there for the gathering. Highbush blueberries grew in a deep swamp where snakes lay on hummocks in the sun. A picker wore boots and a pail on a rope tied round the waist. Children had their daily quota of 10 to 12 quarts.

Wild blackberries were for jam; elderberries for wine. The wild fox grape hung high on vines tangled on roadside trees. An ailing person might eat nothing but grapes for a month and sometimes got cured. At this time, the farm had no cultivated arbor, though the Concord grape, which is related to the wild fox grape, had been developed in Concord, Mass., by 1849.

Tiny tart cranberries grew in the family's own wild bog. The matriarch made sauce by a tedious but effective method that had been taught her great-grandmother by an Indian. Slice each berry in half; soak them overnight. "Play with your hands" in the water, then lift the berries and the seeds all fall out. Cook as usual with sugar and a little water. My mother still makes sauce this way, perhaps needlessly, for the big modern cultivated berries have far fewer seeds.

Everybody kept busy without much letup. After the haying, there was a family picnic at the beach (Charlestown, R.I.) and "sea-bathing." Or more rowdy good times at a fresh-water pond on the Connecticut line. Children and old people didn't go. Farmers from miles around gathered to sharpen their scythes in a special fine sand, though this custom was beginning to die out in my mother's childhood.

The Yankee high holiday was Thanksgiving when all the descendants came back to the farm. Except for sugar, salt, tea and white flour for piecrust, nothing on the table was "bought."

My mother's family in the city gave gifts and celebrated Christmas, but the people on the farm, according to the custom of their colonial ancestors, did not.

"My Family's History Begins in Edmondson, Arkansas"

Norene Dove

The family history that follows is, obviously, much more ambitious than the selection you have just read. The author, a student at The City College of New York, encountered many of the problems that you might face as you try to obtain sufficient data for writing about your family's past. She overcame most of the problems, however, by perseverence and imagination. By using most of the resources we have suggested—oral interviews, questionnaires, family documents, and relevant literature about the times and places under study—she was able to produce her paper, which traces her family from its roots in the black South to its transplantation to an inner city in the North. Significantly, she accomplished her research without leaving New York City.

LIFE IN THE SOUTH

My family's history begins in Edmondson, Arkansas. Edmondson is a one-horse town that could easily be missed or overlooked upon passing through. Population at the last count was 212 and that count I am sure included dogs, chickens, cows, and other living animals. My parents' ancestors had come to Edmondson in the late 1800s. They were able to buy a small farm with money they had saved up as sharecroppers. In this one-horse town that was without any of the conveniences necessary if a person desired to live a normal, healthy life, my mother and father and later their five children were born. My father was born in 1916 and my mother in 1918. They both lived and worked on their parents' farms until they were married. The change in Edmondson from the time of my parents' childhood up until we left was minimal. Edmondson is still without (1) a hospital, (2) doctors, (3) public transportation, (4) industries, (5) paved streets, (6) shopping areas and department stores for the most part, and (7) any of the social institutions found in other towns and cities. Memphis, which was thirty miles away, was the closest city.

My mother and father were married in January 1938. They started out with a small house and twenty-five acres of land that had been left to my father by his father. Compared to some of the other blacks in Edmondson they were pretty lucky and well off. The Great Depression of the thirties affected the entire world, but the people of Edmondson suffered tremendously from it. Many of them fled to the North while others, who could not get their fare, found themselves in servitude, with white farm owners as their overseers. Both my mother and my father lacked extensive educational careers. My father had left school when he was in the eighth grade because his help was needed on the farm. My mother had gone as long as the school system in Edmondson permitted and that was only to the ninth grade. So with hardly any education, no skills other than those associated with farming, and no money to buy equipment necessary to make their first crop, the nightmare began. Like many other blacks, they entered into a semisharecropping agreement with one of the larger white farmers who, together with a few other whites, had succeeded in maintaining complete control over the entire black community.

The black people in Edmondson were mainly of one social class except for the two teachers and the preachers who, although they too were farmers, felt a little superior because of their part-time positions. Most of the people in the community had (1) similar moral attitudes, (2) lots of religious and racial affiliations, (3) no political or economic influence, and (4) little or no formal schooling. Most of them either owned small plots of land or hired themselves out to white farmers, who sometimes permitted them to cultivate small portions of their land. Though there were whites who had economic investments in Edmondson, hardly any of them lived in the predominantly black Edmondson. Those who did live there lived within their own little world and dared the blacks to cross their path.

There were three stores, which were white-owned and -operated in Edmondson. They sold everything from food and clothing to farm supplies and drugs. Housed in one of these three stores were the post office and a small stand where one could buy whiskey, wine, and beer. The stores were located on the only paved street in Edmondson. These stores not only functioned to provide the people of Edmondson a place in which to shop, but you often found many of the black males congregated on their steps, discussing crops and on some occasions talking about the good life that was available in the North. The store owners discouraged the use of money by their customers to purchase goods. Most of them did not have money anyway. The store owners readily charged and kept annual accounts for their customers, gladly settling with them after their crops were gathered. Since no records were being kept by the purchasers, they often found themselves having to pay for goods that they had not purchased.

The people in Edmondson depended on the cotton economy as a source of income. My parents, though they owned a small farm, could not compete with the large, white-owned and -operated farms surrounding them. Because of the inadequate rules and regulations governing the banks and credit unions, they were not permitted to borrow money to make a profit on their crops. They had to indebt themselves to a white farmer, who often managed to claim the entire profit made from a single crop. Each year before planting time my family was given what I will call an allowance. Most of the money was spent for purchases of farm supplies and what was left, which was usually minimal, went toward purchases of clothing and food that was not raised on the farm. After the receipt of this allowance, which did not vary with an increase in family size, there was no other source of income within our household until the end of the year when the crops had been gathered. If the family consisted of many members (and it usually did), the members were often very hungry and without sufficient clothing. Whether the crops were good or bad had little effect upon the plight of my family, who had planted and gathered the crops. The crops, after they were gathered, were turned over to the white suppliers. They sold the crops in Memphis and, often without telling my parents how much the crops sold for, gave them that which was left after all of the incurred expenses had been deducted. Since my parents had not kept their own records or were ignorant about selling prices in Memphis, they often received just enough money to keep them going until they received their next allowance.

In this type of system, it was impossible for them to ever conceive of getting ahead. Not only were the people of Edmondson being exploited individually, they were being denied the right to develop or improve their community. None of the money that was made from the many hours spent in the fields by the people was being invested in the community to make life easier or more fulfilling for them and future generations.

There were only a few places in the South where a black man dared go to bring charges against his white exploiters and Edmondson was not among those places. There was no judicial system in Edmondson. The systems outside town were useful and helpful only for those who were politically and economically in control, and this definitely did not include the poor black farmers. People in the community as a whole were not allowed to vote or to express any of their personal beliefs about many local politicians, who were always white. Occasionally teachers were permitted to vote as long as they voted for the candidate favored by the whites controlling the school system.

The denial of intelligence, ambition, health, education, and economic achievement motivated my parents to move to Cleveland. After having spent the majority of their lives working hard on a farm that no longer belonged to them and having nothing to show for their hard work, they decided to move. They had hopes of a better life for their children if not for themselves.

In September of 1960 we moved to Cleveland, Ohio.

LIFE IN THE NORTH

The North offered my family, if not a totally different life, a more favorable one. In spite of considerable discrimination, it offered them more economic opportunities, more security as citizens, and greater freedom as human beings. Many of my parents' relatives and friends had moved to Cleveland during or after World War I. The fact that they were not completely alone in Cleveland did much to help them adjust without too much unhappiness about the familiar places and friends they had left behind.

My parents had come to Cleveland with a few personal objects and very little money. They did not have enough money to secure a place of their own. My mother's brother permitted us to live with him until we could do better. My uncle at the time lived in a very large, dilapidated apartment building in one of Cleveland's many ghettos. It appeared that among the many people in the building every Southern state in the Union was represented except Arkansas. My family came to their aid by expanding their representation. All of the people were black and appeared to be in no better shape than the black people we had left behind. My uncle had two children of his own, to whom he was acting as both mother and father, since their mother had left for work one morning and never returned home. Although the outside of the building wasn't pleasant to look at, the inside really wasn't that bad. I should say that it wasn't that way until after my mother spent many hours on her hands and knees scrubbing the floors, washing walls, and making it what she considered livable. My mother had always been a fanatic when it came to housework and that apparent need that she had to keep everything spotless created a lot of discomfort for me throughout my entire childhood. There were five rooms in my uncle's apartment, which now served as accommodations for eleven people. During the time that we stayed in his apartment, there was always a fuss at night as to who was sleeping where.

My father managed to get a job working for Ford Motor Company on an assembly line. Although his salary was as much in one week as our entire allowance had been for several months in the South, it wasn't enough to buy the house that my mother was constantly saying we needed. After we had been in Cleveland about nine months my mother decided to go to work in order to get her children out of that neighborhood before they turned bad. Most of the kids including myself attended an all-black school about two blocks away from home. Naturally we walked to school and en route we often had fights with the kids from other blocks who thought or acted as if they were better than us, and occasionally kids from different neighborhoods would try to coax us to try drugs. It was when my younger brother reported these happenings to my mother that she developed an intense dislike for the neighborhood and everyone in it. She complained about how the people in the neighborhood didn't try to look after their children or how they showed a lack of interest about the vicinity in which they lived in general. On several occasions she took it upon herself to act as the sanitation department and cleaned up the entire court surrounding our building.

My mother was also unhappy with the school that we had to attend because, for reasons that were known only by the board of education, it was open for only four hours each day. On nights that we did not have homework she complained and told us that if we only knew how badly she had wanted to go to school and wasn't permitted to do so, we would show a little more concern about school and try to do our best at all times. On a few occasions she made calls to our teachers verifying whether or not we had homework.

During the week our neighborhood was relatively quiet. Most of the adults worked during the day on jobs that left them fatigued by the end of the day and ready for little other than their beds when they returned home. All of the children, if they were of school age, attended school. When we were not in school, we spent the remainder of our time outside in front of the building or strolling around downtown, window shopping, making sure we arrived home before our parents did. Unlike other children in nearby neighborhoods, we could never afford to go to the movies or participate in any activity that required money. There were no free recreational facilities made available for us, so we had little else to do but stroll around town. On Saturday nights it seemed that practically everyone was awake and sort of celebrating. My mother objected and did not permit us to participate in the celebrating. She termed the behavior of the people outrageous and refused to get involved or participate. My father on the other hand seemed to enjoy the loud laughter, the music, and the arguments that usually ended in fights.

The burning and stealing that resulted from the riots of the sixties proved to be a little bit too much for my parents, and besides, our entire neighborhood was almost burned down. When the streets were declared safe again, my parents went out and found a house in a neighborhood that had been, up until blacks began to move in, totally white. My mother for one solid year never stopped thanking the Lord for having answered her prayers.

Partially because she was so wrapped up in her new home, my mother did not find adjusting in the new neighborhood difficult. For myself and the other children it took quite a while to get used to our new peers, both black and white. We didn't seem to have much in common with the blacks or the whites. We had previously lived in areas that were racially and culturally homogeneous; therefore, it was difficult for us to identify with the whites or the blacks who appeared to be imitating their white peers. My mother, as she has always done in the past, came to our rescue. Although we knew we could not afford it, my mother insisted that all five of us join the community center where we took music, swimming, and dancing lessons. She also made sure that those that were young enough were sent off to camp each summer. This new mode of living that mother had adopted for the family put a big strain on my father's wallet. Though my father had since gotten a raise and a promotion, he could not financially afford to live the type of life that my mother had decided upon for the family. He eventually had to take a second job as a cab driver. He really did not seem to mind it that much because all of the other black men in our neighborhood at one time or another worked two jobs in order to maintain the standard of living they had adopted. Most of them tried to give the appearance of being middle class, but this was far from the real truth. None of the workers in our neighborhood held positions that, according to American standards, entitled them to middle-class status. Because they were black they were kept out of certain industries. Most of them were confined because of their educational background to skilled and semiskilled occupations that were unattractive to white workers. In Cleveland, as in other cities in the North, many employers believed that black people are inferior as workers except for dirty, heavy, hot, or otherwise unattractive jobs. In Cleveland, as in the South, the chances of a black man in our neighborhood achieving vocational success and social recognition were minimal. The aspiration that was present in both my father and mother did little to change their position in society but it had a great impact on all of their children. All of their children except me have finished college and are, according to American standards, holding white-collar jobs and would, if they were not black, be allowed to participate in America's economic and social prosperity.

I attended a racially mixed high school. This was beneficial in that it exposed me to people that were of different cultural and economic backgrounds. Some of the children were from families that were economically well off and some were from families that were less fortunate than my parents. Although there was no law that said blacks were not to intermingle with people of other races as there had been in the South, other nonblack groups just avoided the black population, letting it exist separately in its designated black neighborhoods. The school was structurally superior to the one that I had attended in Arkansas, but there was no encouragement for vocational or academic achievement given from the teachers who were predominantly white. The encouragement and aspiration that I possess can be attributed to both my parents and the racist society in which I have been forced to live. The society taught me early in life how important the color of my skin is and my parents taught me that if I was to minimize the obstacles that would present themselves because of my skin color, I would have to work harder and surpass those who desire white over black. It never seemed to bother my parents that they were never able to go on a vacation or that the only place they were really accepted or recognized was within the walls of their black neighborhood.

My mother seemed pretty content as long as she could afford to buy the material conveniences that are enjoyed by the genuinely successful and economically fixed American middle class. My mother never gave up hopes of going back to school. When she could find the time she would attend the Y.W.C.A., taking whatever course they had available at the time. She was forever buying some kind of book that someone had told her about or one that she had heard about in her travels back and forth to work. Because of her active participation in the block unit and numerous church affairs, she seldom got a chance to read any of them. My father, on the other hand, when he was not working, either watched television or tried to engage in a conversation about the local politicians when he could get a listener. The children of the family did not fancy talking about that because it was far removed from poor working-class people. The year that I graduated from high school, my mother became very ill and had to quit work. Unlike my other sisters and brothers, I did not receive a scholarship. Because of the financial situation that had gotten worse since mother had left her job, I was unable to go to college. Depressed about not being able to go to college and my parents' financial situation, I decided to come to New York where I could make some fast money to help my parents and go to college with the rest.

In New York I lived with my father's sister and got a job as a file clerk in the telephone company, making $70 a week. I soon found out that I was not going to be able to help my parents very much, and as for school, I would have to work a long time on that salary. During my stay at the telephone company I experienced what I feel many working-class people experience. The job that I had was meaningless and extremely boring. I had no interest whatsoever in my job. The only meaning that it had was that it provided me with a source of weekly income. Realizing that I could not mentally or physically endure a lifetime of paper pushing, I decided to save as much as possible for the day that I could return to school. On the salary that I was making it took several years. But for me, returning to school was my only hope and salvation. In September 1972 I entered college in hopes of learning to deal with or understand the "society" which I am forced to live in but, because I'm black, have little chance of ever entering.

SKETCHING YOUR FAMILY: QUESTIONS AND QUESTIONNAIRES

NOTE: The following questions are suggestions only. You may want to ask them of yourself and your relatives, but they do not exhaust the possibilities, and not every question may apply to your particular situation.

BASIC INFORMATION

When were you born? How old were you when you married? When did you move to your present residence? Why? What kinds of work have you done?

RACE ETHNICITY

To what racial or ethnic group do you belong? When did you begin to think of yourself as a member of this group? Why? How did this identification influence you? In what ways is your group primarily defined—by religion, ancestry, skin color, or language? Are there general limitations imposed on your group by society? What? How are they imposed? In what economic and social class are most members of your group found? Why? What are society's stereotypes of your group? What stereotypes does your group hold of other groups?

EDUCATION

How many years of schooling have you had? How was your education important in your life? Did you have more schooling than your parents? Did you "do well" in school? How did that affect your life? What do you remember about your teachers?

COMMUNICATION

What are your sources of information about the world outside your community? What folklore about your family or group do you know? What outsider has been most widely respected in your family in the last ten years? Why?

CLASS, STATUS, AND MOBILITY

How do you define your social class—working class, middle class, professional class, country club set, other? What characteristics put you in this class? How do your social contacts influence your life? What contacts do you have with people in other classes? Is your social class different from that of your parents? If so, how was it changed? Is formal education most important in social mobility, that is, moving up in social class? If not, what is? What places outside your community have the reputation for offering a better life? Could you improve your social-class position if you tried? How? What do you like/dislike about your place in society?

STATE, LAW, AND POLITICAL LIFE

What rights does citizenship give you? What burdens come with citizenship? In what areas does the state provide you services? Through what officials are you in contact with the state (e.g., policemen, politicians, tax collectors)? Are representatives of the state generally from the same economic and social class as you? What kinds of laws affect your life? Do you think the law favors any individual or group? How? Where are the political decisions made that affect your life? What kinds of people run for political offices? Could you approach political officials about your problems successfully? How much does voting mean to you? Would you run for office?